國高中英文
單字加深加廣

《Storytelling 英文單字好好記》修訂版

全MP3一次下載

https://globalv.com.tw/mp3-download-9789864544240/

掃描QR碼進入網頁後,請按「全書音檔下載請按此」連結,
可一次性下載全書音檔壓縮檔,也可點選檔名線上播放。
iOS系統請升級至iOS13後版本再行下載,壓縮檔為大型檔案,建議使用
WiFi連線下載,以免占用流量,並請確認連線狀況,以利下載順暢。

Contents

目錄

Day 01 ▶ Day 03

學校與朋友

01.（Story 001-005）..P.009
02.（Story 006-010）..P.018
03.（Story 011-015）..P.027
⭐ 掌握常見字根 01

Day 04 ▶ Day 06

旅遊與冒險

04.（Story 016-020）..P.037
05.（Story 021-025）..P.046
06.（Story 026-030）..P.055
⭐ 掌握常見字根 02

家庭與幸福

07.（Story 031-035）..P.065
08.（Story 036-040）..P.074
09.（Story 041-045）..P.083
⭐ 掌握常見字首 01

Day 10 ▶ Day 12

社會與規範

10.（Story 046-050）..P.093
11.（Story 051-055）..P.102
12.（Story 056-060）..P.111
⭐ 掌握常見字首 02

Day 13 ▶ Day 15

動物世界

13.（Story 061-065）..P.122
14.（Story 066-070）..P.130
15.（Story 071-075）..P.139
⭐ 掌握常見字尾 01

Day 16 ▶ Day 18

日常生活

16.（Story 076-080）..P.148
17.（Story 081-085）..P.157
18.（Story 086-090）..P.166

⭐ 常見常見字尾 02

Day 19 ▶ Day 21

文化與健康

19.（Story 091-095）..P.177
20.（Story 096-100）..P.186
21.（Story 101-105）..P.195

⭐ 掌握常見多義字 01

Day 22 ▶ Day 24

自然與環境

22.（Story 106-110）..P.206
23.（Story 111-115）..P.215
24.（Story 116-120）..P.224

⭐ 掌握常見多義字 02

Day 25 ▶ Day 27

日常生活

25.（Story 121-125）..P.235
26.（Story 126-130）..P.244
27.（Story 131-135）..P.253
★ 掌握常見易混淆字 01

Day 28 ▶ Day 30

文化與健康

28.（Story 136-140）..P.264
29.（Story 141-145）..P.273
30.（Story 146-150）..P.282
★ 掌握常見易混淆字 02

附錄　一起看圖開口說說看吧！................................P.293

How to use this book

使用說明

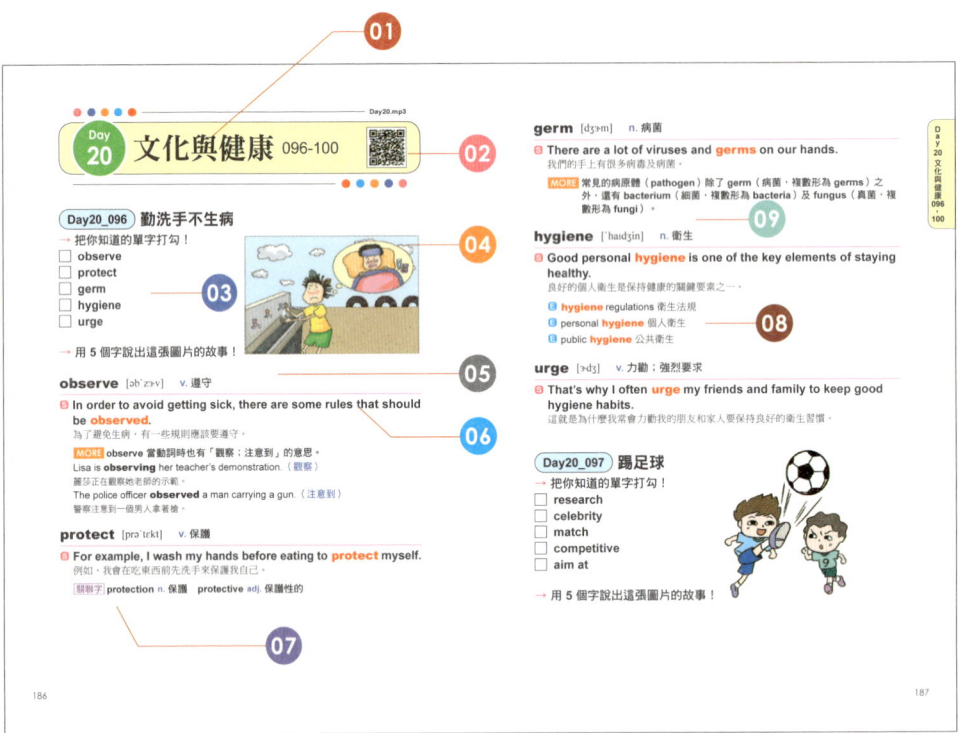

- ① 10 大主題分類，貼近生活的各個層面，學習最實用的主題單字。
- ② 收錄單字英文＋中文字義＋英文主題句音檔，不只複習單字唸法與字義，聽力和實際運用也一併練習！
- ③ 檢視自己認識多少個主題單字，為接下來的學習做好準備。
- ④ 先看圖片刺激視覺印象，為大腦做暖身。
- ⑤ 主題單字搭配音標與字義，不僅懂意思也會唸。
- ⑥ 主題句彼此串聯，構成說明圖片背景的小故事，讓圖片、單字、故事在腦中形成長期記憶。
- ⑦ 額外補充同義字、反義字、關聯字，擴大單字庫最有效率。
- ⑧ 補充經常與主題單字搭配使用的詞彙，更了解實際運用情形。
- ⑨ 補充單字或例句相關的英文知識，學習更深入。

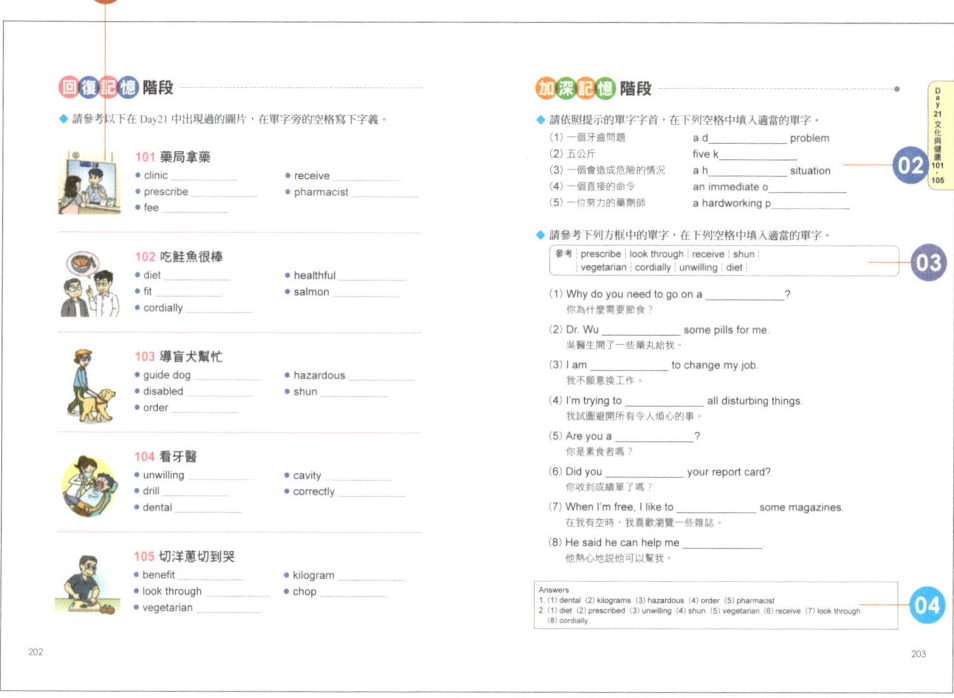

01 先看圖片內容，再回想由主題句構成的背景故事，透過故事回復對單字字義的記憶，將正確字義填入右側空白欄中，填完後翻回前面確認是否正確。

02 搭配左側的中文提示及右側空白欄的字首提示，填入正確的單字，加深運用單字的印象。

03 參考方框中所提示的單字，按照題目翻譯的中文來填入正確的單字，並依照句子內容變化單字的時態、單複數等形態，進一步熟悉單字的使用方式。

04 請對照自己的答案與正確答案，及時檢視學習成果。

01 特別收錄能夠幫助單字記憶與理解的常用字根、字首、字尾，讓單字不再只是無意義的字母組合，進而可以透過字源來拆解及記憶，此外亦收錄易混淆字及多義字的整理，學習範圍更廣！

02 特別將本書主題句完整整理，搭配主題配圖，請試著看圖開口説説看，再搭配純主題句音檔開口説，跟著外籍老師學習最道地的發音，訓練自己看圖説故事的能力，不只會看、會聽，還會開口説，英文能力全面升級！

- **本書附贈三種音檔：**
❶ 單字英文＋中文字義：快速複習單字唸法與字義。
❷ 單字英文＋中文字義＋英文主題句：不只複習單字唸法與字義，一併練習聽力和實際運用。
❸ 英文主題句：搭配附錄的主題句整理，跟著開口看圖説説看，不只學會單字，也能提升口説力。

Day01.mp3

Day 01 學校與朋友 001-005

Day01_001 值得稱讚的優秀學生

→ 把你知道的單字打勾！
- [ ] grade
- [ ] subject
- [ ] praise
- [ ] jealous
- [ ] diligently

→ 用 5 個字說出這張圖片的故事！

grade [gred]　n. 分數

S Mary is so hardworking at school that she always gets good **grades**.
Mary 在學校非常認真，所以她總是能拿到好成績。

同義字 score
關聯字 upgrade v. 升級
We should **upgrade** our computers.
我們應該升級我們的電腦。

subject [ˈsʌbdʒɪkt]　n. 科目

S She is good at almost every **subject**, especially English and math.
她幾乎每一科都擅長，特別是英文和數學。

MORE subject 也有「主題」或是「主格」的意思。

E After talking about some recent events, he went on to another **subject**.
在說了一些最近發生的事之後，他繼續進行了另一個話題。

E We put a **subject** before a verb to make a sentence.
我們會把主詞放在動詞之前來造出句子。

9

praise [prez]　v. 讚賞

S **Mary's teacher always praises her for her good grades.**
瑪莉的老師總是稱讚她的好成績。

同義字 admire、compliment

jealous [`dʒɛləs]　adj. 忌妒

S **A lot of Mary's classmates are jealous of her being praised.**
很多瑪莉的同學都忌妒她被稱讚的這件事。

關聯字 envious adj. 忌妒的；羨慕的　envy v. 忌妒；羨慕

diligently [`dɪlədʒəntlɪ]　adv. 勤勉地

S **Regardless of the ill words from her classmates, she still works diligently at school.**
不管她的同學們所說的那些難聽話，她在學校仍然很認真努力。

同義字 industriously
Those high school students work very **industriously**.
那些高中生非常勤奮努力。

Day01_002　作弊抓包

→ 把你知道的單字打勾！
- [ ] science
- [ ] anxious
- [ ] cheat
- [ ] secretly
- [ ] furious

→ 用 5 個字說出這張圖片的故事！

science [`saɪəns]　n. 科學

S **Yesterday, our science teacher gave us a pop quiz.**
昨天我們的自然老師突然抽考了我們。

MORE 研究科學的人就是 scientist n. 科學家。
I have wanted to be a **scientist** since I was little.
我從小就一直想當一位科學家。

10

anxious [ˈæŋkʃəs]　　adj. 焦慮的

- Most of the students in my class were **anxious** about the quiz.
  我們班上大部分的學生都對這次小考感到很焦慮。

  關聯字 anxiety n. 焦慮　　nervous adj. 緊張的　　restless adj. 不安的　　worried adj. 擔憂的

  MORE 要讓焦慮的人「冷靜下來」，可以說 calm down。
  The police tried to **calm down** those restless people.
  警方試圖讓那些不安的人冷靜下來。

---

cheat [tʃit]　　v. 作弊

- Some of the students decided to **cheat**, because they didn't prepare for this at all.
  有些學生決定要作弊，因為他們完全沒準備。

---

secretly [ˈsikrɪtlɪ]　　adv. 祕密地

- They tried to pass notes to each other **secretly**.
  他們試圖要偷偷傳紙條給彼此。

  關聯字 secret n. 祕密

---

furious [ˈfjʊrɪəs]　　adj. 非常憤怒的

- When our science teacher found they were cheating, he was **furious** and shouted at us angrily.
  當我們的自然老師發現他們在作弊，他非常憤怒並對我們生氣地大吼。

  同義字 mad、angry
  MORE 副詞是 furiously。
  My husband often shouts at me **furiously** with no reason. I can't stand it anymore!
  我的丈夫常無緣無故地對我憤怒大吼。我再也無法忍受了！

Day01_003 大學新生活！

→ 把你知道的單字打勾！
- [ ] notify
- [ ] freshman
- [ ] excitedly
- [ ] ideal
- [ ] elective

→ 用 5 個字說出這張圖片的故事！

notify [ˋnotəˌfaɪ]　v. 通知

When John was **notified** that he had been accepted by a renowned university, he was proud of himself.
當約翰被通知他被知名大學錄取時，他對他自己感到驕傲。

關聯字 notification n. 通知；告示

freshman [ˋfrɛʃmən]　n. 大一生，新鮮人

Being a university **freshman** has always been John's dream.
當一位大學新鮮人，一直都是約翰的夢想。

MORE sophomore n. 大二生　junior n. 大三生　senior n. 大四生

excitedly [ɪkˋsaɪtɪdlɪ]　adv. 興奮地

"It's a whole new start!", said John **excitedly**.
約翰興奮地說：「這是一個全新的開始！」。

反義字 calmly adv. 冷靜地
Even though I was under pressure, I still acted very **calmly**.
即使在壓力之下，我仍然表現得非常冷靜。

ideal [aɪˋdɪəl]　adj. 理想的

John has been thinking about how to have an **ideal** university life.
約翰一直在思考要如何擁有理想的大學生活。

關聯字 idea n. 想法
- **ideal** job 理想的工作
- **ideal** lifestyle 理想的生活型態

A job that can work from home is an **ideal job** for me.
一份能在家工作的工作對我來說是理想工作。
The definition of **ideal lifestyle** varies from person to person.
理想生活型態的定義因人而異。

elective [ɪˋlɛktɪv]　adj. 選修的

🅢 On his first day in the university, he immediately took some **elective** courses he liked very much.
在大學的第一天，他馬上上了一些他非常喜歡的選修課。

關聯字 elect v. 選擇；選舉
　　　　select v. 選擇＝choose＝opt＝pick up
　　　　selection n. 選擇；可供選擇的人（或物）
MORE 其他常見的課程還有：
selective course 精選課程　required course 必修課程
core course 核心課程　online course 線上課程　crash course 速成課程

Day01_004　校園遊

→ 把你知道的單字打勾！
☐ elementary
☐ campus
☐ PE class
☐ bench
☐ jog

→ 用 5 個字說出這張圖片的故事！

elementary [ˌɛləˋmɛntərɪ]　adj. 初級的

🅢 One day, I happened to walk into an **elementary** school.
有一天，我碰巧走進了一所小學。

🅔 **elementary** level 初級
MORE 常見的各級學校的說法：
elementary school＝primary school 小學　junior high school 國中
senior high school 高中　college 學院，大專　university（綜合）大學
graduate school 研究所

campus [ˋkæmpəs]　n. 校園

- The **campus** is spacious, and there were energetic students everywhere.
  這座校園很寬廣，而且到處都是充滿活力的學生。

PE class [ˋpɪˏiˋklæs]　n. 體育課（PE＝physical education）

- I saw some of the students doing exercises in their **PE class**.
  我看見有一些學生正在體育課上做運動。

  關聯字　physical adj. 身體的；生理的　　mental adj. 心理的
  My doctor told me that I needed some **physical** therapy.
  我的醫生告訴我，我需要做一些物理治療。
  If you have **mental** issues, you'll need a professional therapist.
  如果你有心理問題，你會需要專業的治療師。

bench [bɛntʃ]　n. 長椅

- Two girls were sitting on the **bench** chatting.
  兩個女孩子坐在長椅上聊天。

  MORE 其他常見的「椅子」：
  chair 椅子　stool 凳子，高腳椅　armchair 扶手椅　sofa 沙發
  coach（長）沙發　lounge 躺椅　ottoman 軟墊凳

jog [dʒɑg]　v. 慢跑

- What's more, I also saw a boy **jogging** on the track.
  還有，我也看到了一個男孩正在跑道上慢跑。

  MORE 想要講「去慢跑」時，可以說 go jogging，如果是像賽跑般，速度很快的跑步，則要說 go running。

Day01_005　知名教授來了！

→ 把你知道的單字打勾！
- ☐ reputable
- ☐ knowledgeable
- ☐ seminar
- ☐ auditorium
- ☐ well-attended

→ 用 5 個字說出這張圖片的故事！

reputable [ˈrɛpjətəbl]　adj. 有名聲的；有名望的

Mr. Wang is a reputable and very well respected professor.
王先生是一位有名望且備受敬重的教授。

同義字 well-known、renowned、famous

knowledgeable [ˈnɑlɪdʒəbl]　adj. 有知識的；知識淵博的

He is not only knowledgeable but also nice to his students.
他不但知識淵博，也對他的學生很好。

關聯字 knowledge n. 知識
He is a skilled worker with full of **knowledge**.
他是一位充滿知識、技術純熟的員工。

seminar [ˈsɛməˌnɑr]　n. 研討會

He will give a speech on economy in the seminar next month.
他在下個月的研討會上會進行一場與經濟相關的演說。

MORE 除了 seminar 之外，各種「會議」的說法如下：
meeting 小型會議　conference 中大型會議　convention 代表大會
symposium 座談會；討論會　panel discussion 小組討論會

auditorium [ˌɔdəˈtorɪəm]　n. 禮堂

The seminar will be held in the school auditorium.
這場研討會將會在學校的禮堂裡舉辦。

well-attended [wɛl əˈtɛndɪd]　adj. 參加者眾多的

It is expected that this seminar will be well-attended.
這場研討會預期會有很多人參加。

MORE 其他常見的 well- 複合形容詞：
well-mannered 舉止文雅的　well-behaved 規矩的
well-built 體格健美的　well-trained 受過良好訓練的

Day 01 學校與朋友 001-005

回復記憶 階段

◆ 請參考以下在 Day01 中出現過的圖片,在單字旁的空格寫下字義。

001 值得稱讚的優秀學生
- grade _____
- subject _____
- praise _____
- jealous _____
- diligently _____

002 作弊抓包
- science _____
- anxious _____
- cheat _____
- secretly _____
- furious _____

003 大學新生活!
- notify _____
- freshman _____
- excitedly _____
- ideal _____
- elective _____

004 校園遊
- elementary _____
- campus _____
- PE class(= physical education)_____
- bench _____
- jog _____

005 知名教授來了!
- reputable _____
- knowledgeable _____
- seminar _____
- auditorium _____
- well-attended _____

 **階段**

◆ 請依照提示的單字字首,在下列空格中填入適當的單字。

(1) 一位有名望的領導者　　　a r_____ leader
(2) 一個大型的禮堂　　　　　a big a_____
(3) 一位焦慮的母親　　　　　an a_____ mother
(4) 兩堂選修課　　　　　　　two s_____ courses
(5) 一張公園的長椅　　　　　a park b_____
(6) 一個重要的研討會　　　　an important s_____

◆ 請參考下列方框中的單字,在下列空格中填入適當的單字。

參考 | praise | secretly | knowledgeable | furious | freshman | jealous | subject

(1) I am a _____ in this university.
    我是這間大學的新鮮人。

(2) I think English is an interesting _____.
    我認為英文是個有趣的科目。

(3) If you read a lot, you'll become _____.
    如果你的閱讀量很大,你會變得很有知識。

(4) My teacher always _____ me a lot.
    我的老師總是大力稱讚我。

(5) I was _____ because he made a big mistake.
    我因為他犯了大錯而非常憤怒。

(6) He was _____ when his girlfriend chatted with other boys.
    當他的女友和其他男生聊天時,他很忌妒。

(7) My coworker told me some gossips _____.
    我的同事偷偷告訴了我一些八卦。

(8) Nobody _____ me that I have to attend the meeting.
    沒人通知過我說我必須出席那場會議。

Answers:
1. (1) reputable (2) auditorium (3) anxious (4) selective (5) bench (6) seminar
2. (1) freshman (2) subject (3) knowledgeable (4) praises (5) furious (6) jealous (7) secretly (8) notified

Day02.mp3

Day 02 學校與朋友 006-010

Day02_006 我的好朋友

→ 把你知道的單字打勾！
- [ ] encounter
- [ ] friendship
- [ ] appreciate
- [ ] sincerely
- [ ] precious

→ 用 5 個字說出這張圖片的故事！

encounter [ɪn`kaʊntɚ]　v. 遭遇；偶然相遇

S Tom and I are good friends, and he always gives me a hand when I **encounter** difficulties.
湯姆與我是好友，他總是在我遇到困難時伸出援手。

同義字 meet、bump to、come across

friendship [`frɛndʃɪp]　n. 友誼

S The **friendship** between us makes a lot of people impressed.
我們之間的友誼讓很多人印象深刻。

E precious **friendship** 珍貴的友誼

MORE 字尾 -ship 常有著「～的關係」的意味，例如 relationship（人際關係）、membership（會員身分）、kinship（親屬關係），不過也有例外，像是 scholarship（獎學金）。

appreciate [ə`priʃɪ,et]　v. 感激；欣賞

S Last week he came all the way just to give me a birthday present, and I really **appreciated** what he did for me.
上週他大老遠過來送我生日禮物，我真的很謝謝他為我做的事。

關聯字 appreciation n. 感激；欣賞

sincerely [sɪn`sɪrlɪ]　adv. 真誠地

S **I gave him a firm hug and thanked him sincerely.**
我給了他一個緊緊的擁抱，並且真誠地感謝他。

precious [`prɛʃəs]　adj. 珍貴的，貴重的

S **I will definitely cherish the precious friendship forever.**
我絕對會永遠珍惜這段珍貴的友誼。

同義字 priceless、invaluable

Day02_007　暗戀一個人

→ 把你知道的單字打勾！
- [ ] proactive
- [ ] encourage
- [ ] gorgeous
- [ ] admirer
- [ ] hopefully

→ 用 5 個字說出這張圖片的故事！

proactive [`æktɪv]　adj. 積極的；主動的

S **Tina wants to be Charles' girlfriend, but she is not a proactive person.**
蒂娜想成為查爾斯的女友，但是她不是個積極主動的人。

> MORE　proactive 通常用來形容「人格特質」上的積極主動，而生活中常見的 active，雖然也有著「主動」的意味，但只會用在形容「行為上」的積極，更偏向「活躍；積極參與」的意思。

You need to be more proactive to make our team work better.
你必須更主動點來讓我們團隊運作更順暢。

Amy is an active member of our debate team.
艾咪是我們辯論隊裡的活躍成員。

encourage [ɪn`kɝɪdʒ]　v. 鼓勵

S **Many of Tina's friends encourage her to express herself directly to Charles.**
很多蒂娜的朋友都鼓勵她直接去告訴查爾斯她的感覺。

反義字 discourage v. 使氣餒

gorgeous [`gɔrdʒəs]　　adj. 非常漂亮的；極好的

Ⓢ **One time she saw Charles chatting with a gorgeous girl, she felt a little depressed.**
有一次她見到查爾斯在和一位非常漂亮的女孩聊天，她覺得有些沮喪。

admirer [əd`maɪrɚ]　　n. 愛慕者

Ⓢ **In spite of all the hurt feelings she had, she still decided to just be a silent admirer.**
儘管覺得很受傷，她仍然決定只當一個安靜的愛慕者。

> MORE　in spite of＝despite 即使，儘管

hopefully [`hopfəlɪ]　　adv. 抱持希望地；但願

Ⓢ **Hopefully, he would understand her mind sometime in the future.**
但願他在未來的某個時間會了解她的心意。

> MORE　同為副詞的 sometime 和 sometimes，在拼字上只差了一個 s，但意義上卻很不一樣，sometime 是「未來的某個時間」，而 sometimes 則是「有時候」的意思。
> I **sometimes** go fishing on the weekend. 我有時會在週末去釣魚。
> I will go fishing **sometime** next week. 我會在下週的某個時間去釣魚。

Day02_008　患難見真情

→ 把你知道的單字打勾！
- ☐ suburb
- ☐ saying
- ☐ immediately
- ☐ accompany
- ☐ indecisive

→ 用 5 個字說出這張圖片的故事！

20

suburb [ˈsʌbɝb]　n. 市郊

- Eric and I grew up together in the **suburbs**.
  艾瑞克與我在市郊一起長大。

  MORE suburb 是指遠離 city downtown（市中心）的住宅區。
  關聯字 suburban adj. 市郊的　countryside n. 鄉下；鄉村

saying [ˈseɪŋ]　n. 格言，諺語

- Just as a **saying** goes, "A friend in need is a friend indeed."
  就如同格言所說的：「患難見真情」。

  - a wise **saying** 一句明智的格言

immediately [ɪˈmidɪɪtlɪ]　adv. 立刻，馬上

- Whenever I need him, he just shows up **immediately**.
  每當我需要他，他就會立刻出現。

  同義字 right away、at once

accompany [əˈkʌmpənɪ]　v. 陪伴；伴隨

- Yesterday I was frustrated about work, he came to **accompany** me and drank with me.
  昨天我因為工作而感到挫折，他就來陪我喝酒。

  關聯字 company n. 同伴；公司　companion n. 同伴

indecisive [ˌɪndɪˈsaɪsɪv]　adj. 舉棋不定的；不明確的

- Moreover, he always gives me solid suggestions, so I won't be **indecisive** when I have to make a decision.
  此外，當我必須做決定時，他總是會給我有用的建議，讓我不會舉棋不定。

  反義字 decisive adj. 決定性的；確定的
  MORE 英文中帶有「做決定」意味的說法有很多，除了最常見的 decide，還有 make a decision（做決定）、make up one's mind to（某人下定決心做～）、determine（決心做～）等說法，可以依照當下的使用情境，選擇適合的說法。

Day 02 學校與朋友 006–010

21

Day02_009 這種朋友不交也罷！

→ 把你知道的單字打勾！
- [ ] invite
- [ ] celebrate
- [ ] feel like
- [ ] shortly
- [ ] dismay

→ 用 5 個字說出這張圖片的故事！

invite [ɪn`vaɪt]　v. 邀請

S Last night, May **invited** Jessie over for a party, but she said she had to work overtime.
昨晚梅邀了潔西來家裡參加派對，但她說她必須加班。

關聯字 invitation n. 邀請
MORE 一起比較一下和 invite 及 invitation 長得很像的字吧！
invest v. 投資；investment n. 投資
invent v. 發明；invention n. 發明

celebrate [`sɛlə͵bret]　v. 慶祝

S It was May's birthday yesterday, so she really wanted to **celebrate** with her best friend.
昨天是梅的生日，所以她真的很想和她最好的朋友一起慶祝。

關聯字 celebration n. 慶祝　celebratory adj. 慶祝的　celebrated adj. 有名的
There is a **celebratory** party tonight.
今晚有一個慶祝派對。
The restaurant is **celebrated** with its roast ducks.
這間餐廳以它的烤鴨聞名。

feel like　phr. 想要

S After the party, some of May's friends **felt like** singing at a karaoke bar.
在派對之後，梅的一些朋友想去 KTV 唱歌。

同義字 want、would like

shortly [ˈʃɔrtlɪ]　　adv. 不久，立刻

S **Shortly** after they arrived, May saw Jessie was in the lobby too, and she's with a handsome boy!
在他們抵達後不久，梅看到潔西也在大廳裡，而且她和一個帥哥在一起！

dismay [dɪsˈme]　　n. 沮喪，失望

S May was filled with **dismay** and said she would never want to see Jessie again.
梅感到非常失望，並說她永遠都不想再見到潔西。

同義字 disappointment、letdown

Day02_010　從小認識的朋友

→ 把你知道的單字打勾！
- [ ] childhood
- [ ] neighborhood
- [ ] via
- [ ] electronic
- [ ] cherish

→ 用 5 個字說出這張圖片的故事！

childhood [ˈtʃaɪld͵hʊd]　　n. 童年時期

S Jason and Jimmy have known each other since **childhood**.
傑森和吉米從小就認識了。

關聯字 child n. 孩童（單數）　children n. 孩童（複數）
　　　childish adj. 幼稚的　childlike adj. 天真無邪的

I hate my boyfriend's **childish** behavior.
我討厭我男友的幼稚行為。
It's so nice to talk with a **childlike** student.
跟天真無邪的學生說話真好。

neighborhood [ˈnɛbɚˌhʊd]　n. 住家附近的區域

- They used to live in the same **neighborhood**; however, Jason moved out last year.
  他們以前住在同一個社區，然而，傑森在去年搬走了。

  關聯字 neighbor n. 鄰居

via [ˈvaɪə]　prep. 透過；經由

- Now they connect with each other **via** messaging apps.
  現在他們會透過通訊軟體聯絡。

  MORE connect v. 與～建立良好關係

electronic [ɪlɛkˈtrɑnɪk]　adj. 電子的

- They also write to each other, from paper to **electronic**, the only thing unchanged is their friendship.
  他們也會寫信給對方，從紙本到電子，唯一不變的是他們的友誼。

  關聯字 electronic adj. 電子的　electric adj. 有電的
  　　　electricity n. 電力　electrician n. 電工

cherish [ˈtʃɛrɪʃ]　v. 珍惜

- They will **cherish** each other's company forever.
  他們會永遠珍惜彼此的陪伴。

回復記憶 階段

◆ 請參考以下在 Day02 中出現過的圖片，在單字旁的空格寫下字義。

006 我的好朋友
- encounter _____
- friendship _____
- appreciate _____
- sincerely _____
- precious _____

007 暗戀一個人
- proactive _____
- encourage _____
- gorgeous _____
- admirer _____
- hopefully _____

008 患難見真情
- suburb _____
- saying _____
- immediately _____
- accompany _____
- indecisive _____

009 這種朋友不交也罷！
- invite _____
- celebrate _____
- feel like _____
- shortly _____
- dismay _____

010 從小認識的朋友
- childhood _____
- neighborhood _____
- via _____
- electronic _____
- cherish _____

 階段

◆ 請依照提示的單字字首，在下列空格中填入適當的單字。
(1) 一位沮喪的學生　　　　　　a d_____ student
(2) 一個珍貴的項鍊　　　　　　a p_____ necklace
(3) 邀請所有的客戶　　　　　　i_____ all the clients
(4) 一位非常漂亮的女演員　　　a g_____ actress
(5) 一個危險的社區　　　　　　a dangerous n_____

◆ 請參考下列方框中的單字，在下列空格中填入適當的單字。

> 參考 | celebrate | indecisive | suburb | proactive |
> | encounter | immediately | appreciate | via |

(1) The shipment is in transit _____ trucks.
這批貨物正透過卡車運送中。

(2) He has a _____ personality.
他有著積極主動的個性。

(3) I haven't _____ serious problems at work.
我在工作中還沒遭遇過嚴重的問題。

(4) Quiet is an advantage of living in _____.
住在市郊的一個優點是安靜。

(5) Every victim _____ the public's help.
每一位受害者都感謝大眾的協助。

(6) Final exams are over. Let's _____ and have a good time.
期末考結束了。讓我們來慶祝一下並好好去玩。

(7) _____ after he came, Jessica took off without a word.
他來了後不久，潔西卡就不說一聲地離開了。

(8) _____ people always let their opportunities slip away.
優柔寡斷的人總是讓機會溜走。

Answers:
1. (1) dismay (2) precious (3) invite (4) gorgeous (5) neighborhood
2. (1) via (2) proactive (3) encountered (4) suburb (5) appreciate (6) celebrate (7) Immediately (8) Indecisive

Day 03 學校與朋友 011-015

Day03_011 學校社團展

→ 把你知道的單字打勾！
- [ ] fair
- [ ] booth
- [ ] particularly
- [ ] sign up
- [ ] practice

→ 用 5 個字說出這張圖片的故事！

fair [fɛr]　n. 展示會

S Anna went to the school club **fair** a few days ago.
安娜在幾天前去了學校的社團博覽會。

> **MORE** fair 這個字除了「展示會」的意思之外，當形容詞時還有「公平的；晴朗的；白皙的」等涵義，所以看到這個字的時候，要透過上下文和情境來判斷這裡的 fair 是什麼意思喔！

The competition is **fair**.（公平的）
這場競賽是公平的。
The weather was forecast **fair** tomorrow.（晴朗的）
氣象預報說明天天氣晴朗。
All my family are **fair**-skinned.（白皙的）
我們全家人都皮膚白皙。

booth [buθ]　n. 攤位

S Many **booths** were set up on campus to show the students all the benefits they would get if they join a club.
校園裡設立了很多攤位來告訴學生若他們加入社團可以得到的一切好處。

E telephone **booth** 電話亭
E security **booth** 警衛室

27

particularly [pɚˋtɪkjələ‧lɪ]　adv. 特別地；尤其地

S She was **particularly** interested in the debate club and the chess club.
她對辯論社及棋藝社特別感興趣。

> **MORE** 其他常見的社團名稱還有下面這些：
> film club 電影欣賞社　　　　dance club 舞蹈社
> photography club 攝影社　　computer club 電腦社
> 國外大學裡常見的兄弟會則是 fraternity，姐妹會則是 sorority。

sign up　phr. 報名；登記

S After she was introduced to a variety of clubs, Anna decided to **sign up** for the debate club.
在看過各式各樣的社團介紹後，安娜決定要報名辯論社。

practice [ˋpræktɪs]　v. 練習

S She has always hoped that she could express herself better, so she joined the club to **practice** more.
她一直都希望自己能更擅長表達，所以她加入社團來多加練習。

E **Practice** makes perfect. 熟能生巧。

Day03_012　學語言不容易

→ 把你知道的單字打勾！
☐ language
☐ fluently
☐ consequently
☐ enroll
☐ multilingual

→ 用 5 個字說出這張圖片的故事！

language [ˈlæŋgwɪdʒ]　n. 語言

- Ed is always interested in **language** learning.
  愛德一直都對學語言很有興趣。

  - **language** center 語言中心
  - **language** learning program 語言學習計畫

fluently [ˈfluəntlɪ]　adv. 流利地

- He hopes he can speak English **fluently** one day.
  他希望有天他能流利地說英文。

consequently [ˈkɑnsəˌkwɛntlɪ]　adv. 因此

- **Consequently**, he has tried to find the best way to learn English, but he still barely can talk in English.
  因此，他一直試著要找到學英文的最佳方法，但他還是幾乎不會說英文。

  [同義字] as a result、therefore、thus、hence、as a consequence、subsequently

  [MORE] 像 consequently 這種字，就是我們常聽到的「轉折語」，轉折語在寫作時特別重要，用得好的話，就能讓文章顯得條理分明又言之有物。

enroll [ɪnˈrol]　v. 登記；報名

- Some people advise him to **enroll** in a language learning program.
  有些人建議他去報名語言學習計畫。

multilingual [ˌmʌltɪˈlɪŋgwəl]　adj. 使用多國語言的

- Besides English, he also wants to learn other languages, such as French and German; and with proper training methods, he may be **multilingual** one day.
  除了英文，他也想學其他語言，像是法文及德文，有了正確的學習方法，也許有天他就能使用多國語言了

  [關聯字] monolingual adj. 單一語言的　bilingual adj. 雙語言的
  [MORE] 上面的關聯字中，可以看到「-lingual」部分不斷出現，不同的部分只有字首，一起來看看這些常用的字首吧！
  mono-：單一的 → monopoly n. 獨占，壟斷
  bi-：雙的 → bicycle n. 腳踏車
  multi-：多的 → multifunction n. 多功能

Day 03 學校與朋友 011-015

Day03_013 網友

→ 把你知道的單字打勾！
- [ ] net friend
- [ ] forum
- [ ] fashion
- [ ] typical
- [ ] fortunate

→ 用 5 個字說出這張圖片的故事！

net friend [nɛt`frɛnd]　phr. 網友

I have a **net friend** named Jane, who is a really lovely girl.
我有一個叫做珍的網友，她是一個真的很討人喜歡的女孩。

MORE 在還沒有網路的時候，人們會透過寫信來交友，這種朋友就是 **pen pal**（筆友）。此外，**net friend** 是指真的和自己有交情、透過網路認識的朋友，如果是想指沒有真正交情的「網民」，則要用 **netizen** 這個字，這個字是從 **net**（網路）和 **citizen**（公民）組合而來的。

forum [`forəm]　n. 論壇

We often chat in a **forum** on the Internet, but we never meet face-to-face.
我們經常在網路論壇上聊天，但我們從來沒有面對面地見過面。

MORE **Internet** 也可以用 **net** 替代，因為網際網路是專有名詞，所以第一個字母要記得大寫。

fashion [`fæʃən]　n. 流行時尚

We usually talk about **fashion** and share the latest information with each other.
我們通常會討論流行時尚並彼此分享最新消息。

關聯字 in fashion = fashionable adj. 流行時尚的　trendy adj. 流行的
反義字 old-fashioned

typical [ˈtɪpɪkl]　adj. 普通的，典型的

Ⓢ Although we are not the **typical** type of friends, we still care about each other.
儘管我們不是典型的那種朋友，但我們仍然關心彼此。

　Ⓔ a **typical** day 普通的一天
　Ⓔ **typical** weather 典型的天氣

fortunate [ˈfɔrtʃənɪt]　adj. 幸運的

Ⓢ It's truly **fortunate** that I could meet Jane on the Internet and befriend her!
我能在網路上遇見珍並和她做朋友，真的很幸運！

反義字 unfortunate
同義字 lucky
關聯字 fortune n. 命運；財富

Day03_014 好朋友帶你飛！

→ 把你知道的單字打勾！
☐ accommodating
☐ volunteer
☐ wisdom
☐ manage
☐ relationship

→ 用 5 個字說出這張圖片的故事！

accommodating [əˈkɑməˌdetɪŋ]　adj. 隨和的；樂於助人的

Ⓢ Lillian is one of my best friends, and she is **accommodating** and considerate.
莉莉安是我最好的朋友之一，而且她既隨和又體貼。

關聯字 accommodate v. 容納；迎合
　　　accommodation n. 住宿設施；適應

Day 03 學校與朋友 011-015

volunteer [ˌvɑlən`tɪr]　　v. 自願提供；自願做

- When I was facing financial problems, she was the one who **volunteered** to help.
  在我遇到財務問題時，她是那個自願要幫我的人。

wisdom [`wɪzdəm]　　n. 智慧

- She is the kind of friend who is full of **wisdom**.
  她是那種充滿智慧的朋友。

  關聯字　wisdom n. 智慧　　wise adj. 有智慧的

manage [`mænɪdʒ]　　v. 管理；控制

- She often tells me how to **manage** my money for better use.
  她常常告訴我要如何管理和妥善運用我的錢。

  關聯字　management n. 管理
  　　　　business management n. 商業管理
  　　　　human resources management n. 人力資源管理
  　　　　finance management n. 財務管理
  　　　　marketing management n. 行銷管理

relationship [rɪ`leʃənˌʃɪp]　　n. 關係

- The **relationship** between us is very special and close, and I'm lucky to have her as my friend.
  我們之間的關係非常特別又緊密，我很幸運有她當我的朋友。

Day03_015　閨密奪愛

→ 把你知道的單字打勾！
- ☐ cheerful
- ☐ beloved
- ☐ suspiciously
- ☐ lip
- ☐ shocking

→ 用 5 個字說出這張圖片的故事！

32

cheerful [ˈtʃɪrfəl]　adj. 令人愉快的；興高采烈的

- Holly used to be my close friend, and she was a **cheerful** person to me.
  荷莉曾是我很親近的朋友，她以前對我來說是一個令人愉快的人。

  關聯字 cheers n. 歡呼　cheer up phr. 振奮某人　cheerleader n. 啦啦隊隊長

beloved [bɪˈlʌvɪd]　adj. 心愛的；被喜愛的

- One day, I introduced my **beloved** boyfriend to her, and we had an awesome dinner together that night.
  有天我介紹我心愛的男朋友給他認識，並在那天晚上一起吃了一頓很棒的晚餐。

  MORE 在英文裡還有很多可以表達「親近」、「喜愛」的說法，例如 **sweetheart**、**darling**、**dear** 等等。

suspiciously [səˈspɪʃəslɪ]　adv. 可疑地；疑心很重地

- However, yesterday I found my boyfriend talking to someone **suspiciously** on the phone and he went out right away.
  然而，昨天我發現我的男友很可疑地在和某人講電話，而且他立刻就出去了。

  關聯字 suspicious adj. 可疑的　suspect v. 懷疑　suspect n. 嫌疑犯

lip [lɪp]　n. 嘴唇

- I followed him and caught him kissing Holly on her **lips**.
  我跟蹤了他並抓到他正在親吻荷莉的雙唇。

shocking [ˈʃɑkɪŋ]　adj. 令人震驚的

- What a **shocking** sight! My best friend and my dear boyfriend betrayed me!
  這是多麼令人震驚的一幕啊！我最好的朋友和我的愛人背叛了我！

回復記憶 階段

◆ 請參考以下在 Day03 中出現過的圖片,在單字旁的空格寫下字義。

011 學校社團展
- fair ....
- booth ....
- particularly ....
- sign up ....
- practice ....

012 學語言不容易
- language ....
- fluently ....
- consequently ....
- enroll ....
- multilingual ....

013 網友
- net friend ....
- forum ....
- fashion ....
- typical ....
- fortunate ....

014 好朋友帶你飛!
- accommodating ....
- volunteer ....
- wisdom ....
- manage ....
- relationship ....

015 閨密奪愛
- cheerful ....
- beloved ....
- suspiciously ....
- lips ....
- shocking ....

加深記憶 階段

◆ 請依照提示的單字字首，在下列空格中填入適當的單字。

(1) 一種困難的語言　　　　a difficult l_____
(2) 一個令人震驚的意外　　a s_____ accident
(3) 一段友善的關係　　　　a friendly r_____
(4) 一個心愛的男朋友　　　a _____ boyfriend
(5) 一位隨和的主管　　　　an a_____ supervisor
(6) 我普通的一天　　　　　my t_____ day

◆ 請參考下列方框中的單字，在下列空格中填入適當的單字。

參考 | fair | practice | cheerful | manage | particularly | fortunate | consequently

(1) You should learn how to _____ your emotion.
    你應該要學習如何管理你的情緒。

(2) There are many businessmen in this trade _____.
    這次貿易展中有很多商務人士。

(3) She is a girl with a _____ smile.
    她是一個有著令人愉悅微笑的女孩。

(4) My teacher asks us to _____ speaking English every day.
    我的老師要求我們每天練習說英文。

(5) I was so _____ that I won the lottery.
    我真的非常幸運而中了樂透。

(6) Jack really likes seafood, _____ shrimps and octopus.
    傑克真的很喜歡海鮮，尤其是蝦子與章魚。

(7) I was sick in bed, _____, I didn't go to my office today.
    我臥病在床，因此，我今天沒有進辦公室。

(8) The event _____ guided me to the venue.
    活動志工引導我去到了會場。

Answers:
1. (1) language (2) shocking (3) relationship (4) beloved (5) accommodating (6) typical
2. (1) manage (2) fair (3) cheerful (4) practice (5) fortunate (6) particularly (7) consequently (8) volunteer

記單字必備！掌握常見字根 01

01 -spire 呼吸；氣息
ex<u>spire</u> 滿期，屆期；（期限）終止
con<u>spire</u> 共謀，密謀；共同促成
re<u>spire</u> 呼吸
a<u>spire</u> 抱負，嚮往
in<u>spire</u> 啟發；激勵；促使

02 -volve 旋轉；轉動
e<u>volve</u> 逐步形成；發展；進化；引申出
de<u>volve</u> 將～下放；轉移，移交
in<u>volve</u> 使捲入；牽涉；包含
re<u>volve</u> 旋轉，自轉

03 -rupt 斷裂
bank<u>rupt</u> 破產的
inter<u>rupt</u> 打斷（對話或說話的人）
ab<u>rupt</u> 突然的；魯莽的
e<u>rupt</u> 噴出；爆發

04 -scribe 書寫
de<u>scribe</u> 描寫，描繪；敘述
pre<u>scribe</u> 開（藥方）
sub<u>scribe</u> 訂閱
circum<u>scribe</u> 在周圍畫線；限制
tran<u>scribe</u> 抄寫，謄寫

05 -serv 保有
ob<u>serv</u>e 觀察，注意；遵守
re<u>serv</u>e 保存；預訂
de<u>serv</u>e 應受；值得
pre<u>serv</u>e 保存；防腐；維護
con<u>serv</u>e 保存；保護；節省

06 -vac 空的
<u>vac</u>ation 假期
<u>vac</u>ancy 空白
<u>vac</u>uum 真空
e<u>vac</u>uate 撤離

07 -dict 說
pre<u>dict</u> 預測；預言；預報
contra<u>dict</u> 提出論據反駁；反對；與～發生矛盾
in<u>dict</u> 告發；起訴
inter<u>dict</u> 禁制；制止

08 -mit 發送；放出
com<u>mit</u> 犯下（罪行等）；致力於；投入
e<u>mit</u> 發散；射出；發出
per<u>mit</u> 批准，許可
trans<u>mit</u> 傳送，傳達
vo<u>mit</u> 嘔吐

Day 04 旅遊與冒險 016-020

Day04_016 英倫之旅

→ 把你知道的單字打勾！
- [ ] hobby
- [ ] camera
- [ ] memorable
- [ ] landmark
- [ ] recall

→ 用 5 個字說出這張圖片的故事！

hobby [ˋhɑbɪ]　n. 嗜好

S As a backpacker, traveling to foreign countries is my **hobby**.
身為一個背包客，到國外去旅行是我的嗜好。

關聯字 pastime n. 消遣　interest n. 興趣

camera [ˋkæmərə]　n. 相機

S When I go abroad traveling, I always carry a **camera** with me.
當我到國外旅行時，我總是會帶著一台相機。

MORE 這裡補充一些平時常會帶在身上的東西的說法：
cell phone 手機　thermos 保溫瓶　handbag 手提包　wallet 皮夾
keychain 鑰匙圈　coin purse/pouch 零錢包　laptop 筆記型電腦
reusable shopping bag 環保購物袋　earphone 耳機　wet wipe 濕紙巾

memorable [ˋmɛmərəbl]　adj. 難忘的；值得紀念的

S For me, taking pictures is the best way to preserve those **memorable** experiences.
對我而言，拍照是保存那些難忘經驗的最佳方法。

E **memorable** childhood 難忘的童年

關聯字 memory n. 紀念　memorize v. 記憶

landmark [ˈlænd͵mɑrk]　n. 地標

🅢 I will never forget the joy of seeing Big Ben, which is a famous **landmark** in England, for the first time.
我永遠不會忘記第一次見到英國知名地標大笨鐘時的喜悅。

> **MORE** 除了 landmark 之外，還有很多地方是旅行時必去的：
> monument 紀念碑　museum 博物館　aquarium 水族館
> amusement park 遊樂園　botanic garden 植物園　observatory 觀景台

recall [rɪˈkɔl]　v. 回想

🅢 I can just pull up the pictures whenever I want to **recall** those precious memories.
每當我想要回想這些珍貴的回憶時，我只要把照片叫出來就行了。

Day04_017　令人毛骨悚然的景點

→ 把你知道的單字打勾！
- [ ] ancient
- [ ] castle
- [ ] scenic spot
- [ ] creepy
- [ ] apart from

→ 用 5 個字說出這張圖片的故事！

ancient [ˈenʃənt]　adj. 古老的；古代的

🅢 Last summer, our family had a trip to Europe, and we were interested in seeing **ancient** architecture.
去年夏天，我們家去了歐洲旅行，而我們都想去看看古老的建築物。

> 反義字　modern adj. 現代的　contemporary adj. 當代的

castle [ˈkæsl̩]　n. 城堡

🅢 Following the recommendation of the guidebooks, we went to an old **castle** in central Europe.
照著旅遊指南的建議，我們去了中歐的一個古堡。

scenic spot [ˈsinɪk] [spɑt]　n.（有美麗景色的）景點

- According to the guidebooks, it's a beautiful and well-known **scenic spot**.
  根據旅遊指南所說，它是一個漂亮的知名景點。

  > **MORE** scenic 的意思是「風光明媚的」，因此 scenic spot 所說的「景點」，是指以風景如畫為賣點的那種景點，如果不是以景色為賣點，則可以用 attraction 來表達。

  > **關聯字** spot n. 地點；汙點

creepy [ˈkripɪ]　adj. 令人毛骨悚然的

- However, when we finally arrived there, we were all shocked by its **creepy** appearance and weird atmosphere.
  然而，當我們終於抵達那裡時，我們都被它令人毛骨悚然的外表及詭異的氛圍給嚇到了。

apart from　phr. 除了

- **Apart from** that, the weather that day was really terrible, and it made us feel even more uncomfortable.
  除此之外，那天的天氣非常糟糕，而這讓我們覺得更不舒服了。

  > **MORE** 形容「狀態很糟糕」，除了 terrible（糟糕的）之外，也可以簡單用 bad 來形容，horrible（駭人的；恐怖的）、lousy（差勁的）、awful（極糟的）等形容詞也很常用。

  > **同義字** aside from

Day04_018　旅途中看音樂表演

→ 把你知道的單字打勾！
- [ ] concert
- [ ] spectator
- [ ] total
- [ ] especially
- [ ] original

→ 用 5 個字說出這張圖片的故事！

Day 04 旅遊與冒險 016・020

concert [ˈkɑnsɚt]　n. 音樂會，演唱會

S When I was traveling in New York, I went to a wonderful outdoor **concert**.
當我在紐約旅行時，我去看了一個戶外音樂會。

spectator [spɛkˋtetɚ]　n. 觀眾

S There were many **spectators** in front of the stage, and they really enjoyed the show very much, just like me.
在舞台前有很多觀眾，而且他們真的很享受這場表演，就像我一樣。

- **E** **spectator** crowds 觀眾群
- **E** exciting **spectators** 興奮的觀眾

total [ˈtotl]　adj. 總計的，全體的

S On the stage, a **total** of three musicians were playing their instruments beautifully.
在舞台上，總共三位音樂家正在優美地演奏著自己的樂器。

MORE 這裡補充一些常見的樂器名稱：
flute 長笛　violin 小提琴　viola 中提琴　cello 大提琴
double bass 低音大提琴　saxophone 薩克斯風　drums 鼓
oboe 雙簧管　piano 鋼琴　clarinet 單簧管

especially [əˋspɛʃəlɪ]　adv. 尤其，特別

S Among all the musicians, I **especially** liked the double bass player; the tones he played were truly a pleasure to hear.
在這些音樂家之中，我尤其喜歡那個低音大提琴的演奏者，他演奏的曲子真的很好聽。

同義字 particularly、in particular

original [əˋrɪdʒənl]　adj. 有原創性的；原始的

S Even better, the music he played was all **original**!
更厲害的是，他表演的音樂都是原創的！

關聯字 origin n. 起源　originally adv. 原始地　originality n. 原始性

Day04_019 巴黎之旅

→ 把你知道的單字打勾！
- [ ] abroad
- [ ] destination
- [ ] romantic
- [ ] tourist
- [ ] in front of

→ 用 5 個字說出這張圖片的故事！

---

abroad [əˋbrɔd]　adv. 在國外；在海外

🅢 This was the first time that I had been **abroad**.
這是我第一次出國。

同義字 overseas

destination [͵dɛstəˋneʃən]　n. 目的地

🅢 European countries have been always the dream **destinations** for me, especially France.
歐洲國家一直都是我的夢想目的地，尤其是法國。

romantic [rəˋmæntɪk]　adj. 浪漫的

🅢 France is notable for its long history, beautiful scenery, and **romantic** atmosphere.
法國以它的長久歷史、美麗風景及浪漫氛圍聞名。

關聯字 romance n. 風流韻事；浪漫情調

tourist [ˋtʊrɪst]　n. 觀光客

🅢 The most attractive **tourist** spot in Paris is the Eiffel Tower.
巴黎最吸引人的觀光景點是艾菲爾鐵塔。

關聯字 tourism n. 觀光；旅遊業　tour guide n. 導遊

41

in front of　phr. 在～的前方

🅢 See, I was **in front of** the Eiffel Tower to have my photograph taken.
你看，我在艾菲爾鐵塔的前面照了像。

> **MORE** 在描述相對位置時，英文裡有很多不同的常見表達方式，下面是一些一定要會的描述方法，一起來看看吧！

before prep. 在～的前方＝in front of
in back of phr. 在～的後方＝after＝behind
kitty corner to phr. 在～的斜對角
across from phr. 在～的對面＝opposite
next to phr. 在～的旁邊＝beside＝alongside＝by

Day04_020　日本神社之旅

→ 把你知道的單字打勾！
- [ ] when it comes to
- [ ] behave
- [ ] temple
- [ ] pray
- [ ] career

→ 用 5 個字說出這張圖片的故事！

---

when it comes to　phr. 當我們談到～

🅢 **When it comes to** traveling abroad, Japan is my first choice.
當我們談到去國外旅遊，日本是我的第一選擇。

> **MORE** when it comes to（當我們談到～）是一個很常在寫作時用到的開頭，意思相似的還有 speaking of，下次在寫文章時可以用用看。

When it comes to/Speaking of gardening, Kelly is really good at it.
當我們談到園藝，凱莉是真的很擅長。

---

behave　[bɪˋhev]　v. 表現；行為

🅢 Every time I travel to Japan, I always **behave** myself and try to act like a Japanese person.
每次我去日本旅遊，我都會很守規矩並試著表現得像個日本人。

MORE behave oneself 某人守規矩
Tim is a good boy. He **behaves himself** all the time.
提姆是個好男孩。他總是守規矩。

temple [ˋtɛmpl]　n. 廟宇

🅢 Last year I went to a Japanese traditional **temple** in Japan.
去年我去了在日本的一間日式傳統廟宇。

> **MORE** 表示「廟宇」的 temple，不管是拼法還是唸法，都和 tempo（節奏）很像，在使用的時候要小心不要搞混了。

pray [pre]　v. 祈禱；祈求

🅢 Many people there were following a unique procedure for worshipping and **praying**.
在那裡的很多人都在照著一個獨特的步驟來拜拜和祈禱。

career [kəˋrɪr]　n. 職業生涯

🅢 I imitated the people beside me and prayed for gaining good luck in my future **career** and love life.
我模仿了我旁邊人的動作並祈求在未來職涯和愛情上能有好運。

> 關聯字　career planning 職業生涯規劃
> 　　　　career prospect 職業生涯前景

回復記憶 階段

◆ 請參考以下在 Day04 中出現過的圖片，在單字旁的空格寫下字義。

016 英倫之旅
- hobby _____
- camera _____
- memorable _____
- landmark _____
- recall _____

017 令人毛骨悚然的景點
- ancient _____
- castle _____
- scenic spot _____
- creepy _____
- apart from _____

018 旅途中看音樂表演
- concert _____
- spectator _____
- total _____
- especially _____
- original _____

019 巴黎之旅
- abroad _____
- destination _____
- romantic _____
- tourist _____
- in front of _____

020 日本神社之旅
- when it comes to _____
- behave _____
- temple _____
- pray _____
- career _____

加深記憶階段

◆ 請依照提示的單字字首，在下列空格中填入適當的單字。

(1) 一個古老的城市　　　　　an a_____ city
(2) 一首原創的歌曲　　　　　an o_____ song
(3) 一個有名的景點　　　　　a famous s_____ spot
(4) 一些興奮的觀眾　　　　　some exciting s_____
(5) 一場成功的音樂會　　　　a successful c_____

◆ 請參考下列方框中的單字，在下列空格中填入適當的單字。

| 參考 | hobby | memorable | apart from | destination |
| romantic | total | especially | when it comes to |

(1) _____ math, no one in the class can beat Henry.
當我們談到數學，班上沒有人可以比得上亨利。

(2) _____ history, I also like other subjects.
除了歷史之外，我也喜歡其他科目。

(3) Staying in an island for a vacation is the most _____ experience for me.
在一個島上度假對我來說是最難忘的經驗。

(4) Singing at a karaoke bar is my _____.
在 KTV 唱歌是我的嗜好。

(5) I like this small restaurant because its atmosphere is so _____.
我喜歡這間小餐廳，因為它的氣氛非常浪漫。

(6) The _____ amount is too much for me to pay.
總金額對我來說高到付不出來。

(7) Where is your next _____?
你的下一個目的地在哪裡？

(8) I am _____ interested in this topic.
我對這個主題尤其感興趣。

Answers:
1. (1) ancient (2) original (3) scenic (4) spectators (5) concert
2. (1) When it comes to (2) Apart from (3) memorable (4) hobby (5) romantic (6) total
   (7) destination (8) especially

Day 05 旅遊與冒險 021-025

Day05_021 難得的露營之旅

→ 把你知道的單字打勾！
- ☐ camp
- ☐ stuff
- ☐ tent
- ☐ campfire
- ☐ superb

→ 用 5 個字說出這張圖片的故事！

camp [kæmp]　v. 露營

S Jason and I had been looking forward to this **camping** trip since last month.
傑森和我從上個月開始就一直期待著這次的露營之旅。

> 同義字 expect、anticipate
> MORE camp 除了當動詞之外，也可以當名詞，當名詞時是「野營；帳篷」的意思。但若想說的是「露營這件事」，則會在字尾加上 -ing 變成 camping，「去露營」的說法就是 go camping。

stuff [stʌf]　n. 東西，物品

S We had planned it for a while, and we'd prepared a lot of **stuff** before we set off.
我們已經籌劃了一陣子，且我們在出發前準備了很多東西。

> **E** useless **stuff** 無用的東西
> MORE stuff 本身是不可數名詞，而最常見的 thing（東西，物品）則是可數名詞，使用時要特別注意。

tent [tɛnt]　n. 帳篷

S At the campsite, we put up the **tent** quickly and without any problem.
在營地中，我們很快架好帳篷，沒有碰到任何問題。

> **MORE** 這裡補充一些與露營相關的單字：
> campsite n. 營地　　put up phr. 架設　　sleeping bag n. 睡袋
> camping lamp n. 露營燈　　peg n. 固定釘　　flashlight n. 手電筒
> gas stove n. 卡式爐　　grill v. 燒烤　　start a fire phr. 生火

campfire [ˋkæmp͵faɪr]　n. 營火

S At night, we set up the **campfire** to warm us, and we chatted happily all night.
我們晚上的時候升起了營火來取暖並快樂地聊了整晚。

> **MORE** 「升起營火」的英文是 set up the campfire，而「撲滅營火」的說法則是 put out the campfire。

superb [sʊˋpɝb]　adj. 絕佳的；極好的

S We had a **superb** time together, so we immediately decided to start planning for the next camping trip.
我們一起度過了一段美好的時光，所以我們立刻決定要開始規劃下次的露營之旅了。

> 同義字 great、fantastic、fabulous、marvelous、wonderful、terrific

Day05_022 我是背包客

→ 把你知道的單字打勾！
- [ ] backpacker
- [ ] brave
- [ ] effort
- [ ] in advance
- [ ] hostel

→ 用 5 個字說出這張圖片的故事！

Day 05 旅遊與冒險 021-025

47

backpacker [ˈbækˌpækɚ]　n. 背包客

- Lisa has always wanted to be a **backpacker**.
  麗莎一直想要當背包客。

  > **MORE** travel with a group 跟團旅行
  > travel alone = travel by oneself 獨自旅行
  >
  > I never **travel with a group**. I always **travel by myself**.
  > 我從不跟團旅行。我總是一個人旅行。

brave [brev]　adj. 勇敢的

- She is **brave** and has a good sense of direction.
  她勇敢又有很好的方向感。

  > **MORE** sense of humor 幽默感
  > sense of accomplishment 成就感
  > sense of happiness 幸福感
  > sense of relief 解脫感
  > sense of insecurity 不安全感

effort [ˈɛfɚt]　n. 努力

- Every time she plans to travel, she puts a lot of **effort** into doing the research.
  每一次她計畫去旅行時，她都很努力做功課。

in advance　phr. 事先地

- Lisa tells me that she likes to be prepared **in advance**.
  麗莎告訴我說她喜歡事先做好準備。

hostel [ˈhɑstl̩]　n.（青年）旅舍

- To save money, she choose to book **hostels** instead of fancy hotels.
  為了省錢，她選擇訂青年旅舍而不是高級飯店。

  > **MORE** hostel 是設施簡單、且須與其他住宿者共享房間的旅舍，住宿費用較一般的旅館或飯店來得便宜。

Day05_023 坐錯位子啦！

→ 把你知道的單字打勾！
- [ ] instead of
- [ ] historic
- [ ] conductor
- [ ] politely
- [ ] correct

→ 用 5 個字說出這張圖片的故事！

instead of　　phr. 代替，而不是

S **Instead of** taking a train, I always choose to travel by HSR.
我總是選擇搭高鐵而不是台鐵去旅行。

historic　[hɪsˋtɔrɪk]　　adj. 歷史性的；具有歷史價值的

S Today, I went to Tainan to visit **historic** buildings and have great food.
今天我去台南看歷史古蹟和吃美食。

E **historic** site 歷史遺跡，歷史景點

MORE historical 這個字和 historic 長得很像，但意思卻完全不一樣，historical 是「歷史的；有關歷史的」，與無形的價值或意義無關。
historic site：具有歷史性的價值，例如紀念碑、古建築、遺址等等。
historical site：與歷史相關的地點，例如博物館、歷史研究中心等等。

conductor　[kənˋdʌktɚ]　　n. 列車長；指揮

S After I found my seat and sat down, the **conductor** came to me and asked me to show my ticket.
在我找到座位坐下之後，列車長過來要我出示車票。

MORE conductor 除了「列車長」的意思之外，也是「樂團指揮」的意思。

politely　[pəˋlaɪtlɪ]　　adv. 禮貌地

S After checking my ticket, he **politely** said, "Miss, your seat is 26A, not 28A".
在檢查了我的車票之後，他禮貌地說：「小姐，你的座位是 26A，而不是 28A」。

correct [kəˋrɛkt]　adj. 正確的

- I thanked him and stood up right away to move to the **correct** seat.
  我向他道謝並立刻起身換去正確的座位。

Day05_024　可怕的搭機經驗

→ 把你知道的單字打勾！
- [ ] bumpy
- [ ] turbulence
- [ ] vomit
- [ ] flight attendant
- [ ] awful

→ 用 5 個字說出這張圖片的故事！

bumpy [ˋbʌmpɪ]　adj. 顛簸的

- I was flying from Taipei to New York, and it's the **bumpiest** flying experience ever.
  我之前從台北飛紐約，而這是有史以來最顛簸的一次飛行經驗。

  E **bumpy** flight 顛簸的航程

turbulence [ˋtɝbjələns]　n. 亂流

- The **turbulence** made me sick and very uncomfortable.
  亂流讓我覺得噁心又非常不舒服。

  MORE turbulence 指的是紊亂、不規則的氣流，若只是普通的「氣流」則是 air current。

vomit [ˋvɑmɪt]　v. 嘔吐

- The headache and dizziness also made me feel like **vomiting**.
  頭痛和暈眩也讓我很想吐。

  同義字 throw up

MORE feel like 是「想要」的意思，後面會接「V-ing」，意思相同的 want 的後面則是接「to＋原形動詞」。
I **feel like drinking** some water. ＝ I **want to drink** some water.
我想要喝一些水。

flight attendant [flaɪt] [ə`tɛndənt]　n. 空服員

Ⓢ I asked a **flight attendant** to give me an extra blanket to keep myself warm.
我請空服員多給我一張毯子來保暖。

awful [`ɔful]　adj. 可怕的；極糟的

Ⓢ I have truly wished I had never been on this **awful** flight.
我真希望我從來沒上過這班可怕的飛機。

同義字 terrible、horrible、unpleasant
I have to say this is a **terrible/horrible/unpleasant** party.
我必須要說這是個糟糕的派對。

Day05_025　一個人看恐怖片

→ 把你知道的單字打勾！
☐ timid
☐ horror
☐ nominate
☐ persuade
☐ frightened

→ 用 5 個字說出這張圖片的故事！

timid [`tɪmɪd]　adj. 膽小的

Ⓢ Let me tell you a secret, I'm a **timid** person and I'm really afraid of ghosts and darkness.
讓我告訴你一個祕密，我是個膽小的人，而且我非常怕鬼又怕黑。

反義字 brave adj. 勇敢的

horror [ˈhɔrɚ]　n. 恐怖；令人覺得恐怖的事物

S One day, my best friend recommended a **horror** movie to me.
有一天，我最好的朋友推薦了我一部恐怖片。

> MORE　除了恐怖片之外，電影還有很多不同的分類：
> action movie 動作片　　animated movie 動畫片　　romance 愛情片
> thriller 驚悚片　　documentary 紀錄片　　comedy 喜劇片　　drama 劇情片

nominate [ˈnɑməˌnet]　v. 提名

S My friend said it was a popular movie, and the leading actress was **nominated** for the Oscar for best actress.
我朋友說這是一部熱門電影，且女主角被提名了奧斯卡的最佳女主角獎。

> 關聯字　nominee n. 被提名人　　nominator n. 提名人　　nomination n. 提名

persuade [pɚˈswed]　v. 說服

S I was **persuaded** to watch the film alone on Saturday night.
我被說服在週六的晚上自己看了這部電影。

> MORE　persuade 是「說服某人去做某事」的意思，per- 字首帶有「徹底；強烈」的意味，而 -suade 則有「力勸，慫恿」的意思，因此若將 per- 換成表示「否定；遠離」的 dis- 字首，變成 dissuade，字義就會變成「說服某人不去做某事」。

They **persuaded** me **to join** them
他們說服我來加入他們。
They **dissuaded** me **from joining** them
他們說服我不要加入他們。

frightened [ˈfraɪtn̩d]　adj. 害怕的

S I really regret I made this decision, because I was almost **frightened** to death.
我真的很後悔我做了這個決定，因為我幾乎要被嚇死了。

回復記憶 階段

◆ 請參考以下在 Day05 中出現過的圖片，在單字旁的空格寫下字義。

021 難得的露營之旅
- camp _____
- stuff _____
- tent _____
- campfire _____
- superb _____

022 我是背包客
- backpacker _____
- brave _____
- effort _____
- in advance _____
- hostel _____

023 坐錯位子啦！
- instead of _____
- historic _____
- conductor _____
- politely _____
- correct _____

024 可怕的搭機經驗
- bumpy _____
- turbulence _____
- vomit _____
- flight attendant _____
- awful _____

025 一個人看恐怖片
- timid _____
- horror _____
- nominate _____
- persuade _____
- frightened _____

Day 05 旅遊與冒險 021-025

加深記憶階段

◆ 請依照提示的單字字首，在下列空格中填入適當的單字。

(1) 一位被提名的演員　　　　a n_____ actor
(2) 一個可怕的意外　　　　　an a_____ accident
(3) 一位火車列車長　　　　　a train c_____
(4) 一位有經驗的背包客　　　an experienced b_____
(5) 一個有歷史意義的地點　　a h_____ site

◆ 請參考下列方框中的單字，在下列空格中填入適當的單字。

參考 | stuff | persuade | effort | frightened | timid | politely | hostel | in advance

(1) Hank, clean your room quickly and throw away those useless _____.
漢克，快點清理你的房間，把那些沒用的東西丟掉。

(2) _____ are much cheaper than hotels.
青年旅舍比飯店要便宜很多。

(3) The children were _____ by lightning and thunder.
孩子們被閃電與雷聲嚇到了。

(4) We should prepare _____.
我們應該預先準備。

(5) My students talked to me _____.
我的學生禮貌地和我說話。

(6) I can _____ my associates to accept my ideas.
我可以說服我的同事接受我的想法。

(7) Are you too_____ to ask for a raise?
你膽小到不敢要求加薪嗎？

(8) I made _____ to make them believe me.
我努力要讓他們相信我。

Answers:
1. (1) nominated (2) awful (3) conductor (4) backpacker (5) historic
2. (1) stuff (2) Hostels (3) frightened (4) in advance (5) politely (6) persuade (7) timid (8) efforts

Day 06 旅遊與冒險 026-030

Day06_026 好玩的節慶活動

→ 把你知道的單字打勾！
- ☐ festival
- ☐ attend
- ☐ exhibition
- ☐ agriculture
- ☐ energetic

→ 用 5 個字說出這張圖片的故事！

---

festival [ˈfɛstəv!]　**n.** 節慶；（音樂、影視等的）節

S Have you ever been to a **festival** held abroad?
你曾去過辦在國外的節慶活動嗎？

> **MORE** 除了festival，其他常見的活動類型還有：
> fair 集會，市集　carnival 嘉年華會，園遊會　expo 博覽會
> exhibition 展覽　party 派對

---

attend [əˈtɛnd]　**v.** 參與；出席

S My classmate and I **attended** a festival when we were studying abroad.
我和我同學在國外念書時參加了一個節慶活動。

> **關聯字** attendee **n.** 參與者　attendant **n.** 服務人員　attentive **adj.** 專注的

---

exhibition [ˌɛksəˈbɪʃən]　**n.** 展示；展覽

S There were many different **exhibitions** and interesting shows held there.
那裡有很多不同的展覽和有趣的表演。

E special **exhibition** 特展

E permanent **exhibition** 常設展
E solo **exhibition** 個展
E group **exhibition** 聯展
E traveling **exhibition** 巡迴展

agriculture [ˈægrɪˌkʌltʃɚ]　n. 農業

S The festival was about **agriculture**, so we saw a lot of unique vegetables and fruits.
因為這個節慶活動和農業有關，所以我們看到了很多獨特的蔬菜和水果。

energetic [ˌɛnɚˈdʒɛtɪk]　adj. 有活力的；精力旺盛的

S Although the venue was really large, we still felt **energetic** and not tired at all.
儘管場地真的很大，但我們仍然覺得很有活力，而且一點也不累。

反義字 listless、tired

Day06_027　老鼠的復仇

→ 把你知道的單字打勾！
☐ cabin
☐ irritate
☐ revenge
☐ ambush
☐ tail

→ 用 5 個字說出這張圖片的故事！

cabin [ˈkæbɪn]　n. 小屋；（飛機等的）艙

S In a little wooden **cabin**, there is a cat, a mouse and their owner.
在一個小木屋中，有一隻貓、一隻老鼠以及他們的主人。

irritate [ˈɪrəˌtet]　v. 激怒

🅢 The cat likes to chase the mouse for fun, which **irritates** the mouse very much.
這隻貓喜歡追這隻老鼠來取樂，這讓老鼠非常憤怒。

> **MORE** irritate 這個字也有「使發炎；刺激」的意思。過去式的 irritated 則可以當作形容詞「被激怒的；發炎的」。

The smoke **irritated** my eyes.（刺激）
煙霧刺激到我的雙眼。
I am **irritated** by his rude attitude.（被激怒的）
我被他的無理態度給激怒。

revenge [rɪˈvɛndʒ]　n. 報復

🅢 The mouse wants to seek **revenge** on the cat.
這隻老鼠想要找機會報復這隻貓。

ambush [ˈæmbʊʃ]　v. 伏擊

🅢 It is difficult for a mouse to fight back facing a cat, so he decides to **ambush** the cat.
對一隻老鼠來說，很難在面對一隻貓時反擊回去，所以他決定要伏擊那隻貓。

> **MORE** ambush 是動詞和名詞同形的單字，意思都是「躲起來等待目標物出現，再出其不意地進行攻擊」，如 lie in ambush（進行埋伏）或 wait in ambush（等待進行埋伏）都是很常用到的表達方式。這邊一併補充一些與「攻擊」相關的字彙。

attack v. 攻擊　　strike v. 猛擊　　slaughter v. 屠殺　　bombard v. 轟炸
shell v. 砲擊　　raid v. 突襲　　slay v. 殘殺　　assault v. 毆打　　siege v. 圍攻
invade v. 入侵　　offense v. 冒犯

tail [tel]　n. 尾巴

🅢 One day, the mouse jumps out of nowhere and bites the cat's **tail** really hard.
有一天，這隻老鼠突然跳出來並狠狠咬了那隻貓的尾巴。

> **MORE** out of nowhere 如果照字面翻譯，就是「出自不知名的地方」，衍生出來的意思就是「非常突然；出乎預料」，這是相當常用的表達方式。

Day06_028 滑雪之旅

→ 把你知道的單字打勾！
- [ ] passion
- [ ] strengthen
- [ ] attentive
- [ ] resort
- [ ] acclaim

→ 用 5 個字說出這張圖片的故事！

passion [ˋpæʃən]　n. 熱情；對～的熱愛

S Both Stephanie and Oliver have a great **passion** for skiing.
史蒂芬妮與奧利佛兩人都對滑雪非常熱愛。

關聯字　passion fruit n. 百香果　passionate adj. 有熱情的

strengthen [ˋstrɛŋθən]　v. 強化

S They have continued **strengthening** their skills for a skiing trip in the future.
為了未來的滑雪之旅，他們一直持續強化著他們的技巧。

關聯字　strength n. 力量，力氣　strong adj. 強壯的

attentive [əˋtɛntɪv]　adj. 專注的

S People sometimes ask them how they can ski so well, and they always say the key is being **attentive**.
人們有時會問他們怎麼能滑雪滑得那麼好，他們總說關鍵在於保持專注。

resort [rɪˋzɔrt]　n. 渡假村

S Finally, they have left for a ski **resort** to fulfill their dream of going on a ski trip.
終於，他們出發前往滑雪渡假村來實現他們滑雪之旅的夢想。

MORE　除了渡假村之外，還有一些出去玩時會待的地方，像是 guesthouse（民宿）、inn（小旅館）、hostel（青年旅舍）或是 motel（汽車旅館）。

acclaim [əˋklem]　v. （公眾）稱讚；喝采

- Their skiing skills were highly **acclaimed** by people around them.
  他們的滑雪技巧備受身旁的人的稱讚。

Day06_029　健行很棒！

→ 把你知道的單字打勾！
- [ ] overseas
- [ ] humid
- [ ] hike
- [ ] exclaim
- [ ] trail

→ 用 5 個字說出這張圖片的故事！

overseas [ˋovɚˋsiz]　adv. 海外地，國外地

- I had been living **overseas** before I changed my job.
  在我換工作之前，我一直住在國外。

humid [ˋhjumɪd]　adj. 潮濕的

- The **humid** climate in Taiwan makes me suffer from allergies all the time.
  台灣潮濕的氣候讓我飽受過敏之苦。

> **MORE** 英文中表達「濕」的說法有很多，但卻有著一些差異，**humid** 是指「空氣中濕熱的水氣很重」，**damp** 則是「陰陰冷冷的濕潤感」，「濕到滴水的狀態」則是 **wet**。

hike [haɪk]　v. 健行

- I often go **hiking** on weekends, hoping the fresh air can relieve my allergies.
  我週末常去健行，希望新鮮空氣能緩解我的過敏。

> **關聯字** mountain climbing　n. 爬山

exclaim [ɪksˋklem]　v. 驚呼

🅢 The views in the mountains are so marvelous that I even **exclaim** with joy sometimes.
山中的景色美不勝收到讓我有時甚至會因為開心而驚呼出聲。

trail [trel]　n.（荒野中的）小徑，步道

🅢 Every time when I am strolling along the **trails**, I feel the joy of being surrounded by nature.
每次當我走在步道上，我就感受到被大自然圍繞的喜悅。

> **MORE** 英文裡的「道路」有很多種說法，雖然都是給人或車通行的通道，但還是略有不同，一起來看看吧。
> road 馬路　street 街道　alley 巷弄　path 小徑　passage 通道
> sidewalk 人行道　crosswalk 行人穿越道　track 步道；跑道

Day06_030　在飛機上

→ 把你知道的單字打勾！
- ☐ board
- ☐ step
- ☐ compartment
- ☐ pretty
- ☐ gently

→ 用 5 個字說出這張圖片的故事！

board [bord]　v. 登上（交通工具）

🅢 I had been waiting at the airport for quite a while before I could **board** the plane.
在我登機之前，我已經在機場等了好一陣子。

同義字 get on、embark

step [stɛp]　v. 踏上

S With my passport and boarding pass, I finally **stepped** onto the plane.
帶著我的護照與登機證,我終於踏上飛機了。

> MORE　step 也可以當作名詞,意思是「腳步;步驟」。
> We should learn the tips **step** by **step**.（步驟）
> 我們應該一步一步地學習訣竅。
> He is just a few **steps** away from me.（腳步）
> 他離我只有幾步的距離。

compartment [kəm`pɑrtmənt]　n. 具特定用途的分隔空間

S I was standing in the aisle, trying to put my baggage into the overhead **compartment**, but I was too short to do it.
我站在走道上試著把我的行李放進頭上的置物櫃裡,但我因為太矮了而做不到。

- **E** overhead **compartment** 頭上的置物櫃
- **E** first-class **compartment** 頭等車廂

pretty [`prɪtɪ]　adj. 漂亮的

S "Could you help me put my baggage up there?" I asked a **pretty** flight attendant.
「妳可以幫我把行李放上去嗎?」我詢問了一位漂亮的空服員。

> MORE　pretty 也可以當作副詞,這時是「相當,非常」的意思。
> The prize money is one million, it's **pretty** much.
> 獎金是一百萬,真的滿多的。

gently [`dʒɛntlɪ]　adv. 溫和地;溫柔地

S She replied to me **gently**, "No problem, let's do it together."
她溫柔地回覆我:「沒問題,我們一起來吧。」

> 關聯字　gentle adj. 溫和的;溫柔的　　gentleman n. 紳士

Day 06 旅遊與冒險 026-030

回復記憶 階段

◆ 請參考以下在 Day06 中出現過的圖片，在單字旁的空格寫下字義。

026 好玩的節慶活動
- festival _____
- attend _____
- exhibition _____
- agriculture _____
- energetic _____

027 老鼠的復仇
- cabin _____
- irritate _____
- revenge _____
- ambush _____
- tail _____

028 滑雪之旅
- passion _____
- strengthen _____
- attentive _____
- resort _____
- acclaim _____

029 健行很棒！
- overseas _____
- humid _____
- hike _____
- exclaim _____
- trail _____

030 在飛機上
- board _____
- step _____
- compartment _____
- pretty _____
- gently _____

加深記憶階段

◆ 請依照提示的單字字首，在下列空格中填入適當的單字。

(1) 頭上的置物櫃　　　　　overhead c_____
(2) 一個專注的學生　　　　an a_____ student
(3) 一個精緻的小木屋　　　a fine wooden c_____
(4) 一隻貓的尾巴　　　　　a cat's t_____
(5) 遲來的報復　　　　　　late r_____

◆ 請參考下列方框中的單字，在下列空格中填入適當的單字。

參考 | board | gently | strengthen | irritate | attend | hike | passion | exhibition

(1) I sometimes go _____ as a good way to exercise.
我有時會去健行做為一個運動的好方法。

(2) _____ your work skills, or you will be fired.
強化你的工作技能，不然你會被開除。

(3) There are many _____ in the museum.
博物館裡有許多展覽。

(4) I am a man with lots of _____.
我是一個很有熱忱的人。

(5) My lazy husband's behavior _____ me a lot.
我懶惰丈夫的行為讓我非常火大。

(6) Do I have to _____ the symposium?
我必須參加這場座談會嗎？

(7) All passengers please get ready _____ the plane.
所有乘客請準備好登機。

(8) He whispered _____ by my side.
他在我身旁溫柔細語。

Answers:
1. (1) compartment (2) attentive (3) cabin (4) tail (5) revenge
2. (1) hiking (2) Strengthen (3) exhibitions (4) passion (5) irritates (6) attend (7) board (8) gently

記單字必備！掌握常見字根 02

01 -ply（摺疊）
re**ply** 回答，答覆
im**ply** 暗指；暗示
sup**ply** 供給，提供
ap**ply** 申請，請求
multi**ply** 相乘；使成倍增加

02 -pose（放置）
pur**pose** 目的；意圖
im**pose** 強加；課徵
ex**pose** 揭露
com**pose** 作曲；構成
de**pose** 罷黜

03 -cide（殺死）
sui**cide** 自殺
homi**cide** 兇殺
geno**cide** 種族滅絕
herbi**cide** 除草劑
pesti**cide** 殺蟲劑

04 spec-（注視；觀察）
re**spec**t 尊敬
sus**spec**t 懷疑
in**spec**t 監看
pro**spec**t 展望
spectator 觀眾

05 -press（按壓）
de**press** 使蕭條；使沮喪
ex**press** 表達；傳達
im**press** 使印象深刻
op**press** 壓迫
sup**press** 鎮壓

06 -aud（聽）
audience 聽眾，觀眾
audit 稽核
audition 試鏡
audio 聽覺的，聲音的
auditorium 禮堂

07 -cur（奔跑；流動）
oc**cur** 發生
in**cur** 招致，帶來
current 目前的；流動
currency 貨幣
ex**cur**sion 郊遊遠足

08 -ject（投射；丟）
pro**ject** 投射
re**ject** 拒絕
in**ject** 注射；打針
e**ject** 逐出；轟出
ob**ject** 反對

Day 07 家庭與幸福 031-035

Day07_031 老公來做飯

→ 把你知道的單字打勾！
- [ ] complain
- [ ] contented
- [ ] microwave
- [ ] explode
- [ ] embarrassed

→ 用 5 個字說出這張圖片的故事！

complain [kəm`plen]　v. 抱怨

Henry's wife, Emma, sometimes **complains** that he never cooks for the family.
亨利的太太艾瑪，有時會抱怨他從未替家人煮過飯。

MORE 不像 explain 的名詞是 explanation，complain 的名詞是 complaint，請特別注意。

The customer filed a **complaint** about late delivery.
顧客投訴延遲到貨。

contented [kən`tɛntɪd]　adj. 滿意的

In order to make his wife feel **contented**, Henry decided to cook a meal for her.
為了讓他太太滿意，亨利決定要為她煮一餐。

contented with ~ 對～感到滿意

MORE 除了 contented 之外，content 也是「滿意的」的意思，不過 contented 會比較偏向是因為當下情境所造成的心滿意足，而 content 所指的滿意則沒有特定成因。另外，當 content 唸成 [`kɑntɛnt] 時，意思是「內容，內容物」。

microwave [ˈmaɪkroˌwev]   n. 微波爐

S Henry didn't know how to use the gas stove, so he chose to use the **microwave**.
因為亨利不知道要怎麼用瓦斯爐。於是他選擇使用微波爐。

MORE 字首 micro- 是「微小」的意思。
microscope n. 顯微鏡   microphone n. 麥克風   microchip n. 微晶片

explode [ɪkˈsplod]   v. 爆炸

S Just as Henry was microwaving some food, the food he put inside suddenly **exploded** and made a mess.
就在亨利微波一些食物的時候，他放到裡面的食物突然爆炸了，弄得一團糟。

E A volcano **explodes** 火山爆發

關聯字 explosion n. 爆炸   explosive adj. 爆炸性的 n. 炸藥；爆裂物
5 people were killed in the **explosion**.
5 人在這場爆炸中死亡。
Angie's divorce is the most **explosive** news today.
安吉離婚是今天最爆炸性的新聞了。
The terrorists put **explosives** in the mall.
恐怖分子在商場裡放了爆裂物。

embarrassed [ɪmˈbærəst]   adj. 尷尬的；不好意思的

S Henry felt really **embarrassed** and he ended up calling for food delivery instead.
亨利真的覺得很不好意思，結果他最後改叫了外送。

Day07_032 哥哥捉弄弟弟

→ 把你知道的單字打勾！
- [ ] sibling
- [ ] nevertheless
- [ ] tease
- [ ] fake
- [ ] can't help but

→ 用 5 個字說出這張圖片的故事！

sibling [ˋsɪblɪŋ]　n. 手足；兄弟姊妹

S Edison and Edward are **siblings**, and their parents want Edison, the older one, to take care of Edward.
愛迪生和愛德華是手足。他們的父母想要哥哥愛迪生照顧弟弟愛德華。

> MORE　siblings 是親兄弟姊妹的意思，若是堂表兄弟姊妹，則可以用 cousin 這個字。
> My uncle's son is my **cousin**.
> 我叔叔的兒子是我的堂弟。

nevertheless [͵nɛvɚðəˋlɛs]　adv. 然而

S **Nevertheless**, naughty Edison always does the opposite.
然而，頑皮的愛迪生總是唱反調。

> 同義字　nonetheless、however
> MORE　opposite 是「相反的」的意思，當介系詞時則是「對面」的意思，這時和 across from 同義。

tease [tiz]　v. 捉弄；嘲弄

S What's more, Edison likes to **tease** Edward, and he often tries to scare him.
此外，愛迪生喜歡捉弄愛德華也常常試圖要嚇他。

fake [fek]　adj. 假的；冒充的

S He even spooked his younger brother with a **fake** snake yesterday.
昨天他甚至用了條假蛇去嚇他弟弟。

can't help but　phr. 忍不住做～

S Although Edison knows he is supposed to take care of Edward, he just **can't help but** keep making fun of him.
儘管愛迪生知道他應該要照顧愛德華，但他就是忍不住一直作弄他。

> MORE　can't help but 的後面要接「原形動詞」，若 can't help 的後面沒有 but，則接「動名詞（V-ing）」
> Every time I see the picture, I can't help **but laugh**.
> = Every time I see the picture, I can't help **laughing**.
> 每次我看到那張圖，我都忍不住大笑。

Day 07　家庭與幸福　031-035

67

Day07_033 全家去動物園

→ 把你知道的單字打勾！
- [ ] leisure
- [ ] preferable
- [ ] alive
- [ ] tame
- [ ] spend

→ 用 5 個字說出這張圖片的故事！

leisure [ˋliʒɚ]　adj. 休閒的；空閒的

S What kind of **leisure** activities does your family do on weekends?
你們家在週末會做哪種休閒活動呢？

- **E** **leisure** time 閒暇時間＝free time＝spare time
- **E** **leisure** wear 休閒服＝casual wear

preferable [ˋprɛfərəbl̩]　adj. 較偏好的；較適合的

S One of our **preferable** choices is to go to the City Zoo.
我們比較喜歡的其中一個選擇是去市立動物園。

- **E** a **preferable** candidate 一個較適合的候選人
- **E** a **preferable** applicant 一個較適合的應徵者
- **E** a **preferable** choice 一個較偏好的選擇

alive [əˋlaɪv]　adj. 活著的；現存的

S There are many kinds of animals **alive** in the zoo.
動物園裡有很多種動物。

tame [tem]　adj. 溫馴的

S Giraffes and zebras are **tame** animals, and they are well-liked by people.
長頸鹿和斑馬都是溫馴的動物，而且牠們深受人們的喜愛。

spend [spɛnd]　v. 花費

Every time we go to the zoo, we always spend a whole day browsing thoroughly.
我們每次去動物園,我們總是會花上一整天徹底逛過。

> **MORE** spend 花費的可以是金錢或時間,但同樣可以解釋為花費的 cost 卻只能用來表示「花錢」,而 take 則是和 spend 一樣,可以用來表示花時間或錢,只是 spend 後面出現的動詞必須要用「動名詞」,而 take 後面出現的動詞則要使用「不定詞」。

I spent three hundred dollars **buying** the book.
= It cost me three hundred dollars **to buy** the book.
我花了 300 元買這本書。

I spent three hours **reading** the book.
= It took me three hours **to read** the book.
我花了三小時看這本書。

Day07_034　在遊樂園約會

→ 把你知道的單字打勾!
- [ ] amusement
- [ ] considerate
- [ ] promptly
- [ ] vendor
- [ ] comparable

→ 用 5 個字說出這張圖片的故事!

amusement [ə`mjuzmənt]　n. 娛樂;樂趣

Alan and I had a date at an amusement park last weekend.
上個週末艾倫和我去了遊樂園約會。

關聯字 theme park n. 主題公園

considerate [kən`sɪdərɪt]　adj. 體貼的

Alan is a considerate boyfriend.
艾倫是個很體貼的男朋友。

反義字 inconsiderate

promptly [ˋprɑmptlɪ]　adv. 立即地；很快地

- After I told him that I'd wanted to go to an amusement park, he **promptly** bought the tickets.
  在我告訴他我想去遊樂園後，他就立刻買了門票。

  同義字 shortly、right away、immediately

vendor [ˋvɛndɚ]　n. 小販，攤販

- We bought some snacks from the **vendors** in the park.
  我們向園內的攤販買了一些小吃。

comparable [ˋkɑmpərəbl̩]　adj. 可比較的；比得上的

- It was an amazing date, and no one else can be **comparable** to Alan in my mind.
  那是一次很棒的約會，且在我心中沒有其他人可以比得上艾倫。

  關聯字 compare v. 比較　comparison n. 比較

Day07_035 家庭主婦忙忙忙

→ 把你知道的單字打勾！
- [ ] exhausting
- [ ] multitasking
- [ ] daily
- [ ] flexibility
- [ ] organize

→ 用 5 個字說出這張圖片的故事！

exhausting [ɪgˋzɔstɪŋ]　adj. 令人筋疲力盡的

- Being a full-time housewife is an **exhausting** job.
  當一位全職家庭主婦是一件令人筋疲力盡的工作。

  關聯字 exhaust v. 使筋疲力盡　exhausted adj. 感到筋疲力盡的
  Taking exams all day **exhausted** me completely.
  考一整天的試讓我完全筋疲力盡。
  I am **exhausted** after the whole day work.
  一整天工作下來我感到筋疲力盡。

multitasking [ˌmʌltɪˈtæskɪŋ]　n. 同時做超過一件事的能力

- After years, my **multitasking** skills have been polished.
  在幾年後，我同時做超過一件事的技能已經爐火純青了。

daily [ˈdelɪ]　adj. 每日的；日常的

- Cleaning the house, preparing meals and taking care of my kids are my basic **daily** jobs.
  打掃屋子、準備三餐和照顧小孩是我基本的日常工作。

  關聯字　weekly adj. 每周的　biweekly adj. 每兩週的　monthly adj. 每月的
  　　　　quarterly adj. 每季的　yearly adj. 每年的　annual adj. 每年的

flexibility [ˌflɛksəˈbɪlətɪ]　n. 彈性；靈活

- My schedule is so tight that there's no **flexibility** to make time for myself.
  我的時間安排緊湊到沒有任何彈性可以空出時間給我自己。

organize [ˈɔrgəˌnaɪz]　v. 組織；籌劃

- To **organize** a family and make it work smoothly is really difficult!
  要組織一個家庭並讓它能順利運作真的好難！

  關聯字　organization n. 組織　organized adj. 條理分明的

回復記憶階段

◆ 請參考以下在 Day07 中出現過的圖片，在單字旁的空格寫下字義。

031 老公來做飯
- complain ....
- contented ....
- microwave ....
- explode ....
- embarrassed ....

032 哥哥捉弄弟弟
- sibling ....
- nevertheless ....
- tease ....
- fake ....
- can't help but ....

033 全家去動物園
- leisure ....
- preferable ....
- alive ....
- tame ....
- spend ....

034 在遊樂園約會
- amusement ....
- considerate ....
- promptly ....
- vendor ....
- comparable ....

035 家庭主婦忙忙忙
- exhausting ....
- multitasking ....
- daily ....
- flexibility ....
- organize ....

加深記憶 階段

◆ 請依照提示的單字字首，在下列空格中填入適當的單字。

(1) 一個每日的例行公事　　　a d_____ routine
(2) 一個大型的遊樂園　　　　a huge a_____ park
(3) 一個特別的休閒活動　　　a special l_____ activity
(4) 一張假的紙鈔　　　　　　a f_____ bill
(5) 一隻溫馴的動物　　　　　a t_____ animal

◆ 請參考下列方框中的單字，在下列空格中填入適當的單字。

> 參考 | alive | siblings | contented | organize |
> | explode | spend | nevertheless | embarrassed |

(1) How are you going to _____ your summer vacation?
　　你打算怎麼度過你的暑假？

(2) It is your turn to _____ a new working group.
　　這回輪到你組織一個新的工作小組了。

(3) Brothers and sisters are _____.
　　兄弟姊妹就是手足。

(4) Your outstanding performance made the boss _____.
　　你出色的績效讓老闆很滿意。

(5) The fireworks are about to _____ in several hours.
　　這些煙火將在幾小時後引爆。

(6) I felt _____ when I had a wrong number.
　　當我打錯電話時我覺得很尷尬。

(7) He is rich, _____, he is not happy.
　　他很有錢，然而，他並不快樂。

(8) Only few people were still _____ under the attack.
　　只有很少的人在攻擊之下還活著。

Answers:
1. (1) daily (2) amusement (3) leisure (4) fake (5) tame
2. (1) spend (2) organize (3) siblings (4) contented (5) explode (6) embarrassed (7) nevertheless (8) alive

Day 08 家庭與幸福 036-040

Day08_036 全家來野餐

→ 把你知道的單字打勾！
- [ ] picnic
- [ ] sunny
- [ ] value
- [ ] awesome
- [ ] enthusiastically

→ 用 5 個字說出這張圖片的故事！

---

picnic [ˋpɪknɪk]　n. 野餐

S Every weekend, the Chen family always goes on a **picnic** in a neighborhood park.
陳家人每個週末都會去社區公園野餐。

> MORE　go on a picnic 是「去野餐」的意思，也可以用 go picnicking 來表達，picnic 本身可以當動詞，特別要注意的是 picnic 在變化成動名詞時要先在字尾加上一個 k 才能接 -ing，寫成 picnicking。

---

sunny [ˋsʌnɪ]　adj. 晴朗的

S Today is a **sunny** day, so they sit on the grass and enjoy the food Mrs. Chen prepared.
今天天氣晴朗，所以他們坐在草地上享受陳太太準備好的食物。

> MORE　其他常見的天氣形容詞還有：
> windy 颱風的　rainy 下雨的　cloudy 多雲的　snowy 下雪的
> warm 溫暖的　cool 涼爽的　freezing cold 非常寒冷的
> scorching hot 非常炎熱的　foggy 起霧的　humid 潮溼的

value [ˈvælju]　　v. 重視，珍惜

🅢 Mr. and Mrs. Chen **value** the time that the whole family gets together very much.
陳先生與陳太太非常珍惜全家人聚在一起的時光。

關聯字 valuable adj. 珍貴的，貴重的　　valuation n. 評鑑，評估

awesome [ˈɔsəm]　　adj. 極佳的

🅢 With the nice weather and the **awesome** food, everyone enjoys the atmosphere and chats with each other.
天氣很好食物又很棒，每個人都享受著這種氛圍並彼此閒聊。

enthusiastically [ɪnˌθjuzɪˈæstɪklɪ]　　adv. 熱烈地

🅢 The kids are discussing what they want to bring for their next picnic **enthusiastically**.
孩子們正在熱烈討論著下一次他們想要帶什麼來野餐。

關聯字 enthusiastic adj. 熱烈的；充滿熱忱的

Day08_037　媽媽的早晨

→ 把你知道的單字打勾！
- ☐ homemaker
- ☐ various
- ☐ dress up
- ☐ sweep
- ☐ worthwhile

→ 用 5 個字說出這張圖片的故事！

homemaker [ˈhomˌmekɚ]　　n. 持家的人，家庭主婦（夫）

🅢 Being a **homemaker** is a tough job for every mother in the world.
當家庭主婦對世界上所有母親來說都是件很棘手的工作。

MORE 只要是負責操持家務、照顧家庭生活，而非外出工作賺取金錢的角色，皆可用 homemaker 這個字，無關性別。

75

various [`vɛrɪəs]　adj. 各式各樣的；許多的

ⓢ I have two kids, so I have to do **various** things every morning.
我有兩個孩子，所以每天早上我都必須做很多事。

　ⓔ **various** activities 各式各樣的活動
　ⓔ **various** exhibitions 各式各樣的展覽

關聯字 **vary** v. 使不同；使多樣化　**variety** n. 變化；多種
Living expenses **vary** from state to state.
生活開支每一州都不同。
Variety is the spice of life.
變化是生命的香料。

dress up　phr. 打扮；著裝

ⓢ My kids have to go to school today, so I **dress** them **up**.
我的孩子們今天在學校有個頒獎典禮，所以我替他們穿衣打扮。

　MORE dress up 所穿的不是一般沒有考量場合和對象、未經挑選的休閒服，而是指「盛裝打扮」或穿「特殊服裝」的情況。

sweep [swip]　v. 清掃

ⓢ After my kids leave for school, I start to **sweep** and clean the house all by myself.
在我的孩子們去上學後，我開始獨自一個人掃地和清理房子。

　MORE 除了掃地之外，這裡再補充幾個清潔相關的動詞：
　vacuum 吸塵　mop 拖地　rinse 沖洗　dust 撢塵

worthwhile [`wɝθ`hwaɪl]　adj. 值得花費金錢或時間的

ⓢ Cleaning house is always tiring, but it's **worthwhile** when I see my floors are shiny.
打掃房子總是很累人，但當我看到我的地板閃閃發光，我就覺得很值得。

Day08_038　我想買鋼琴！

→ 把你知道的單字打勾！
- [ ] musician
- [ ] catch one's eye
- [ ] enormous
- [ ] instrument
- [ ] full of

→ 用 5 個字說出這張圖片的故事！

---

musician　[mjuˋzɪʃən]　n. 音樂家

S When Kelly was a kid, she dreamed of becoming a **musician** in the future.
在凱莉小時候，她曾夢想在未來成為一位音樂家。

> **MORE** musician 和 magician（魔術師）長得有點像，請小心別搞混了。

catch one's eye　phr. 引起某人的注意

S One day, Kelly and her daughter were walking down the street and there was something shiny that **caught her daughter's eye**.
有一天，當凱莉和她女兒走在街上時，有個閃亮的東西引起了她女兒的注意。

> **MORE** shiny 所指的「閃閃發亮」，是因為表面很光滑或乾淨而「反光」，所造成的那種閃亮的感覺，而不是自己「發光」，而與閃亮相對的「黯淡」則可用 dull 這個字來形容。

The kitchen floor is dirty and **dull**, not **shiny** at all.
廚房地板又髒又黯淡，一點都不閃閃發亮。

enormous　[ɪˋnɔrməs]　adj. 巨大的

S An **enormous** but beautiful piano was displayed inside a store.
一台巨大但美麗的鋼琴被擺在店內展示。

> **同義字** huge、giant、large

77

instrument [ˈɪnstrəmənt]　n. 器具；樂器

- Kelly's daughter liked the **instrument** very much and asked her to buy the piano.
  凱莉的女兒非常喜歡這項樂器，並要她買這台鋼琴給她。

full of　phr. 充滿～

- Kelly was **full of** surprise when her daughter told her that she also has wanted to be a musician in the future.
  凱莉在她女兒告訴自己說她未來也想成為音樂家時充滿驚訝。

Day08_039 倒數計時做功課

→ 把你知道的單字打勾！
- [ ] strict
- [ ] strike a balance
- [ ] executive
- [ ] assignment
- [ ] obedient

→ 用 5 個字說出這張圖片的故事！

strict [strɪkt]　adj. 嚴格的

- I was born in a single-parent family, and I have a **strict** mother.
  我出生於一個單親家庭，且我有一個嚴格的母親。

  反義字 lenient adj. 寬容的
  MORE 現代社會中出現了許多有著不同特色的家庭類型，一起來看看要怎麼用英文說吧！
  single-parent family 單親家庭
  double-income family 雙薪家庭
  nuclear family 核心家庭（小家庭）
  extended family 延伸家庭（大家庭）

strike a balance　　phr. 在～之中取得平衡

- As a career woman, she is very good at **striking a balance** between family and work.
  身為一位職業婦女，她非常擅長在工作和家庭之間取得平衡。

executive　[ɪɡˋzɛkjʊtɪv]　　n. 行政主管

- She is a senior **executive** in her company, so she is used to giving orders.
  她在她公司裡是高級行政主管，所以她習慣發號施令。

  關聯字　supervisor n. 主管　superior n. 上級　management n. 管理階層

assignment　[əˋsaɪnmənt]　　n.（分派的）作業，任務

- She asks me to finish all my school **assignments** before she comes back from work.
  她要求我在她下班回來前把所有的學校作業都做完。

  關聯字　assign v. 分派

obedient　[əˋbidjənt]　　adj. 順從的

- I always do my best to be **obedient** to her orders.
  我總是盡我所能地順從她的命令。

  關聯字　obey v. 遵守　obedience n. 順從

Day08_040　有人求婚好幸福

→ 把你知道的單字打勾！
- [ ] date
- [ ] in addition
- [ ] propose
- [ ] touched
- [ ] blessed

→ 用 5 個字說出這張圖片的故事！

date [det]　v. 約會

🅢 Lisa and her boyfriend have been **dating** for years.
麗莎與她的男友已經約會好幾年了。

> **MORE** date 也可以當作名詞使用，這時會是「日期」的意思。
> What **date** is today?
> 今天是幾月幾號？

in addition　phr. 此外

🅢 They are serious to each other; **in addition**, their family members get along with one another.
他們對彼此很認真；此外，他們的家庭成員彼此也相處融洽。

> **同義字** additionally、moreover、besides、further、furthermore
> **MORE** each other 是指「兩者之間的彼此」，而 one another 則是「多者之間的彼此」，但其實在實際運用上，這兩種表達方式常常會混用。

propose [prə`poz]　v. 求婚

🅢 On a beautiful Sunday, Lisa's boyfriend **proposed** to her, and gave her a big diamond ring.
在一個美麗的星期日，麗莎的男友向她求婚，並給了她一個大鑽戒。

> **關聯字** proposal n. 提議；求婚
> **MORE** propose 這個字也有「提案，提議」的意思。
> The manager **proposed** to extend opening hours.
> 經理提議要延長營業時間。

touched [tʌtʃt]　adj. 感動的

🅢 Lisa was deeply **touched**, and she exclaimed, "Yes, I do!"
麗莎非常感動並開心大叫說：「好，我願意！」。

> **MORE** touched 是「感動的」的意思，但 touchy 則是「易怒的；棘手的」的意思，小心別搞錯了。

blessed [`blɛsɪd]　adj. 幸福的；受祝福的

🅢 She felt she was the most **blessed** woman in the world.
她覺得她是世界上最幸福的女人了。

> **關聯字** bless v. 祝福　blessing n. 祝福；幸運的事

回復記憶 階段

◆ 請參考以下在 Day08 中出現過的圖片，在單字旁的空格寫下字義。

036 全家來野餐
- picnic _____
- sunny _____
- value _____
- awesome _____
- enthusiastically _____

037 媽媽的早晨
- homemaker _____
- various _____
- dress up _____
- sweep _____
- worthwhile _____

038 我想買鋼琴！
- musician _____
- catch one's eye _____
- enormous _____
- instrument _____
- full of _____

039 倒數計時做功課
- strict _____
- strike a balance _____
- executive _____
- assignment _____
- obedient _____

040 有人求婚好幸福
- date _____
- in addition _____
- propose _____
- touched _____
- blessed _____

Day 08 家庭與幸福 036・040

81

加深記憶階段

◆ 請依照提示的單字字首，在下列空格中填入適當的單字。

(1) 一位偉大的音樂家　　　　a great m_____
(2) 一位負責任的行政主管　　a responsible e_____
(3) 一個昂貴的樂器　　　　　an expensive i_____
(4) 一個巨大的建築物　　　　an e_____ architecture
(5) 一位嚴格的母親　　　　　a s_____ mother

◆ 請參考下列方框中的單字，在下列空格中填入適當的單字。

參考	value	touched	propose	full of
	awesome	in addition	sweep	various

(1) There are _____ flowers in the garden.
　　花園裡有多種花朵。

(2) It is my turn to _____ the classroom floor.
　　輪到我掃教室的地板了。

(3) The food I'm eating is _____.
　　我正在吃的食物超棒。

(4) The trainee is _____ confidence.
　　這位受訓人員充滿信心。

(5) He _____ to me a few days ago, but I didn't agree.
　　他在幾天前向我求婚，但是我沒有同意。

(6) I am a college student; _____, I have a part time job.
　　我是大學生；此外，我有一份兼職工作。

(7) He was _____ because his daughter gave him a birthday card.
　　他很感動，因為他的女兒送了他一張生日卡片。

(8) My boss _____ his employees.
　　我的老闆重視他的員工們。

Answers:
1. (1) musician (2) executive (3) instrument (4) enormous (5) strict
2. (1) various (2) sweep (3) awesome (4) full of (5) proposed (6) in addition (7) touched (8) values

Day 09 家庭與幸福 041-045

Day09_041 什麼是幸福

→ 把你知道的單字打勾！
- [ ] definition
- [ ] own
- [ ] gather
- [ ] in short
- [ ] tedious

→ 用 5 個字說出這張圖片的故事！

definition [ˌdɛfəˋnɪʃən]　n. 定義

- Have you ever asked yourself what's the **definition** of happiness?
  你曾經問過自己幸福的定義是什麼嗎？

own [on]　v. 擁有

- People say that being rich or having their **own** business is happiness.
  人們會說有錢或是有自己的事業就是幸福。

  關聯字 owner n. 擁有者
  Who's the **owner** of the house?
  誰是這間房子的擁有者？

gather [ˋgæðɚ]　v. 召集；使聚集

- However, true happiness for me is to **gather** my family and have some quality time together.
  不過，對我來說真正的幸福，就是把家人們聚在一起度過一些寶貴的時光。

  MORE　quality time 裡的 quality，意思是「優質的」，也就是那些「把注意力全然放在重視的人身上，一起相處所度過的時間」。

in short　adv. 總而言之

🅢 **In short**, no matter what we do, as long as I stay with my family, I am happy.
總而言之，無論我們在做什麼，只要與我的家人在一起，我就很快樂。

tedious [ˋtidɪəs]　adj. 乏味的

🅢 Life with them is never **tedious** but marvelous.
和他們在一起的生活從來不會乏味，而是非常美好的。

🅔 a **tedious** speech 一場乏味的演講

Day09_042　好孕到

→ 把你知道的單字打勾！
☐ pregnant
☐ unpredictable
☐ leave
☐ approve
☐ regret

→ 用 5 個字說出這張圖片的故事！

---

pregnant [ˋprɛgnənt]　adj. 懷孕的

🅢 Allison has been **pregnant** for eight months.
艾莉森已經懷孕八個月了。

unpredictable [ˌʌnprɪˋdɪktəb!]　adj. 無法預測的

🅢 This is her first baby, so everything for her is new and **unpredictable**.
這是她的第一個小孩，所以所有事情對她來說都是新的且無法預測的。

關聯字　predictable adj. 可預測的
He is careless, so his failure is **predictable**.
他很粗心，所以他的失敗在預料之中。

leave [liv]　**n.** （長時間的）休假

S Now Allison is meeting with her supervisor and talking about her maternity **leave**.
艾莉森正在和她的主管面談並討論她的產假。

- **E** maternity **leave** 產假
- **E** paternity **leave** 陪產假
- **E** sick **leave** 病假
- **E** personal **leave** 事假

approve [əˋpruv]　**v.** 批准，准許

S Her supervisor is nice and **approves** her leave request at once.
她的主管人很好，而且立刻准了她的休假申請。

MORE 除了 at once 之外，可以表達「立刻」的還有 immediately、right away、instantly、promptly 等等。

regret [rɪˋgrɛt]　**v.** 後悔

S Allison is uncertain what her life will be in the future, but she's certain that she won't **regret** having a baby.
艾莉森不確定她未來的人生會如何，但她確定她不會後悔有個小孩。

Day09_043　一家人的週末

→ 把你知道的單字打勾！
- ☐ vital
- ☐ trim
- ☐ grocery
- ☐ feast
- ☐ to sum up

→ 用 5 個字說出這張圖片的故事！

Day 09　家庭與幸福　041-045

vital [ˈvaɪtl̩]   adj. 極為重要的

- **Every Saturday is vital to the Wang family.**
  每個週六對於王家人來說都是極為重要的。

  > **MORE** vital 帶有「因為要活下去而不可缺少」的意味，因此除了衍生出「極為重要的」這個意思之外，也有「充滿生氣的」的意思，當名詞時則有「重要器官；生命徵象」等意義。

trim [trɪm]   v. 修剪

- **On Saturday mornings, they usually trim the bushes and take care of their beautiful garden.**
  在週六早上，他們通常會修剪灌木並照顧他們的美麗花園。

  > **MORE** 如果只是稍微修剪，而不是有很大的變化（例如長頭髮剪成短頭髮），那麼也可以用 trim 來表達剪頭髮的意思。

  I need to **trim** my bangs.
  我的瀏海得修一下。

grocery [ˈɡrosərɪ]   n. 食品雜貨

- **On Saturday afternoons, they go to the supermarket to buy groceries together.**
  在週六下午，他們會一起去超市買一些食品雜貨。

feast [fist]   n. 大餐；饗宴

- **A Saturday night feast is also the Wang family's ritual.**
  週六晚上的大餐也是王家人的固定習慣。

  > **MORE** feast 會比普通的一餐還要更豐盛，也就是我們說的「大餐」。

to sum up   phr. 結論是，總而言之

- **To sum up, Saturdays are their family day and they all enjoy each other's company.**
  總而言之，週六是他們的家庭日，而且他們都很享受彼此的陪伴。

  > 同義字 in sum、in short、in conclusion、to conclude、in brief

Day09_044 雙胞胎不一樣

→ 把你知道的單字打勾！
- [ ] twin
- [ ] alike
- [ ] personality
- [ ] telepathy
- [ ] nauseous

→ 用 5 個字說出這張圖片的故事！

twin [twɪn]　n. 雙胞胎之一，雙胞胎（pl.）

S Vic and Nick are **twins**.
維克與尼克是雙胞胎。

關聯字　triplets n. 三胞胎

alike [ə`laɪk]　adj. 相像的

S Though they look **alike**, they act very differently.
儘管他們看起來很相像，但他們的表現卻非常不同。

同義字　similar、identical、akin
MORE　alike（相像的）和 like 長得很像、意思也很像，但是 like 除了形容詞的「相像的；類似的」之外，也可以當介系詞，表示「和～一樣；如同～」的意思，請特別注意用法上的差異。

Harry and his brother look **alike**.
哈利與他的兄弟看起來很像。
Harry is **like** his brother, they all like baseball very much.
哈利和他的兄弟一樣，他們都非常喜歡棒球。

personality [͵pɝsn̩`ælətɪ]　n. 人格特質，個性

S They have different **personalities**; Vic is shy, and Nick is outgoing.
他們有著不同的個性，維克很害羞，而尼克很外向。

telepathy [təˋlɛpəθɪ]　　n. 心電感應

- People sometimes ask them whether they have the so-called "twin **telepathy**".
  人們有時會問他們有沒有所謂的「雙胞胎心電感應」。

  MORE 字首 tele- 有「遠方；遙遠」的意思，一起利用這個字首記一些單字吧！
  telescope 望遠鏡　television 電視　telegraph 電報

nauseous [ˋnɔʃɪəs]　　adj. 噁心反胃的，覺得作嘔的

- They say; they don't know if it's telepathy or not, but if one is uncomfortable, the other sometimes will feel **nauseous**, too.
  他們說他們不知道到底是不是心電感應，不過如果一個人覺得不舒服，另一個人有時也會覺得噁心反胃。

Day09_045　懷念阿嬤

→ 把你知道的單字打勾！
- [ ] carefully
- [ ] adept
- [ ] masterpiece
- [ ] pass away
- [ ] legend

→ 用 5 個字說出這張圖片的故事！

carefully [ˋkɛrfəlɪ]　　adv. 小心翼翼地；仔細地

- Tim remembers his grandmother took care of him **carefully** when he was little.
  提姆記得在他小時候，他的祖母都小心翼翼地照顧他。

  關聯字 careful adj. 小心翼翼的；仔細的
  反義字 carelessly

adept [əˋdɛpt]　adj. 擅長的

S Tim also remembers that his grandmother was **adept** at painting.
提姆也記得他的祖母很擅長繪畫。

> **MORE** adept 和另外兩個字長得很像，分別是表示「適應」的 adapt，和表示「採納」的 adopt，在使用這些字時必須特別注意，小心不要搞混字義而用錯了。

I slowly **adapted** to the new environment.
我慢慢適應了這個新的環境。
My boss decided to **adopt** my suggestions.
我的老闆決定採納我的建議了。

masterpiece [ˋmæstɚ͵pis]　n. 傑作

S She created many **masterpieces**, and she was well-known for her talent.
她創造出許多傑作，且因她的才華而出名。

E a renowned **masterpiece** 知名的傑作

pass away　phr. 去世

S A few years ago, Tim's grandmother **passed away** peacefully one night.
幾年前，提姆的祖母在一個晚上安詳地去世了。

|同義字| perish、die

legend [ˋlɛdʒənd]　n. 傳奇

S For Tim, his grandmother is a **legend** and always lives in his mind.
對於提姆而言，他的祖母是一個傳奇且永遠活在他的心中。

回復記憶 階段

◆ 請參考以下在 Day09 中出現過的圖片，在單字旁的空格寫下字義。

041 什麼是幸福
- definition _____
- own _____
- gather _____
- in short _____
- tedious _____

042 好孕到
- pregnant _____
- unpredictable _____
- leave _____
- approve _____
- regret _____

043 一家人的週末
- vital _____
- trim _____
- grocery _____
- feast _____
- to sum up _____

044 雙胞胎不一樣
- twin _____
- alike _____
- personality _____
- telepathy _____
- nauseous _____

045 懷念阿嬤
- carefully _____
- adept _____
- masterpiece _____
- pass away _____
- legend _____

加深記憶 階段

◆ 請依照提示的單字字首，在下列空格中填入適當的單字。

(1) 一位懷孕的女子　　　　a p_____ woman
(2) 一件有名的傑作　　　　a famous m_____
(3) 一個特別的人格特質　　a special p_____
(4) 一對雙胞胎　　　　　　a couple of t_____
(5) 不可思議的心電感應　　incredible t_____

◆ 請參考下列方框中的單字，在下列空格中填入適當的單字。

> 參考 | own | nauseous | pass away | regret |
> | approve | grocery | unpredictable | tedious |

(1) After smelling the disgusting smoke, I felt _____.
在聞到這令人作嘔的煙後，我覺得噁心反胃。

(2) If you don't quit smoking, you will _____ for the rest of your life.
假如你不戒菸，你會後悔一輩子的。

(3) We always shop at a _____ store nearby.
我們總是在附近的雜貨店購物。

(4) My supervisor _____ my personal leave.
我的主管批准了我的事假。

(5) My 90-year-old grandfather _____ peacefully last night.
我九十歲的祖父昨晚安詳地過世了。

(6) The outcome is _____.
結果是無法預測的。

(7) His speech was _____, and many people fell asleep.
他的演說冗長沉悶，所以很多人都睡著了。

(8) He is the man who _____ ten mansions in Taipei.
他就是那位在台北擁有十間豪宅的人。

Answers:
1. (1) pregnant (2) masterpiece (3) personality (4) twins (5) telepathy
2. (1) nauseous (2) regret (3) grocery (4) approved (5) passed away (6) unpredictable (7) tedious
　(8) owns

Day 09 家庭與幸福 041-045

記單字必備！掌握常見字首 01

★ 常見常用的字首

1. **sub**（在～之下）
   subway 地下鐵
   submarine 潛艇
   subordinate 下屬

2. **tele**（遠方；遙遠）
   telephone 電話
   telescope 望遠鏡
   telecommute 遠距辦公

3. **ex**（向外；外面；超過）
   exit 出口
   expire 到期
   expensive 昂貴的

4. **trans**（跨越；穿過；克服）
   transfer 移轉
   translate 翻譯
   transform 改變

5. **anti**（對抗；在～之前）
   antibiotics 抗生素
   antique 古董
   antibody 抗體

6. **post**（在～之後）
   postpone 延後
   postwar 戰後
   postscript 附筆

7. **fore**（在～之前）
   foresee 預測
   forefront 最前線
   foremost 最重要的

8. **up**（向上；在～之上）
   upbeat 令人愉快的
   upcoming 即將來到的
   upgrade 升級

9. **out**（向外；超過）
   outing 郊遊
   outdated 過時的
   outgoing 外向的

10. **pre**（在～之前）
    prevent 防止
    predict 預測
    prescription 處方箋

11. **com**（一起）
    company 公司
    combat 對抗
    combine 合併

12. **con**（一起）
    consolidate 合併
    consider 考慮
    congestion 阻塞

13. **auto**（自己）
    autonomy 自治
    automobile 汽車
    autobiography 自傳

14. **counter**（相反；對抗）
    counteraction 抵銷
    counterpart 對應物
    counterattack 反擊

Day 10 社會與規範 046-050

Day10_046 抓到小偷了！

→ 把你知道的單字打勾！
- [ ] righteous
- [ ] core
- [ ] con artist
- [ ] for the sake of
- [ ] break into

→ 用 5 個字說出這張圖片的故事！

righteous [ˈraɪtʃəs]　adj. 公正的；正直的

S Michael is a **righteous** policeman and he is respected by everyone.
麥克是一位公正的警察，且大家都很尊敬他。

關聯字 justice n. 正義

core [kor]　n. 核心

S The **core** of police work is to protect people.
警察工作的核心就是要保護人們。

E a **core** course 一門核心課程
E an apple **core** 一個蘋果核

con artist [kɑn] [ˈɑrtɪst]　n. 騙子，精於詐騙的人

S He does his best to put burglars, thieves, and **con artists** behind bars.
他盡力要把闖空門的人、小偷和騙子關進牢裡。

E a cunning **con artist** 一個狡猾的騙子

93

MORE 除了騙子之外，社會上還有很多犯下了不同罪行的人，如 burglar（闖空門的人）、thief（小偷）、robber（搶劫犯）、shoplifter（順手牽羊的人）、pickpocket（扒手）等等。

for the sake of　phr. 為了～

🅢 These bad guys are not allowed **for the sake of** safety.
為了安全，這些壞人都是不被允許的。

break into　phr. 闖入

🅢 Michael caught a thief today, who had once **broken into** someone's house; he's happy to keep him off the streets.
今天麥克抓到了一個小偷，他曾闖入過別人的家中，他很高興能把他關起來。

Day10_047 手機不見去報案

→ 把你知道的單字打勾！
- [ ] long
- [ ] mobile
- [ ] missing
- [ ] crime
- [ ] assure

→ 用 5 個字說出這張圖片的故事！

long　[lɔŋ]　v. 渴望

🅢 Jenny bought a new cell phone, which she has **longed** for for months.
珍妮買了一支她想要了好幾個月的新手機。

🅔 **long** for 渴望～
同義字 desire、crave、want

mobile [`mobəl]　　**adj.** 可移動的，移動式的

🅢 In fact, the new **mobile** phone cost her an arm and a leg.
事實上，這支新手機花了她很多錢。

> MORE　手機的說法除了最常見的 cell phone 之外，還有 mobile phone 和 cellular phone。另外，例句中出現的 cost an arm and a leg，是一個非常常用的慣用語，其實就是 cost a lot of money（花大錢）的意思。

missing [`mɪsɪŋ]　　**adj.** 找不到的；缺少的

🅢 Although she was really careful, her phone went **missing** today!
儘管她非常小心，但她的手機今天不見了！

crime [kraɪm]　　**n.** 犯罪

🅢 She believed her phone was definitely stolen, so she went to the police to report the **crime**.
她認為她的手機一定是被偷了，所以她去和警方報了案。

> 🅔 report the **crime** 報案
>
> 關聯字　criminal n. 罪犯　criminal law n. 刑法
> The judge has sentenced the **criminal** to death.
> 法官判了這個罪犯死刑。

assure [ə`ʃʊr]　　**v.** 向～保證；使放心

🅢 The police officer **assured** her that he would try his best to find it.
警察向她保證，他會盡力找到她的手機。

Day10_048　視而不見沒禮貌

→ 把你知道的單字打勾！
- ☐ courtesy
- ☐ norm
- ☐ unwritten
- ☐ nod
- ☐ greet

→ 用 **5** 個字說出這張圖片的故事！

Day 10 社會與規範 046‧050

courtesy [ˈkɝtəsɪ]　n. 禮貌；禮數

S As a saying goes, "**Courtesy** costs nothing."
俗語說：「禮多人不怪」。

同義字 politeness
關聯字 courteous adj. 禮貌的
MORE "Courtesy costs nothing." 照字面翻譯就是「禮貌不用任何成本」，表示「對別人禮貌或友善，不會造成任何壞處」，也就是中文所說的「禮多人不怪」。

norm [nɔrm]　n. 規範

S However, there are no standard **norms** about courtesy.
然而，禮貌規範是沒有標準的。

MORE 在英文裡，與「規則」有關的字除了 norm 之外還有很多，如 principle（原則）、rule（規則）、regulation（規定）、law（法律）、standard（標準）、guideline（方針）、code（規範）等字。

unwritten [ʌnˈrɪtn̩]　adj. 不成文的

S People can only follow those **unwritten** rules of courtesy to act.
人們只能按照那些不成文的禮貌規則來行動。

反義字 written adj. 成文的，白紙黑字的

nod [nɑd]　v. 點頭

S For example, **nodding** one's head when a person sees another is a common way to say hi.
舉例來說，人們在見到彼此時點頭，是個常見的打招呼方式。

E a **nodding** acquaintance 一位點頭之交

greet [grit]　v. 問候；打招呼

S But some of my classmates don't think so, in fact, they don't even **greet** me.
但我有些同學不這樣覺得，事實上，他們根本就不會向我打招呼。

Day10_049 別遲到了

→ 把你知道的單字打勾！
- [ ] ignore
- [ ] rule
- [ ] delay
- [ ] absence
- [ ] collaborate

→ 用 5 個字說出這張圖片的故事！

ignore [ɪgˋnor]　v. 忽略

An office is like a small society, and some regulations mustn't be **ignored**.
辦公室就是一個小社會，而有些規則是絕不能被忽略的。

同義字 neglect、omit

rule [rul]　n. 規矩，規則

Rule number one, "Don't be late for meetings."
規則第一條：「開會不要遲到」。

delay [dɪˋle]　v. 延誤；延遲

If you're late, the agenda will be **delayed**.
如果你遲到了，議程就會延誤。

MORE delay 這個字的動詞和名詞（也是「延誤；延遲」的意思）同形，使用時請特別注意詞性。
- flight **delay** 班機延誤
- without **delay** 立刻

absence [ˋæbsn̩s]　n. 缺席；不在

Moreover, you should also avoid **absence** without any notice.
此外，你也應該避免在沒有任何通知的情況下缺席。

關聯字 absent adj. 缺席的

collaborate [kə`læbə,ret]　v. 協同合作

- Otherwise, your coworkers will think you're difficult to **collaborate** with.
  不然，你的同事們會認為你很難合作。

  同義字 cooperate、coordinate、work with

Day10_050 餐桌禮儀

→ 把你知道的單字打勾！
- ☐ manner
- ☐ orderly
- ☐ certain
- ☐ spread
- ☐ wipe

→ 用 5 個字說出這張圖片的故事！

manner [`mænɚ]　n. 規矩，禮貌

- Table **manners** are important and should be followed.
  餐桌禮儀很重要，而且應當被遵守。

  E good **manners** 好習慣，有規矩

  MORE manner 在作「規矩，禮貌」的字義時一定會是複數，可以想成「規矩或禮貌的行為一定不會只有一個」，所以一定是複數。

orderly [`ɔrdɚ·lɪ]　adv. 依序地

- For example, we should know how to use tableware **orderly**.
  例如，我們應該要知道如何依序使用餐具。

  MORE orderly 這個字看起來很像是單純的副詞，但其實它也可以當作名詞「勤務員，勤務兵」，或是形容詞「整齊的」，使用時一定要特別注意。

certain [`sɝtən]　adj. 確定的

- When eating soup, be **certain** that you use the right spoon.
  當在喝湯時，要確定你用的是正確的湯匙。

  關聯字 certainly adv. 當然地

spread [sprɛd]　v. 塗抹

🅢 When **spreading** butter onto bread, use butter knife instead of your spoon.
當在抹奶油到麵包上時，要用奶油刀而不是你的湯匙。

> **MORE** spread 這個字最常見的意思是「擴散；傳播」，但也有「展開；攤開」的意思，因此把奶油「抹開」的動作，也就會用 spread 這個字來表達了。

wipe [waɪp]　v. 擦拭；抹除

🅢 After having your meal, don't use a napkin to **wipe** your mouth, just blot it.
在吃完你的餐點之後，別用餐巾紙擦嘴，只要輕拭就好。

> **MORE** wipe 的動作是「滑過整個表面」，所以 wipe mouth 指的是「擦過整個嘴唇的表面」，也就是「抹嘴」，這個動作在用餐時被視為比較不禮貌，因此應該要做的是 blot（按乾，輕拭）而不是 wipe 的動作。

回復記憶 階段

◆ 請參考以下在 Day10 中出現過的圖片，在單字旁的空格寫下字義。

046 抓到小偷了！
- righteous ....
- core ....
- con artist ....
- for the sake of ....
- break into ....

047 手機不見去報案
- long ....
- mobile ....
- missing ....
- crime ....
- assure ....

048 視而不見沒禮貌
- courtesy ....
- norm ....
- unwritten ....
- nod ....
- greet ....

049 別遲到了
- ignore ....
- rule ....
- delay ....
- absence ....
- collaborate ....

050 餐桌禮儀
- manner ....
- orderly ....
- certain ....
- spread ....
- wipe ....

加深記憶 階段

◆ 請依照提示的單字字首，在下列空格中填入適當的單字。

(1) 一個正直的男子　　　　　a r_____ man
(2) 一個重要的規則　　　　　an important r_____
(3) 一個核心價值　　　　　　a c_____ value
(4) 一個不成文的規定　　　　an u_____ rule
(5) 一個被遵守的規範　　　　a followed n_____

◆ 請參考下列方框中的單字，在下列空格中填入適當的單字。

參考 | ignore | for the sake of | spread | greet | long | wipe | missing | break into

(1) Some strangers tried to _____ the apartment.
一些陌生人試圖要闖入這間公寓。

(2) Why do you always _____ me?
你為何總是忽視我？

(3) They are _____ each another.
他們正在彼此問候。

(4) Please _____ the table after dinner.
請在晚餐後擦桌子。

(5) Don't _____ for what you can't get.
不要渴望你無法得到的。

(6) Where is my _____ key?
我遺失的鑰匙在哪裡？

(7) Please _____ the jam onto the bread for me.
請幫我在麵包上抹上果醬。

(8) _____ your own health, you should exercise more.
為了你自己的健康，你應該多運動。

Answers:
1. (1) righteous (2) rule (3) core (4) unwritten (5) norm
2. (1) break into (2) ignore (3) greeting (4) wipe (5) long (6) missing (7) spread (8) For the sake of

Day 11 社會與規範 051-055

Day11_051 霸凌就不對

→ 把你知道的單字打勾！
- [ ] bully
- [ ] harass
- [ ] rookie
- [ ] abuse
- [ ] threaten

→ 用 5 個字說出這張圖片的故事！

bully [`bʊlɪ]　v. 霸凌

S **Bullying** is wrong, but unfortunately it's common in today's society.
霸凌是不對的，但不幸的是，這在現今社會上很普遍。

MORE bully 除了當動詞，也可以當名詞，這時字義就變成「霸凌別人的人」。
Jason is the **bully** in my school.
傑森是我學校裡霸凌別人的人。

harass [`həræs]　v. 騷擾

S Some students like to tease or **harass** their classmates at school.
有些學生在學校喜歡捉弄或是騷擾他們的同學。

關聯字 harassment n. 騷擾　sexual harassment n. 性騷擾

rookie [`rʊkɪ]　n. 菜鳥；新手

S At work, senior workers like to give impossible tasks to **rookies**.
在公司裡，資深員工喜歡把不可能的任務推給菜鳥們。

同義字 apprentice、freshman、beginner、starter

abuse [ə`bjus]　n. 虐待

- Bullying exists in families too, physical or mental **abuse** happens all the time.
  霸凌也存在於家庭之中，身體或心靈上的虐待總是會發生。

threaten [`θrɛtn̩]　v. 威脅

- As a result, we should take measures to stop people **threatening** others.
  因此，我們應該要採取措施來阻止人們威脅其他人。

Day11_052　遲到非好事

→ 把你知道的單字打勾！
- [ ] behavior
- [ ] crawl
- [ ] make up
- [ ] get used to
- [ ] breath

→ 用 5 個字說出這張圖片的故事！

behavior [bɪ`hevjɚ]　n. 行為，舉止

- Being late is not a good **behavior** when you're meeting someone.
  當你要和別人見面的時候，遲到不是個好行為。

  關聯字 behave v. 使守規矩
  Behave yourself, John! Don't speak while I'm talking.
  約翰！規矩一點。我說話時不要講話。

crawl [krɔl]　v. 爬行；緩慢地移動

- Take my boyfriend as an example, he is often late for our date, and I sometimes wonder if he's "**crawling**" to see me.
  拿我男友來說，我們約會的時候他常常遲到，我有時都好奇他是不是用「爬」得來見我。

  關聯字 climb v. 向上爬　creep v. 慢慢爬行；匍匐前進

103

make up　phr. 編造

🅢 Every time he is late, he always **makes up** ridiculous excuses.
每次他遲到，他總是會編造荒謬的藉口。

> **MORE** make up 是一個有很多意義與用法的片語，除了「編造」的意思之外，還有「和解」、「組成」、「補償」等意思，一定要從前後文來解讀 make up 的意思喔！

We had a fight last night, but we **made up** this morning.（和解）
我們昨晚吵架了，但今天早上和好了。
The team is **made up** of 6 engineers.（組成）
這個團隊由 6 個工程師組成。
I will **make** it **up** to you.（補償）
我會補償你的。

get used to　phr. 逐漸習慣

🅢 Today he made me wait for half an hour, and I was kind of **getting used to** it.
今天他讓我等了半個小時，但我有點習慣這種事了。

breath　[brɛθ]　n. 呼吸；氣息

🅢 I just took a deep **breath**, watching as he ran to me and said sorry.
我只是做了一次深呼吸，看著他跑向我並道歉。

> 關聯字　breathe v. 呼吸

Day11_053　騎車記得戴安全帽

→ 把你知道的單字打勾！
- [ ] helmet
- [ ] urban
- [ ] rural
- [ ] force
- [ ] safety

→ 用 5 個字說出這張圖片的故事！

helmet [ˋhɛlmɪt]　n. 安全帽

In accordance with traffic rules, we should wear a **helmet** when riding a motorcycle.
按照交通規則，我們騎機車時應該要戴安全帽。

> **MORE** helmet 泛指一般的安全帽、頭盔等，若要講的是「在工地戴的那種安全帽」，英文則是 hard hat。

urban [ˋɝbən]　adj. 城市的

In Taiwan, people living in **urban** areas tend to follow this regulation.
在台灣，住在城市地區的人們通常會遵守這項規定。

> 關聯字　city n. 城市　downtown n. 市中心　suburban adj. 市郊的
> suburb n. 市郊　outskirt n. 郊區

rural [ˋrʊrəl]　adj. 鄉村的

However, people living in **rural** areas often ignore it.
然而，住在鄉村地區的人們卻經常忽視它。

force [fors]　v. 強迫

In fact, I think the police should **force** them to put on their helmets.
事實上，我認為警方應該強迫他們把他們的安全帽戴上。

> **MORE** force 也可以當成名詞，表示「力量；武力；有影響力的人事物」。

safety [ˋseftɪ]　n. 安全

After all, observing traffic rules can not merely protect yourself but also ensure others' **safety**.
畢竟，遵守交通規則不只能保護你自己，也能確保其他人的安全。

Day11_054 騙子房東

→ 把你知道的單字打勾！
- [ ] landlord
- [ ] deceitful
- [ ] tenant
- [ ] expensive
- [ ] leak

→ 用 5 個字說出這張圖片的故事！

landlord [ˋlænd͵lɔrd]　n. 房東

- There are many bad **landlords** in the rental market.
  在租賃市場上有很多惡房東。

deceitful [dɪˋsitfəl]　adj. 欺騙的；詐欺的

- These **deceitful** landlords rent out their houses with false descriptions.
  這些騙人的房東會用假的描述來把他們的房子租出去。

  關聯字 deceive v. 欺騙　deceit n. 欺騙

tenant [ˋtɛnənt]　n. 房客

- Peter was a new **tenant** moving into an apartment.
  彼得是剛搬進一間公寓的新房客。

expensive [ɪkˋspɛnsɪv]　adj. 昂貴的

- The landlord had told Peter that the apartment was just renovated, so the rent would be more **expensive**.
  房東告訴彼得這間公寓剛裝修過，所以房租會比較貴。

  同義字 pricy、costly
  關聯字 overpriced adj. 售價過高的
  The new released cell phones are **overpriced**.
  新推出的手機售價過高。

leak [lik]　v. 漏水

S Peter rented it anyway, but he soon found the ceiling was **leaking**!
彼得還是租了下去，但他很快就發現天花板在漏水！

E **leaking** water 漏水

E **leaking** pipe 漏水的水管

Day11_055　收件人百百種

→ 把你知道的單字打勾！
- [ ] perceive
- [ ] recount
- [ ] apprehension
- [ ] gentle
- [ ] contempt

→ 用 5 個字說出這張圖片的故事！

perceive [pə`siv]　v. 領悟；察覺

S After years of delivering packages, Johnny **perceives** that calling recipients is just like rolling dice.
在送了幾年包裹之後，強尼領悟到打電話給收件人就像是在擲骰子。

E **perceive** hypocrisy 察覺到虛情假意

同義字 realize、understand

recount [ˌri`kaʊnt]　v. 詳述

S One day, he **recounted** what he had observed to his friends.
有一天，他向他的朋友們詳述了他所觀察到的事。

同義字 state、explain、describe

apprehension [ˌæprɪ`hɛnʃən]　n. 擔心

S Out of **apprehension** for no one being home, he would make a call before he delivered the packages.
因為擔心會沒人在家，所以他會在送包裹之前先打電話。

關聯字 apprehend v. 逮捕　apprehensive adj. 憂慮的；領悟的

gentle [`dʒɛntḷ]　adj. 溫和的；和善的

🇸 Sometimes he was lucky, the recipients were **gentle**, and they would thank him for checking in advance.
有時他很幸運，收件人很和善，而且他們會謝謝他事先確認。

關聯字 gently adv. 溫柔地；溫和地

contempt [kən`tɛmpt]　n. 輕蔑

🇸 On the other hand, some of the recipients would treat him with **contempt** or be impolite.
另一方面，有些收件人會用輕蔑或不禮貌的態度對待他。

> MORE　on the other hand 是十分常用的轉折語，用來表達「另一方面」，在提出兩個相反的意見時可以說「on the one hand ..., on the other hand」，表示「一方面～，另一方面～」。

On the one hand, Jason was really mad at his parents, **on the other hand**, he was somehow looking forward to going to the amusement park with them.
一方面，傑森真的很氣他的爸媽，但另一方面，他卻有點期待和他們一起去遊樂園。

回復記憶 階段

◆ 請參考以下在 Day11 中出現過的圖片，在單字旁的空格寫下字義。

Day 11 社會與規範 051-055

051 霸凌就不對
- bully _____
- harass _____
- rookie _____
- abuse _____
- threaten _____

052 遲到非好事
- behavior _____
- crawl _____
- make up _____
- get used to _____
- breath _____

053 騎車記得戴安全帽
- helmet _____
- urban _____
- rural _____
- force _____
- safety _____

054 騙子房東
- landlord _____
- deceitful _____
- tenant _____
- expensive _____
- leak _____

055 收件人百百種
- perceive _____
- recount _____
- apprehension _____
- gentle _____
- contempt _____

加深記憶 階段

◆ 請依照提示的單字字首，在下列空格中填入適當的單字。

(1) 一個好的房客　　　　a good t_____
(2) 一個昂貴的商品　　　an e_____ product
(3) 一個鄉村地區　　　　a r_____ area
(4) 一個騙人的商人　　　a d_____ businessman
(5) 一個不好的行為　　　a bad b_____

◆ 請參考下列方框中的單字，在下列空格中填入適當的單字。

參考 | harass | landlord | rookie | force | gentle | perceive | make up | threaten

(1) His _____ voice make me calm.
他溫和的嗓音使我平靜。

(2) Have you ever met a bad _____?
你曾經遇過惡房東嗎？

(3) I _____ his purposes.
我查覺到他的目的。

(4) He _____ to hit me.
他威脅要打我。

(5) Don't _____ ridiculous excuses.
不要編造荒謬的藉口。

(6) My boss _____ me to accept his ideas.
我的老闆強迫我接受他的想法。

(7) Are you a _____ in your company?
你在你公司裡是菜鳥嗎？

(8) The male supervisor _____ his female colleague.
這位男性主管騷擾他的女性同事。

Answers:
1. (1) tenant (2) expensive (3) rural (4) deceitful (5) behavior
2. (1) gentle (2) landlord (3) perceived (4) threatened (5) make up (6) forced (7) rookie
   (8) harassed

Day 12 社會與規範 056-060

Day12_056 買花送人

→ 把你知道的單字打勾！
- [ ] sweet
- [ ] remember
- [ ] etiquette
- [ ] harmonious
- [ ] zeal

→ 用 5 個字說出這張圖片的故事！

sweet [swit]　adj. 貼心的；溫柔的

🅢 Hank is a **sweet** person, and he never hesitates to show his care for others.
漢克是一個貼心的人，他從不吝嗇表達對他人的關心。

同義字 considerate、thoughtful
反義字 inconsiderate、thoughtless、sour

remember [rɪ`mɛmbɚ]　v. 記得

🅢 He **remembers** everyone's birthday and the special days worth celebrating.
他記得每一個人的生日和值得慶祝的特別日子。

etiquette [`ɛtɪkɛt]　n. 禮節；禮儀

🅢 He thinks giving flowers is a kind of proper social **etiquette** for celebrating special moments.
他認為送花是一種用來慶祝特別時刻的恰當社交禮節。

🅔 a traditional **etiquette** 一個傳統的禮節

harmonious [hɑr`monɪəs]　adj. 和諧的

S His care let him build **harmonious** relationships with people around him.
他的關心讓他能與他周圍的人建立和諧的關係。

關聯字 harmony n. 和諧

zeal [zil]　n. 熱忱

S His **zeal** for helping others also makes him well-liked.
他對幫助他人的熱忱也讓他備受喜愛。

關聯字 zealot n. 熱心者　zealous adj. 熱心的　zealotry n. 狂熱的行為

Day12_057　醫院禁止吸菸

→ 把你知道的單字打勾！
- [ ] forbid
- [ ] taboo
- [ ] inhale
- [ ] tolerate
- [ ] swell

→ 用 5 個字說出這張圖片的故事！

forbid [fɚ`bɪd]　v. 禁止

S Some behavior must be **forbidden** strictly.
有些行為必須被嚴格禁止。

同義字 ban、prohibit
Camping in a public park should be **forbidden/banned/prohibited**.
在公共公園裡露營應該被禁止。
反義字 allow、permit
MORE forbid 的動詞時態變化屬於不規則變化：
forbid → forbade → forbidden，使用時要特別注意。

taboo [tə`bu]　n. 禁忌

S For example, smoking in the hospital is one of the big **taboos**.
舉例而言，在醫院內抽菸是一大禁忌。

inhale [ɪn`hel]　v. 吸入

🅢 **Nobody wants to inhale secondhand smoke, and the smoke may cause lung cancer.**
沒人想要吸二手菸，而且這些煙霧可能會造成肺癌。

反義字 exhale

MORE smoke 當動詞時是「抽菸」的意思，但 smoke 同時也能當名詞，這時指的是「煙霧」而不是「香菸」，如果想要講的是「香菸」，英文是 cigarette。

You can't **smoke** here. 你不能在這裡抽菸。（抽菸）

The **smoke** is really disgusting. 這個煙霧真的很噁心。（煙霧）

Do you have a **cigarette**? 你有菸嗎？（香菸）

tolerate [`tɑlə͵ret]　v. 忍受

🅢 **A man is smoking in the ward, and the nurse doesn't want to tolerate his behavior.**
一位男子正在病房裡抽菸，而護士不打算忍受他的行為。

同義字 bear、stand、put up with

swell [swɛl]　v.（情緒等）高漲

🅢 **The embarrassment swells in the man's mind, so he puts out his cigarette right away.**
這名男子覺得非常尷尬，所以他立刻把菸熄掉。

MORE 要描述「把菸熄掉」的動作時，會用 put out（熄滅）這個動詞片語。

Day12_058　別打擾別人

→ 把你知道的單字打勾！
- ☐ element
- ☐ principle
- ☐ fray
- ☐ diligent
- ☐ intimate

→ 用 5 個字說出這張圖片的故事！

element [ˈɛləmənt]　n. 要素

🅢 One of the basic **elements** of keeping good relationships is not to disturb others when they're busy.
維持良好關係的基本要素之一是不要在別人忙碌時打擾。

> 🅔 a basic **element** 一個基本的要素

關聯字 elemental adj. 自然力的；基本的　elementary adj. 初級的

principle [ˈprɪnsəpl]　n. 原則；信條

🅢 This **principle** can be applied to almost every circumstance.
這項原則可以適用於幾乎所有的情境之中。

fray [fre]　v. 磨損；使惱火

🅢 If you often disturb others for trivial things, your personal relationships will be **frayed** easily.
假如你常常因為不重要的事而打擾別人，你的人際關係會很容易發生摩擦。

> 同義字 wear away
> Constant dropping **wears away** the stone.
> 滴水穿石。

diligent [ˈdɪlədʒənt]　adj. 勤勉的

🅢 Take **diligent** Eden as an example, his classmate Tom often disturbs him no matter how busy he is.
拿勤奮的艾登舉個例子，不論他有多忙，他的同學湯姆常常會打擾他。

> 關聯字 diligence n. 勤勉
> **Diligence** is the key to success.
> 勤勉是成功的關鍵。

intimate [ˈɪntəmɪt]　adj. 親密的

🅢 If the situation keeps on like this, no matter how **intimate** they are now, their relationship won't keep long.
若情況一直這樣，無論他們現在有多親密，他們的關係也不會維持長久。

Day12_059 接待客人很難

→ 把你知道的單字打勾！
- [ ] receptionist
- [ ] generic
- [ ] quiver
- [ ] nuisance
- [ ] graciously

→ 用 5 個字說出這張圖片的故事！

receptionist [rɪ`sɛpʃənɪst]　n. 接待人員

S I am a **receptionist** at the information desk of a department store.
我是一間百貨公司的服務台接待人員。

> **MORE** 除了 receptionist 之外，會提供接待服務的還有 desk lady（櫃台小姐）、agent（服務專員）、usher（餐廳或電影院等的帶位人員）、doorman（門房）、parking valet（泊車人員）。

generic [dʒɪ`nɛrɪk]　adj. 普通的，一般的

S This is a **generic** job, but I have to meet different customers every day.
這份工作沒什麼特別的，但我每天必須面對不同的客人。

[同義字] common、general

quiver [`kwɪvɚ]　v. 顫抖

S Sometimes I even **quiver** with anger when I encounter unreasonable customers.
當我遇到不講理的客人時，我有時甚至會氣到發抖。

[同義字] shiver、tremble

nuisance [`njusn̩s]　n. 惱人的事

S Those **nuisances** make me want to quit sometimes, but nice customers are the reason for me to stay on the job.
這些惱人的事讓我有時想辭職，但好客人是我繼續堅守崗位的理由。

graciously [ˈgreʃəslɪ]　adv. 親切禮貌地

S Like the lady in front of me, she **graciously** asked me where the restrooms were, and her politeness makes me happy to help her.
就像在我眼前的這位小姐，她禮貌地問了我廁所在哪裡，她的禮貌讓我很開心為她服務。

Day12_060　不接受陌生人的食物

→ 把你知道的單字打勾！
- [ ] beware
- [ ] acquainted
- [ ] kidnap
- [ ] disastrous
- [ ] unbearable

→ 用 5 個字說出這張圖片的故事！

---

beware [bɪˈwɛr]　v. 當心；留意

S Children should **beware** of certain kinds of crimes.
孩子們應當要留意某些犯罪型態。

| 同義字 | watch out、be careful

---

acquainted [əˈkwentɪd]　adj. 認識的

S Some bad guys would pretend they are **acquainted** with your parents, and provide snacks to lure you.
有些壞人可能會假裝他們認識你的父母，並給你零食來誘惑你。

| 同義字 | familiar
| 反義字 | unacquainted、unfamiliar
He is **unacquainted/unfamiliar** with his neighbors.
他與他的鄰居不熟。

kidnap [ˋkɪdnæp]　　v. 綁架

🅢 They may take you in their car and **kidnap** you for ransom.
他們可能會把你帶到他們的車上，並綁架你來要求贖金。

disastrous [dɪzˋæstrəs]　　adj. 災難性的，悲慘的

🅢 To avoid something **disastrous** happening, you should say no to strangers, no matter how you want to eat the snacks they offer.
為了避免發生這種悲慘的事，你應該對陌生人說不，不論你有多想吃他們給的零食。

關聯字 disaster n. 災難

unbearable [ʌnˋbɛrəbl]　　adj. 難以承受的

🅢 Otherwise, the outcome will be **unbearable**.
否則，後果將會是難以承受的。

回復記憶 階段

◆ 請參考以下在 Day12 中出現過的圖片，在單字旁的空格寫下字義。

056 買花送人
- sweet ....
- remember ....
- etiquette ....
- harmonious ....
- zeal ....

057 醫院禁止吸菸
- forbid ....
- taboo ....
- inhale ....
- tolerate ....
- swell ....

058 別打擾別人
- element ....
- principle ....
- fray ....
- diligent ....
- intimate ....

059 接待客人很難
- receptionist ....
- generic ....
- quiver ....
- nuisance ....
- graciously ....

060 不接受陌生人的食物
- beware ....
- acquainted ....
- kidnap ....
- disastrous ....
- unbearable ....

加深記憶階段

◆ 請依照提示的單字字首，在下列空格中填入適當的單字。

(1) 一個難以承受的消息　　　an u_____ news
(2) 一個認識的人　　　　　　an a_____ person
(3) 一幅普通的畫作　　　　　a g_____ painting
(4) 一個親密的伙伴　　　　　an i_____ partner
(5) 一個可怕的禁忌　　　　　a scary t_____

◆ 請參考下列方框中的單字，在下列空格中填入適當的單字。

參考 | forbid | sweet | etiquette | element |
　　 | remember | receptionist | harmonious | graciously |

(1) Gambling should be _____.
　　賭博應該被禁止。

(2) Do you understand telephone _____?
　　你了解電話禮儀嗎？

(3) We have a _____ family.
　　我們有個和諧的家庭。

(4) He _____ answered my questions.
　　他親切有禮地回答了我的問題。

(5) Ask the _____ how to buy the tickets.
　　去問接待人員要如何買票。

(6) He is such a _____ guy! Look what he gave me!
　　他真是一個貼心的人！看看他給了我什麼！

(7) What are the _____ of success?
　　成功的要素是什麼？

(8) Did you _____ to lock the door?
　　你有記得鎖門嗎？

Answers:
1. (1) unbearable (2) acquainted (3) generic (4) intimate (5) taboo
2. (1) forbidden (2) etiquette (3) harmonious (4) graciously (5) receptionist (6) sweet (7) elements
　 (8) remember

Day 12 社會與規範 056-060

記單字必備！掌握常見字首 02

★ 表示否定的字首

in-

肯定	否定
expensive 昂貴的	**in**expensive 不貴的
complete 完整的	**in**complete 不完整的
convenient 方便的	**in**convenient 不方便的

im-

肯定	否定
possible 可能	**im**possible 不可能
polite 禮貌的	**im**polite 不禮貌的
balance 平衡	**im**balance 不平衡

ir-

肯定	否定
resistible 可以抵擋的	**ir**resistible 無法抵擋的
responsible 負責的	**ir**responsible 不負責的
rational 有理性的	**ir**rational 不理性的

il-

肯定	否定
legal 合法的	**il**legal 不合法的
literate 識字的	**il**literate 不識字的
logical 合邏輯的	**il**logical 不合邏輯的

non-

肯定	否定
violent 暴力的	**non**violent 非暴力的
stop 停止	**non**stop 不休止的
sense 道理；益處；意義	**non**sense 無道理或不重要的東西

un-

肯定	否定
doubted 存疑的	**un**doubted 無疑的
common 平凡的	**un**common 不凡的
usual 通常的	**un**usual 不尋常的

mis-

肯定	否定
understanding 理解	**mis**understanding 誤解
apply 應用	**mis**apply 誤用
arrange 安排	**mis**arrange 做錯誤的安排

dis-

肯定	否定
cover 覆蓋	**dis**cover 發現
agree 同意	**dis**agree 不同意
like 喜歡	**dis**like 不喜歡

Day 13 動物世界 061-065

Day13.mp3

Day13_061 所謂的能動能靜

→ 把你知道的單字打勾！
- [ ] adorable
- [ ] even-tempered
- [ ] rest
- [ ] patio
- [ ] vigorous

→ 用 5 個字說出這張圖片的故事！

adorable [əˋdorəb!]　　adj. 可愛的

S Jim has an **adorable** beagle.
吉姆有一隻可愛的米格魯。

> **MORE** 這裡補充一些常見的狗種名稱，一起記下來吧！
> Beagle 米格魯　Labrador 拉不拉多　Boxer 拳師犬
> Golden Retriever 黃金獵犬　Poodle 貴賓犬　Bulldog 鬥牛犬
> Shiba Inu 柴犬　Border Collie 邊境牧羊犬

even-tempered [ˋivənˋtɛmpɚd]　　adj. 性情平和的；冷靜的

S His beagle is different, instead of being feisty, he's rather **even-tempered**.
他的米格魯很特別，比起躁動不安，他還滿冷靜的。

> **E** an **even-tempered** man 一個性情平和的男人
> 反義字 bad-tempered、feisty
> **MORE** 因為現代人多把寵物視為家人，因此在使用代名詞時多半會使用 he/she 而不是 it，這點要特別注意。

rest [rɛst]　　v. 休息

S They even can **rest** or sleep on the same bed without any mess.
他們甚至可以一起在同一張床上休息或睡覺，而不會造成任何麻煩。

patio [ˈpɑtɪˌo]　n. 露臺

- Today, Jim and his dog are playing fetch on the **patio**.
  今天,吉姆與他的狗在露臺上玩拋接。

vigorous [ˈvɪgərəs]　adj. 精力充沛的

- He is really **vigorous** and excited during their play time.
  他在他們的玩樂時間裡非常精力充沛且興奮。

  同義字 energetic、spirited

Day13_062　就是喜歡狗！

→ 把你知道的單字打勾！
- [ ] variety
- [ ] altogether
- [ ] domesticated
- [ ] loyal
- [ ] function

→ 用 5 個字說出這張圖片的故事!

variety [vəˈraɪətɪ]　n. 多樣化；種種

- Last time when I went to a dog park, I saw a **variety** of dogs.
  上次我去狗公園的時候,我看到了各式各樣的狗。

  關聯字 vary v. 變化；使多樣化　various adj. 多變的；各式各樣的

altogether [ˌɔltəˈgɛðɚ]　adv. 總計,全部

- **Altogether** I saw beagles, Labradors, poodles and bulldogs.
  我總共看到了米格魯、拉不拉多、貴賓與鬥牛犬。

domesticated [dəˈmɛstəˌketɪd]　adj. 被馴養的

- Unlike wild animals, dogs are **domesticated** animals and it is difficult for them to survive without human beings.
  不像野生動物,狗是被馴養的動物,且牠們在沒有人類的情況下很難生存。

  關聯字 domestic adj. 國內的；家庭的

123

loyal [ˋlɔɪəl]　adj. 忠誠的

S People like dogs because they are friendly and **loyal**.
人們喜歡狗，因為牠們既友善又忠誠。

function [ˋfʌŋkʃən]　n. 功能

S Dogs also perform different **functions** in human society, such as hunting, investigating and leading the blind.
狗也在人類社會中發揮了不同的功能，像是打獵、調查及引導盲人。

Day13_063 我的膽小貓

→ 把你知道的單字打勾！
- [ ] kitten
- [ ] on the contrary
- [ ] hurricane
- [ ] lightning
- [ ] hide

→ 用 5 個字說出這張圖片的故事！

kitten [ˋkɪtṇ]　n. 小貓，幼貓

S I have a **kitten**, and her name is "Tiger".
我有一隻小貓，她的名字是「老虎」。

> **MORE** 有些動物的幼年時期擁有自己的單字，例如這裡的 kitten，其他常見的還有 puppy（小狗）、duckling（小鴨）、piglet（小豬）、chick（小雞；雛鳥）、calf（小牛）、lamb（小羊）等。

on the contrary　phr. 正好相反

S Tiger is nothing like a real tiger, **on the contrary**, she is very timid.
老虎和真的老虎一點也不像，正好相反，她非常膽小。

關聯字 contrary n. 相反 adj. 相反的　contrast v. 對照 n. 差異

hurricane [ˈhɜ˞ɪˌken]   n. 颶風，暴風雨

- The weather today is terrible, because there is a **hurricane** striking.
  今天的天氣很糟，因為有個颶風襲來。

  > **MORE** 除了 hurricane（颶風）之外，還有一些常見的劇烈天氣現象，如 typhoon（颱風）、gust（強風）、tornado（龍捲風）可以一併記住。

lightning [ˈlaɪtnɪŋ]   n. 閃電

- Thunder and **lightning** make Tiger scared.
  雷聲和閃電讓老虎很害怕。

  - flashy **lightning** 閃亮的閃電

hide [haɪd]   v. 隱藏

- She is so scared that she **hides** herself under an armchair.
  她害怕到把自己藏在了扶手椅底下。

  - **hide**-and-seek 捉迷藏

Day13_064　寵物看醫生

→ 把你知道的單字打勾！
- [ ] seek
- [ ] veterinarian
- [ ] infect
- [ ] injection
- [ ] bark

→ 用 5 個字說出這張圖片的故事！

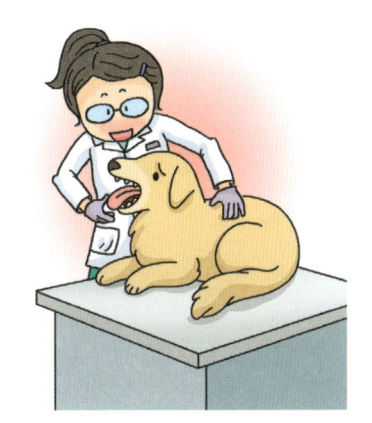

seek [sik]   v. 尋求

- If people are sick, they will **seek** a doctor's help.
  如果人們生病了，他們會尋求醫生的協助。

  同義字 look for

Day 13 動物世界 061-065

125

veterinarian [ˌvɛtərəˈnɛrɪən]　　n. 獸醫

- On the other hand, animals do need doctors too, their doctors are called "**veterinarians**".
  另一方面，動物們當然也需要醫生，牠們的醫生叫做「獸醫」。

  MORE 因為 veterinarian 這個字比較長，一般更常使用 vet 來簡稱。

infect [ɪnˈfɛkt]　　v. 感染

- My dog vomited last night, and I thought he might be **infected** by a flu virus.
  我的狗昨天晚上吐了，我認為他也許感染了流感病毒。

  關聯字 infectious adj. 受感染的　infection n. 感染

injection [ɪnˈdʒɛkʃən]　　n. 注射

- The vet gave him a thorough checkup and decided to give him an **injection**.
  獸醫幫他做了徹底的檢查，並決定幫他打一針。

  關聯字 inject v. 注射　injector n. 注射器

bark [bɑrk]　　v. 吠叫

- After the injection, he **barked** at the vet for a while like he was complaining.
  在打完針之後，他對著獸醫吠了一陣子，像在抱怨似的。

  - **bark** at ~ 對～吠叫
  - be **barking** up the wrong tree 用錯方法；找錯原因

Day13_065　青蛙真有趣

→ 把你知道的單字打勾！
- [ ] fairy tale
- [ ] evil
- [ ] reality
- [ ] species
- [ ] lay

→ 用 5 個字說出這張圖片的故事！

fairy tale [ˈfɛrɪ] [tel]　n. 童話故事

- I have been so interested in frogs since I heard the **fairy tale**, "The Frog Prince".
  從我聽了「青蛙王子」的童話故事之後，我就一直對青蛙非常感興趣。

evil [ˈivl̩]　adj. 邪惡的

- In the story, a prince was turned into a frog by an **evil** fairy.
  在故事之中，一個王子被一個邪惡的精靈變成了青蛙。

  反義字 kind、sacred

reality [rɪˈælətɪ]　n. 現實

- In **reality**, frogs are rather fascinating and interesting.
  在現實中，青蛙是很有意思、很有趣的。

  關聯字 real adj. 真實的　　really adv. 真地；非常

species [ˈspiʃiz]　n. 物種；種類

- Adult frogs can live in fresh water or on dry land, and some **species** can even live underground.
  成年的青蛙可以住在淡水裡或乾燥的陸地上，且有些種類甚至可以在地下生活。

  MORE species 這個字的單複數是同形的，使用時要特別注意。

lay [le]　v. 產卵

- Based on where they live, they also **lay** eggs in different places.
  根據牠們居住的地方，牠們也會在不同地方產卵。

  MORE lay 這個字除了是「產卵」，也是 lie（躺臥）的過去式，下面補充三個長的很像的動詞三態比較，使用時要特別注意。
  lay-laid-laid v. 產卵；放置
  lie-lay-lain v. 躺臥；置於
  lie-lied-lied v. 說謊

Day 13 動物世界 061-065

回復記憶 階段

◆ 請參考以下在 Day13 中出現過的圖片，在單字旁的空格寫下字義。

061 所謂的能動能靜
- adorable _____
- even-tempered _____
- rest _____
- patio _____
- vigorous _____

062 就是喜歡狗！
- variety _____
- altogether _____
- domesticated _____
- loyal _____
- function _____

063 我的膽小貓
- kitten _____
- on the contrary _____
- hurricane _____
- lightning _____
- hide _____

064 寵物看醫生
- seek _____
- veterinarian _____
- infect _____
- injection _____
- bark _____

065 青蛙真有趣
- fairy tale _____
- evil _____
- reality _____
- species _____
- lay _____

128

加深記憶 階段

◆ 請依照提示的單字字首，在下列空格中填入適當的單字。

(1) 一隻可愛的米格魯　　　　an a_____ beagle
(2) 一個邪惡的女巫　　　　　an e_____ witch
(3) 一個特別的童話故事　　　a special f_____
(4) 不同的物種　　　　　　　different s_____
(5) 一位親切的獸醫　　　　　a kind v_____

◆ 請參考下列方框中的單字，在下列空格中填入適當的單字。

| 參考 | patio | even-tempered | infect | seek | loyal | hurricane | rest | reality |

(1) We often _____ at home on Saturday evenings.
我們週六的晚上經常在家裡休息。

(2) The _____ is large, isn't it?
這個露臺很大，不是嗎？

(3) _____ hurts.
現實很傷人。

(4) I am _____ more donations.
我正在尋求更多的捐獻。

(5) The wound is _____.
這傷口被感染了。

(6) My pet dogs are very _____.
我的寵物狗們的性情都非常冷靜。

(7) The employees are all _____ to the company.
員工們全都對公司很忠誠。

(8) You should be prepared for the _____.
你應該要為這個颶風做好準備。

Answers:
1. (1) adorable (2) evil (3) fairy tale (4) species (5) veterinarian
2. (1) rest (2) patio (3) Reality (4) seeking (5) infected (6) even-tempered (7) loyal (8) hurricane

Day 14 動物世界 066-070

Day14_066 我的好夥伴

→ 把你知道的單字打勾！
- [ ] stray
- [ ] adoption
- [ ] establish
- [ ] refreshing
- [ ] no doubt

→ 用 5 個字說出這張圖片的故事！

stray [stre]　　adj. 流浪的；走失的

S Mimi and Fufu were originally **stray** dogs before I adopted them.
咪咪與福福在我領養他們之前是流浪狗。

E a **stray** dog 一隻流浪狗

MORE 如果想要講「流浪漢」，不能用 stray 這個字，而是要用 homeless（無家可歸的）這個字，以 homeless man 來表達。

Many **homeless men** gather in this area.
很多流浪漢聚集在這一區。

adoption [əˋdɑpʃən]　　n. 領養

S The **adoption** process was long and complicated, but it was necessary to make sure the adopter was a suitable one.
領養程序又長又複雜，但確保領養者是適合的人是必要的。

E **adoption** process/procedure 領養程序

關聯字 adopt v. 領養；採納　adopter n. 領養者；採納者

establish [ə`stæblɪʃ]　**v.** 建立

S Since they came, I have fed and played with them every day to **establish** the bond between us.
自從他們來了，我每天都餵他們及和他們玩來建立我們之間的連結。

E **establish** a bond 建立一段連結
同義字 build
關聯字 establishment n. 建立；機構

---

refreshing [rɪ`frɛʃɪŋ]　**adj.** 令人耳目一新的

S They bring joy to my life and it's **refreshing** to be with them.
他們為我的生活帶來樂趣，和他們在一起讓我覺得耳目一新。

關聯字 refresh v. 使提振精神　refreshment n. 精神提振；茶點
Tasty **refreshments refreshes** me.
好吃的茶點讓我精神為之一振。

---

no doubt　**phr.** 無疑地

S Their company is **no doubt** the best gift of my life.
他們的陪伴無疑是我生命中最棒的禮物。

Day 14 動物世界 066・070

Day14_067　獅子生病了

→ 把你知道的單字打勾！
- [ ] beg
- [ ] shout
- [ ] as well as
- [ ] zookeeper
- [ ] muscular

→ 用 5 個字說出這張圖片的故事！

131

beg [bɛg]　v. 乞求，懇求

🅢 My kids **begged** me to take them to the zoo last weekend.
上週末我的孩子們懇求我帶他們去動物園。

關聯字 beggar n. 乞丐

shout [ʃaʊt]　v. 大叫；大聲說

🅢 As we were walking in the zoo, one of my kids **shouted**, "Look at that lion!"
正當我們走在動物園裡時，我其中一個孩子大叫：「看那隻獅子！」。

MORE 英文裡的「叫」有好幾種說法，這裡的 shout 是「放大音量希望自己被聽到」，而 yell 通常是「因為生氣、疼痛或激動而叫」，scream 則是「因恐懼、憤怒等情緒而尖叫」。

as well as　phr. 而且；也

🅢 The lion was surprisingly thin **as well as** spiritless.
這隻獅子令人意外地又瘦又沒精神。

同義字 not only... but also...、both A and B
MORE 如果想要表達「A 和 B 都～」，在英文裡有三種最常用的表達方式，例如想說「麗莎又聰明又漂亮」時，可以有下面三種講法：

1. both A and B：Lisa is **both** smart **and** pretty.
2. A as well as B：Lisa is smart **as well as** pretty.
3. not only A but also B：Lisa is **not only** smart **but also** pretty.

zookeeper [ˋzuˌkipɚ]　n. 動物園飼育員

🅢 "He is sick," a **zookeeper** passing by explained to us.
「他生病了」一位經過的動物園飼育員向我們解釋。

muscular [ˋmʌskjəlɚ]　adj. 肌肉發達的

🅢 "In fact, lions are normally strong and **muscular**," he continued.
他繼續說：「事實上，獅子正常是強壯又肌肉發達的。」

關聯字 muscle n. 肌肉

Day14_068 猴子掉下來了！

→ 把你知道的單字打勾！
- ☐ naughty
- ☐ bright
- ☐ evolve
- ☐ imagine
- ☐ accidentally

→ 用 5 個字說出這張圖片的故事！

naughty [ˈnɔtɪ]　　adj. 頑皮的

🅢 Most people think monkeys are **naughty** animals.
大部分人認為猴子是頑皮的動物。

bright [braɪt]　　adj. 聰明的

🅢 Their **bright** minds and interesting behaviors make them special.
他們聰明的心智與有趣的行為讓牠們很特別。

MORE 除了「聰明的」，bright 也有「明亮的」的意思。
We should look on the **bright** side.
我們應該要看光明面。

evolve [ɪˈvɑlv]　　v. 演化；逐步演進

🅢 It is said that monkeys and human beings **evolved** from the same ancestors.
據說猴子和人類是由相同的祖先演化而來。

imagine [ɪˈmædʒɪn]　　v. 想像

🅢 Looking at them, it's hard to **imagine** that we were once monkeys.
看著牠們，很難想像我們曾經是猴子。

關聯字　imagination n. 想像　　image n. 形象　　imaginary adj. 幻想的

Day 14 動物世界 066-070

accidentally [ˌæksəˋdɛntḷɪ]　adv. 意外地；不小心地

- Just when I was staring at them, there was a monkey that **accidentally** fell from a tree!
就在我盯著牠們瞧時，有一隻猴子不小心從一棵樹上掉下來了！

同義字 by accident
反義字 on purpose

Day14_069 鄰居的狗

→ 把你知道的單字打勾！
☐ mixed-breed
☐ emotional
☐ bury
☐ now and then
☐ compensate

→ 用 5 個字說出這張圖片的故事！

mixed-breed [ˋmɪkstˌbrid]　adj. 混種的

- My neighbor has a **mixed-breed** dog, which was given to him by his friend.
我的鄰居有隻米克斯，這隻狗是他朋友送的。

emotional [ɪˋmoʃən!]　adj. 容易激動的；情緒化的

- He is an **emotional** dog, and he gets really excited when seeing food.
他是一隻容易激動的狗，而且他在看到食物的時候會變得非常興奮。

關聯字 emotion n. 情緒　sentimental adj. 多愁善感的

bury [ˋbɛrɪ]　v. 掩埋

- He likes to dig a hole and **bury** his bones under the ground.
他喜歡挖洞並將他的骨頭埋在地底下。

now and then　phr. 不時，偶爾

- However, **now and then** he buries bones in my yard, which upsets me every time.
  但是，偶爾他會把骨頭埋在我的院子裡，這件事每次都會讓我覺得不高興。

  MORE 一起來看看常用的「頻率片語」吧！
  all the time 總是　more often than not 通常（＝usually）
  now and then 不時地（＝sometimes＝at times＝from time to time）

compensate　[ˈkɑmpənˌset]　v. 補償

- My neighbor apologizes and **compensates** me by giving me some gifts.
  我的鄰居會道歉並送我一些禮物當作補償。

  關聯字　compensation n. 補償；薪資福利
  　　　　compensation management n. 薪酬管理

Day14_070　貓狗不合

→ 把你知道的單字打勾！
- [ ] hostile
- [ ] foe
- [ ] question
- [ ] documentary
- [ ] interaction

→ 用 5 個字說出這張圖片的故事！

hostile [ˋhɑstɪl]　adj. 充滿敵意的

🅢 Are dogs and cats necessarily **hostile** to each other?
狗和貓一定會對彼此充滿敵意嗎？

|同義字| antagonistic
|反義字| friendly

foe [fo]　n. 敵人

🅢 If you ask me, I would say cats see dogs as real **foes**.
如果你問我的話，我會說貓會把狗當成真正的敵人。

|同義字| enemy

question [ˋkwɛstʃən]　v. 質疑

🅢 I know people would **question** my opinion, but my cats reject my dog all the time.
我知道大家可能會對我的意見有所質疑，但我的貓們總是很排斥我的狗。

|MORE| question 的動詞和名詞同形，使用時要注意。

documentary [͵dɑkjəˋmɛntərɪ]　n. 紀錄片

🅢 I remember I once watched a **documentary** about the relationships between dogs and cats.
我記得我曾看過一部與狗貓關係有關的紀錄片。

|關聯字| document n. 文件

interaction [͵ɪntəˋrækʃən]　n. 互動

🅢 In the documentary, the hostile **interactions** between them are mostly started by the hissing cats.
在紀錄片中，牠們之間充滿敵意的互動多半是由正在威嚇的貓開始的。

回復記憶階段

◆ 請參考以下在 Day14 中出現過的圖片，在單字旁的空格寫下字義。

066 我的好夥伴
- stray _____
- adoption _____
- establish _____
- refreshing _____
- no doubt _____

067 獅子生病了
- beg _____
- shout _____
- as well as _____
- zookeeper _____
- muscular _____

068 猴子掉下來了！
- naughty _____
- bright _____
- evolve _____
- imagine _____
- accidentally _____

069 鄰居的狗
- mixed-breed _____
- emotional _____
- bury _____
- now and then _____
- compensate _____

070 貓狗不合
- hostile _____
- foe _____
- question _____
- documentary _____
- interaction _____

Day 14 動物世界 066-070

加深記憶階段

◆ 請依照提示的單字字首，在下列空格中填入適當的單字。

(1) 友善的互動　　　　　　friendly i_____
(2) 一個卑鄙的敵人　　　　a mean f_____
(3) 一個容易激動的女人　　an e_____ woman
(4) 一個頑皮的學生　　　　a n_____ student
(5) 一個肌肉發達的男子　　a m_____ man

◆ 請參考下列方框中的單字，在下列空格中填入適當的單字。

| 參考 | bright | refreshing | establish | accidentally |
| | hostile | no doubt | imagine | as well as |

(1) I dialed a wrong number _____.
    我不小心撥錯了電話號碼。

(2) Are the two firms _____ to each other?
    這兩家公司是敵對的嗎？

(3) Can you _____ what will happen in a decade?
    你能想像十年後會發生什麼事嗎？

(4) Amy is studying _____ her sisters.
    艾咪和她的姊妹們正在念書。

(5) Susie is a _____ girl.
    蘇西是個聰明的女孩。

(6) My boss _____ a new rule for us.
    我的老闆為我們建立了一個新規則。

(7) _____ he is your Mr. Right.
    他無疑是你的夢中情人。

(8) _____ cold drinks make us happy in hot days.
    清爽的冷飲讓我們在炎熱的日子裡覺得開心。

Answers:
1. (1) interaction (2) foe (3) emotional (4) naughty (5) muscular
2. (1) accidentally (2) hostile (3) imagine (4) as well as (5) bright (6) established (7) No doubt
   (8) Refreshing

Day 15 動物世界 071-075

Day15_071 被狗追超可怕

→ 把你知道的單字打勾！
- [ ] chase
- [ ] fierce
- [ ] come across
- [ ] cowardice
- [ ] stammer

→ 用 5 個字說出這張圖片的故事！

chase [tʃes]　v. 追趕

Ben has been afraid of dogs since he was **chased** by a barking dog.
自從班被吠叫的狗追了之後，他就一直很怕狗。

fierce [fɪrs]　adj. 兇猛的

He said what he had encountered then was not a dog but a **fierce** monster.
他說他那時遇到的不是狗而是兇猛的怪獸。

fierce battle 激戰

come across　phr. 碰巧遇到

Now, every time he **comes across** a dog, he always walks away quickly.
現在，每次他碰到狗時，他都會快速走開。

同義字 run into、bump into

cowardice [ˋkaʊɚdɪs]　n. 膽小

🅢 Sometimes Ben's friends laugh at his **cowardice**.
有時班的朋友們會嘲笑他的膽小。

關聯字 **coward** adj. 膽小的 n. 懦夫
The **coward** husband only dares to bully his wife.
這個膽小的丈夫只敢欺負他的老婆。
Don't be a **coward**, you need to fight for what you want!
別當個懦夫，你必須為自己想要的奮鬥！

stammer [ˋstæmɚ]　v. 結巴地說

🅢 Ben always **stammers**, "I'm not afraid of them. I just don't like dogs!" 班總是會結巴地說：「我不是怕牠們。我只是不喜歡狗！」。

Day15_072　好命的貓

→ 把你知道的單字打勾！
☐ treasure
☐ stride
☐ proud
☐ fur
☐ rather

→ 用 5 個字說出這張圖片的故事！

treasure [ˋtrɛʒɚ]　n. 寶藏

🅢 My cat is my **treasure**, and she is spoiled by the whole family.
我的貓是我的寶貝，而且全家都很溺愛她。

　MORE **treasure** 也可以當作動詞，當動詞時的字義和 cherish 相同，都是「珍惜」的意思。

stride [straɪd]　v. 大步走

🅢 She often **strides** about our house with a proud look on her face.
她常常會臉上帶著得意的表情大步走在我們家裡。

　MORE **stride** 特別指的是「邁開腳步大步走」，而不單純只是 walk（走）。

140

proud [praʊd]　adj. 得意的；驕傲的

- She seems to know everyone in my family loves her, and she is **proud** of herself.
  她似乎知道家裡所有人都愛她，而且她對自己感到驕傲。

  反義字 ashamed

fur [fɝ]　n. 毛皮

- She has sleek and soft **fur**.
  她有著光滑又柔軟的毛皮。

  關聯字 furry adj. 毛皮的；毛茸茸的

rather [`ræðɚ]　adv. 相當，有點

- Every time I pet her, I can feel the **rather** comforting feeling filling my mind.
  每次我摸她的時候，我都能感覺到那種有點療癒的感覺充滿了我的心中。

  同義字 quite

Day15_073　逝去的狗

→ 把你知道的單字打勾！
- ☐ die of
- ☐ sorrow
- ☐ pet
- ☐ miserable
- ☐ decline

→ 用 5 個字說出這張圖片的故事！

die of　phr. 因～死亡

- Karen's dog **died of** cancer last month.
  凱倫的狗在上個月因為癌症而死了。

  > **MORE** die of 的 of 之後接的是死因，這裡的死因通常會是疾病或傷心、憂鬱等情緒，有一個類似的片語是 die from，但 from 後面接的死因通常是「外力」，像是車禍或失足等原因。

Day 15 動物世界 071-075

141

sorrow [ˋsaro]　n. 悲傷

- After her dog died, Karen lived in **sorrow**.
  在她的狗死後，凱倫活在了悲傷之中。

  關聯字 sorrowful adj. 悲傷的

pet [pɛt]　v. 拍撫；輕摸

- She would sometimes dream about **petting** her dog.
  她有時候會夢到她在拍撫她的狗。

  MORE pet 當名詞時是「寵物」的意思。

miserable [ˋmɪzərəbl]　adj. 痛苦的

- Sometimes she would feel **miserable**, and have a sleepless night.
  她有時會覺得很痛苦，然後整個晚上都睡不著。

decline [dɪˋklaɪn]　v. 婉拒

- Karen **declined** her parents' offer to have another dog, because she didn't think she was ready for that.
  凱倫婉拒了她父母說要再養一隻狗的提議，因為她不覺得自己準備好要這樣做了。

Day15_074 恐龍時代

→ 把你知道的單字打勾！
- [ ] dinosaur
- [ ] diverse
- [ ] best-selling
- [ ] fossil
- [ ] mysterious

→ 用 5 個字說出這張圖片的故事！

dinosaur [ˋdaɪnəˌsɔr]　n. 恐龍

- **Dinosaurs** appeared during the Triassic period.
  恐龍出現在三疊紀。

142

diverse [daɪˋvɝs]　adj. 多樣化的

- Most of them belong to a group of **diverse** reptiles.
  牠們大部分都屬於一群多樣化的爬蟲類。

  同義字 various

best-selling [ˋbɛstˋsɛlɪŋ]　adj. 最暢銷的

- It's impossible for us to see real dinosaurs, and most people have only seen them in the **best-selling** Jurassic Park movies.
  我們沒辦法看到真正的恐龍，而且大部分的人只會在最暢銷的侏儸紀公園系列電影裡看到牠們。

fossil [ˋfɑsl̩]　n. 化石

- Scientists have learnt about dinosaurs through studying **fossils**.
  科學家們藉由研究化石來習得與恐龍有關的知識。

  MORE　fossil 除了指真正的化石之外，也可以拿來說某人是「食古不化的人」，做為形容詞時則是「化石的；守舊的」的意思。

mysterious [mɪsˋtɪrɪəs]　adj. 神祕的

- But until now, dinosaurs were still rather **mysterious** due to the lack of study materials.
  但直到現在，恐龍還是因為缺乏研究素材而相當神祕。

  關聯字　mystery n. 神祕的事物　　mysteriously adv. 神祕地

Day15_075　人類常吃的動物

→ 把你知道的單字打勾！
- [ ] product
- [ ] pork chop
- [ ] eatable
- [ ] nugget
- [ ] bar

→ 用 5 個字說出這張圖片的故事！

product [ˈprɑdəkt]　n. 產品

🅢 The cattle farming business provides beef and dairy **products** for us.
畜牛產業為我們提供了牛肉及乳製品。

> 關聯字 produce v. 生產 n. 農產品　productive adj. 有生產力的
> productivity n. 生產力
>
> MORE 如果想要特別指「農產品」的話，可以使用 produce 這個字。cattle 這個字是「牛的總稱」，cow 是「乳牛」、bull 是「未閹割的公牛」、ox 是「已閹割的公牛」、calf 則是「小牛」

pork chop [pork] [tʃɑp]　n. 豬排

🅢 Bacon and **pork chops** are from pigs; eggs and chicken are from chickens.
培根與豬排來自豬，而雞蛋與雞肉來自雞。

> MORE pork chop 裡的 chop，當動詞時的意思是「砍；剁」，名詞時則是「排骨」的意思。

eatable [ˈitəb!]　adj.（味道上）可以吃的

🅢 Among all the **eatable** animals, I like chickens best.
在所有這些可以吃的動物之中，我最喜歡雞。

> MORE eatable 所說的「可以吃」是指「味道上過得去的」，字義相似的 edible 則是指「安全考量上可以吃的」。

nugget [ˈnʌgɪt]　n. 雞塊

🅢 Because I like chicken **nuggets** and fried chicken very much.
因為我非常喜歡雞塊與炸雞。

bar [bɑr]　n. 酒吧

🅢 Every time I go to a **bar**, I would definitely order chicken nuggets and fried chicken with a cold beer, what a life!
每次我去酒吧，我一定會點雞塊與炸雞和一杯冰啤酒，人生多美好啊！

回復記憶 階段

◆ 請參考以下在 Day15 中出現過的圖片，在單字旁的空格寫下字義。

071 被狗追超可怕
- chase _____
- fierce _____
- come across _____
- cowardice _____
- stammer _____

072 好命的貓
- treasure _____
- stride _____
- proud _____
- fur _____
- rather _____

073 逝去的狗
- die of _____
- sorrow _____
- pet _____
- miserable _____
- decline _____

074 恐龍時代
- dinosaur _____
- diverse _____
- best-selling _____
- fossil _____
- mysterious _____

075 人類常吃的動物
- product _____
- pork chop _____
- eatable _____
- nugget _____
- bar _____

Day15 動物世界 071・075

145

加深記憶 階段

◆ 請依照提示的單字字首，在下列空格中填入適當的單字。

(1) 被藏起來的寶藏　　　　hidden t_____
(2) 一個有瑕疵的產品　　　a defective p_____
(3) 一個古老的化石　　　　an ancient f_____
(4) 一個雞塊　　　　　　　a chicken n_____
(5) 一塊大豬排　　　　　　a big p_____

◆ 請參考下列方框中的單字，在下列空格中填入適當的單字。

參考 ｜ eatable ｜ come across ｜ chase ｜ decline ｜
　　 ｜ miserable ｜ rather ｜ best-selling ｜ mysterious ｜

(1) After knowing the bad news, I was feeling _____ all the time.
　　在知道這個壞消息後，我一直覺得很痛苦。

(2) Are these books the _____?
　　這些書是最暢銷的嗎？

(3) The police are _____ after the thieves.
　　警察正在追小偷。

(4) He is _____ noisy today.
　　他今天滿吵的。

(5) Don't _____ my assistance.
　　不要拒絕我的協助。

(6) Something _____ happened between them.
　　在他們之間發生了某件神祕的事。

(7) Are you sure these dishes _____?
　　你確定這些菜可以吃嗎？

(8) I _____ my classmates on my way to date.
　　我在去約會的路上碰巧遇到了我的同學。

Answers:
1. (1) treasure (2) product (3) fossil (4) nugget (5) pork chop
2. (1) miserable (2) best-selling (3) chasing (4) rather (5) decline (6) mysterious (7) eatable
　 (8) came across

記單字必備！掌握常見字尾 01

★ 常見常用的字尾

01
-ic（多做為形容詞的結尾）
enthusiast**ic** 具有熱忱的
automat**ic** 自動的
academ**ic** 學術的
energet**ic** 有活力的

02
-ous（形容詞結尾）
danger**ous** 危險的
gener**ous** 慷慨的
mysteri**ous** 神秘的
harmoni**ous** 和諧的

03
-sion（名詞結尾）
divi**sion** 部門
comprehen**sion** 理解
supervi**sion** 監督
revi**sion** 修正

04
-tion（名詞結尾）
regula**tion** 規則
educa**tion** 教育
produc**tion** 生產
pollu**tion** 污染

05
-ent（多做為名詞或形容詞的結尾）
entertainm**ent** 娛樂
encouragem**ent** 鼓勵
evid**ent** 明顯的
confid**ent** 自信的

06
-ive（形容詞結尾）
comparat**ive** 比較的
attent**ive** 專注的
progress**ive** 漸進的
impress**ive** 印象深刻的

07
-al（多做為形容詞結尾）
nation**al** 國家的
fundament**al** 基礎的
digit**al** 數字的
profession**al** 專業的

08
-ate（多做為動詞結尾）
termin**ate** 終結
elimin**ate** 排除
cre**ate** 創造
transl**ate** 翻譯

Day 16 日常生活 076-080

Day16_076 來不及追劇

→ 把你知道的單字打勾！
- [ ] bank teller
- [ ] soap opera
- [ ] continuously
- [ ] drive sb. crazy
- [ ] upset

→ 用 5 個字說出這張圖片的故事！

bank teller [bæŋk] [ˋtɛlɚ]　n. 銀行櫃員

S Joyce is a **bank teller** working in a bank nearby.
喬伊斯是一個在附近銀行工作的銀行櫃員。

關聯字 banking n. 銀行業務　banker n. 銀行家

soap opera [sop] [ˋɑpərə]　n. 肥皂劇

S Just like her colleagues, she likes to watch Korean **soap operas**.
就和她的同事一樣，她喜歡看韓國肥皂劇。

continuously [kənˋtɪnjʊəslɪ]　adv. 連續地

S Believe it or not, she can watch them **continuously** for ten hours without a break.
信不信由你，她可以連續看十個小時不用休息。

關聯字 continuous adj. 連續的　continue v. 繼續
MORE continuous 和 continuously 都是源自 continue 這個字，表示中間毫無停頓或中斷地進行。

Just **continue** your discussion. I didn't mean to interrupt you.
你們繼續討論吧。我不是故意要打斷你們的。

148

drive sb. crazy phr. 讓某人陷入瘋狂；把某人逼到牆角

S The romantic plots always **drive** Joyce **crazy**; she even watches every episode over and over.
浪漫的情節總是會讓 Joyce 陷入瘋狂，她甚至會重複看每一集。

> **MORE** drive 一般最常看到的意思是「駕駛」，但這裡的 drive 是「逼使～，強迫去做～」的意思。

Mike was **driven** by despair to rob the bank.（迫使）
麥克迫於絕望而去搶銀行。

> 不過 drive 也可以當名詞，當名詞時除了「車程」的意思之外，也有「驅使的動力；慾望」的意思。

It needs a 15-minute **drive** to get to the lake.（車程）
去那座湖需要 15 分鐘的車程。
His **drive** for success is so strong that he works overtime every day.（慾望）
他對成功的慾望強烈到讓他每天都加班。

upset [ʌpˋsɛt] adj. 心情煩悶的

S Joyce went back home late today, and she was really **upset** that she missed the finale.
喬伊斯今天回家晚了，她非常不高興自己錯過了最後一集。

Day16_077 做不完的功課

→ 把你知道的單字打勾！
- [ ] primary
- [ ] punctually
- [ ] quiz
- [ ] stay up
- [ ] cruel

→ 用 5 個字說出這張圖片的故事！

primary [ˈpraɪˌmɛrɪ]　adj. 初級的

🅢 Being a **primary** school student is not easy now.
現在當一個小學生不容易。

同義字 basic、elementary

punctually [ˈpʌŋktʃʊəlɪ]　adv. 準時地

🅢 I have to get up very early in the morning to catch my school bus **punctually**.
我必須一大早起床以準時趕上校車。

> MORE　punctually 和常見的片語 on time（準時）意義相近，而另一個常見的片語 in time 是指「來得及」，而不是準時，使用時請特別注意。

I went to the bus stop **punctually/on time**.
我準時到了公車站。
The bus arrived **in time** to prevent me being late.
公車及時抵達讓我沒有遲到。

quiz [kwɪz]　n. 臨時考；小考

🅢 What's more, I have to earn good grades in numerous **quizzes** and tests.
還有，我必須在眾多的小考和大考裡拿到好成績。

> MORE　quiz 指的是課堂小考或是隨堂測驗的抽考，若是像月考或段考這種比較重要的考試，則會用 test 或 exam 這種表示「正式測驗」的字。

stay up　phr. 熬夜

🅢 That is to say, I have to **stay up** late to burn the midnight oil.
也就是說，我必須熬夜到很晚來挑燈夜戰。

同義字 sit up
> MORE　burn the midnight oil 的字面翻譯是「燃燒午夜的油」，這邊的油是指油燈使用的油，因此衍生出「挑燈夜戰」的意思。

cruel [ˈkruəl]　adj. 殘忍的

🅢 It's **cruel** for a kid like me to have so much work to do every day!
對於像我這樣的小孩來說，每天有那麼多事情要做真的很殘忍啊！

Day16_078 來電傳情

→ 把你知道的單字打勾！
- ☐ sight
- ☐ branch
- ☐ distance
- ☐ remote
- ☐ transfer

→ 用 5 個字說出這張圖片的故事！

Day 16 日常生活 076.080

sight [saɪt] n. 看見；視野

S Bill and Dora fell in love at first **sight**.
比爾與朵拉是一見鍾情的。

E love at first **sight** 一見鍾情

branch [bræntʃ] n. 分行

S They were seeing each other before Bill was transferred to the **branch** in Australia.
在比爾被轉調到澳洲分公司之前，他們兩個一直在約會。

MORE branch 除了是「分行，分公司」，也是「樹枝，分支」的意思。

distance [ˋdɪstəns] n. 距離

S Since then, they have had long **distance** calls every day.
從那時起，他們每天都會打長途電話。

關聯字 distant adj. 遙遠的

remote [rɪˋmot] adj. 遙遠的

S Although the distance between them is **remote**, it cannot stop their love.
儘管他們之間的距離很遙遠，但這阻擋不了他們的愛。

E a **remote** control 一個遙控器

151

transfer [træns`fɝ]　　v. 轉調；調動

- Bill is trying to get the opportunity to **transfer**, hoping he can be back home soon.
  比爾正在試圖拿到轉調的機會，希望他可以很快回家。

Day16_079 花錢如流水

→ 把你知道的單字打勾！
- [ ] newlywed
- [ ] relative
- [ ] delicacy
- [ ] frequently
- [ ] broke

→ 用 5 個字說出這張圖片的故事！

---

newlywed [`njulɪˌwɛd]　　n. 剛結婚的人

- Peter and Amy are **newlyweds**.
  彼得與艾咪是新婚夫妻。

---

relative [`rɛlətɪv]　　n. 親戚

- Peter always tells his friends and **relatives** that they live in happiness.
  彼得總是告訴他的親朋好友們說他們過得很快樂。

---

delicacy [`dɛləkəsɪ]　　n. 昂貴精緻的食物

- But the truth is, Peter is kind of unsettled by Amy's desire for eating **delicacies**.
  但事實上，彼得對於艾咪想要吃昂貴精緻的食物的這件事感到有點不安。

frequently [ˋfrikwəntlɪ]　adv. 經常地

S Amy can't stand average foods and asks to go to expensive restaurants very **frequently**.
艾咪受不了普通的食物，而且常常要求去昂貴的餐廳用餐。

> **MORE** 補充一些常見的頻率副詞：
> always 總是　usually 通常　often 經常（＝frequently）　sometimes 有時
> occasionally 偶爾　seldom 很少（＝rarely）　hardly ever 幾乎不　never 從不

broke [brok]　adj. 沒錢的

S Peter is worried that he will go **broke** and will not be able to afford the restaurants one day.
彼得擔心他有天會沒錢而吃不起那些餐廳了。

> **MORE** broke 是表達「沒錢的，破產的」的口語說法，法律上的正式說法則會用 bankrupt（破產的）這個字。

Day16_080　我愛打電動

→ 把你知道的單字打勾！
- [ ] interest
- [ ] clever
- [ ] opponent
- [ ] blame
- [ ] waste

→ 用 5 個字說出這張圖片的故事！

interest [ˋɪntərɪst]　n. 興趣

S Speaking of **interests**, playing online games is my number-one choice.
談到興趣，打線上遊戲是我的第一選擇。

> **關聯字** interested adj.（人）感興趣的　interesting adj.（事物）有趣的
> I am **interested** in learning more about you.
> 我有興趣知道更多與你有關的事。
> Teaching English is an **interesting** job.
> 教英文是件有趣的工作。

Day 16 日常生活 076‧080

clever [`klɛvɚ]　adj. 靈巧的；聰明的

- Playing online games is not easy, you need to acquire every skill to make **clever** moves.
  打線上遊戲並不簡單，你必須要學會所有技巧才能做出聰明的決定。

  反義字 clumsy

opponent [ə`ponənt]　n. 對手

- Sometimes you have to predict what your **opponents** will do next.
  有時你必須預測你的對手接下來會做什麼。

  同義字 rival、competitor

blame [blem]　v. 責備

- But my mother always **blames** me for spending too much time playing online games.
  但是我的母親總是責備我花太多時間打線上遊戲。

waste [west]　v. 浪費

- She says I **waste** too much time playing them, but I think the opposite.
  她說我浪費太多時間在打遊戲上，但我不這樣認為。

  MORE waste 也可以當名詞「廢棄物」的意思。

回復記憶 階段

◆ 請參考以下在 Day16 中出現過的圖片，在單字旁的空格寫下字義。

076 來不及追劇
- bank teller ___
- soap opera ___
- continuously ___
- drive sb. crazy ___
- upset ___

077 做不完的功課
- primary ___
- punctually ___
- quiz ___
- stay up ___
- cruel ___

078 來電傳情
- sight ___
- branch ___
- distance ___
- remote ___
- transfer ___

079 花錢如流水
- newlywed ___
- relative ___
- delicacy ___
- frequently ___
- broke ___

080 我愛打電動
- interest ___
- clever ___
- opponent ___
- blame ___
- waste ___

Day 16 日常生活 076-080

155

加深記憶 階段

◆ 請依照提示的單字字首，在下列空格中填入適當的單字。

(1) 一個認真的銀行櫃員　　　a hardworking b＿＿＿＿＿＿
(2) 一個聰明的女孩　　　　　a c＿＿＿＿＿＿ girl
(3) 一間當地分公司　　　　　a local b＿＿＿＿＿＿
(4) 在我的視野之中　　　　　within my s＿＿＿＿＿＿
(5) 一個殘忍的殺手　　　　　a c＿＿＿＿＿＿ killer

◆ 請參考下列方框中的單字，在下列空格中填入適當的單字。

> 參考 | punctually | primary | interest | soap opera |
> | frequently | continuously | waste | relative |

(1) I always come to work ＿＿＿＿＿＿.
　　我總是準時到班。

(2) Do you like to watch ＿＿＿＿＿＿?
　　你喜歡看肥皂劇嗎？

(3) The course is for ＿＿＿＿＿＿ school students.
　　這個課程是給小學生上的。

(4) He has been on the phone ＿＿＿＿＿＿ for fifty minutes.
　　他持續不斷地講電話五十分鐘了。

(5) Don't ＿＿＿＿＿＿ your time on complaining.
　　不要把你的時間浪費在抱怨上。

(6) I get along well with my ＿＿＿＿＿＿.
　　我與我的親戚們相處的很好。

(7) What is your sister's ＿＿＿＿＿＿?
　　你姐姐的興趣是什麼？

(8) I ＿＿＿＿＿＿ go out with my friends.
　　我經常和朋友出去。

Answers:
1. (1) bank teller (2) clever (3) branch (4) sight (5) cruel
2. (1) punctually (2) soap operas (3) primary (4) continuously (5) waste (6) relatives (7) interest
   (8) frequently

Day 17 日常生活 081-085

Day17_081 烤肉趣

→ 把你知道的單字打勾！
- [ ] barbecue
- [ ] ingredient
- [ ] aluminum foil
- [ ] purchase
- [ ] cozy

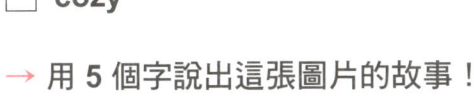

→ 用 5 個字說出這張圖片的故事！

barbecue [ˋbɑrbɪkju]　n. 烤肉

S Kevin likes to have a **barbecue** in his front yard every weekend.
凱文喜歡每個週末都在他的前院裡來場烤肉。

ingredient [ɪnˋgridɪənt]　n.（料理的）材料

S He likes to make his own barbecue sauce with the **ingredients** and tools he bought before.
他喜歡用他之前買的材料和工具來做他自己的烤肉醬。

aluminum foil [əˋlumɪnəm] [fɔɪl]　n. 鋁箔紙

S He usually prepares coal, grill racks, **aluminum foil** and tongs.
他通常會準備木炭、烤網、鋁箔紙及夾子。

> **MORE** aluminum 是「鋁」的意思，其他常見的材質還有：
> wood 木材　steel 鋼　steel 鐵　brass 黃銅　copper 紅銅　gold 黃金
> silver 白銀　platinum 白金　stainless steel 不鏽鋼　plastic 塑膠

purchase [ˈpɝtʃəs]　v. 購買

S He also goes to the supermarket nearby to **purchase** some chicken wings, sausages, meat and seafood.
他也會去附近的超市採購一些雞翅、香腸、肉和海鮮。

同義字 buy

cozy [ˈkozɪ]　adj. 舒適的；愜意的

S The **cozy** atmosphere of having a barbecue always makes him relaxed and happy.
烤肉的愜意氛圍總是讓他覺得放鬆又快樂。

同義字 comfortable、snug

Day17_082 來釣魚吧

→ 把你知道的單字打勾！
☐ partner
☐ lively
☐ taste bud
☐ concerned
☐ perfectly

→ 用 5 個字說出這張圖片的故事！

partner [ˈpɑrtnɚ]　n. 夥伴

S Ed often goes fishing with his fishing **partner** David.
愛德常常和他的釣魚夥伴大衛一起去釣魚。

關聯字 partnership n. 合夥關係；合作關係

lively [ˈlaɪvlɪ]　adj. 充滿生氣的

S Today was a lucky day for them; they caught two **lively** fish in only ten minutes.
今天他們很幸運的在十分鐘之內就抓到了兩條活跳跳的魚。

MORE lively 是「充滿生氣、精力旺盛」的樣子，而意思相似的 alive 還有「活著的」的意思，必須透過上下文來判斷單字字義。

He is **alive** after the car accident.（活著的）
他在車禍後還活著。
The new therapy works, so he's very much **alive** now.（精力旺盛的）
新的治療法起作用了，所以他現在精力非常旺盛。

taste bud [test] [bʌd]　n. 味蕾；口味

🅢 The grilled fish they made by themselves really blew away their **taste buds**.
他們自己烤的烤魚真的非常好吃。

MORE taste bud 雖然可數，但會用到單數的情境很少，幾乎都是以複數形的 taste bud**s** 出現，如例句中的 blow away the taste buds（觸動味蕾；美味好吃）就是常見的表達方式。

concerned [kən`sɜ·nd]　adj. 擔心的

🅢 When they went fishing together the first time, they were **concerned** about how to deal with the fish they caught.
當他們第一次一起去釣魚時，他們曾擔心要怎麼處理釣到的魚。

perfectly [`pɜ·fɪktlɪ]　adv. 完美地

🅢 Gladly, they could always cook it quite **perfectly**.
很高興的是，他們總是能把魚烹調得十分完美。

關聯字 perfect adj. 完美的 v. 使完美

Day17_083　餐廳訂位

→ 把你知道的單字打勾！
☐ candlelit
☐ beneath
☐ atmosphere
☐ uniformed
☐ disappointedly

→ 用 5 個字說出這張圖片的故事！

candlelit [ˈkændḷlɪt]　adj. 點燃燭火的

- One day, William made a phone call to a restaurant to reserve a **candlelit** dinner.
有一天，威廉打了通電話去一間餐廳預訂燭光晚餐。

beneath [bɪˈniθ]　prep. 在～的下方

- William liked the restaurant very much because it had a patio, and customers could have meals **beneath** the stars.
威廉非常喜歡這間餐廳，因為它有一個露臺，而且客人們可以在星星下用餐。

atmosphere [ˈætməsˌfɪr]　n. 氣氛，氛圍

- The **atmosphere** there was romantic, so William thought it was a good place to have a candlelit dinner
那裡的氣氛很浪漫，所以威廉認為那裡是吃燭光晚餐的好地方。

    MORE　atmosphere 也是「大氣層」或「特定地點裡的空氣」的意思。

uniformed [ˈjunəˌfɔrmd]　adj. 穿著制服的

- The **uniformed** staff answered the phone and told William that all their tables were booked.
穿著制服的員工接起了電話並告訴威廉說他們所有的桌位都已經被預訂了。

    MORE　uniform（制服）是 uniformed 這個字的來源，uniform 這個字可以當作名詞（制服）、形容詞（相同的）及動詞（使穿著制服），必須要透過上下文來判斷字義。

disappointedly [ˌdɪsəˈpɔɪntɪdlɪ]　adv. 感到失望地

- William **disappointedly** hung up and started to think which restaurant he should call next.
威廉失望地掛斷電話，並開始思考他接下來應該要打給哪間餐廳。

    關聯字　disappointed adj. 感到失望的　disappoint v. 使失望
    disappointment n. 失望；令人失望的人事物

Day17_084 手機不離身

→ 把你知道的單字打勾！
- [ ] necessary
- [ ] impression
- [ ] operate
- [ ] deal with
- [ ] senior citizen

→ 用 5 個字說出這張圖片的故事！

---

necessary [ˋnɛsəˌsɛrɪ]　adj. 必要的

S In terms of convenience, smartphones are **necessary** for modern people.
就便利性而言，智慧型手機對現代人來說是必要的。

同義字 essential、indispensable

---

impression [ɪmˋprɛʃən]　n. 印象

S I have a strong **impression** that people nowadays are using their cellphones anytime and anywhere.
我印象很強烈的是現在的人隨時隨地都在用他們的手機。

E make a good **impression** 留下好印象
關聯字 impressive adj. 令人留下深刻印象的；令人欽佩的

---

operate [ˋɑpəˌret]　v. 操作

S Now, there are three people in front of me, and they are all **operating** their cell phones.
現在有三個人在我的面前，而他們都正在操作他們的手機。

關聯字 operation n. 操作；手術　operator n. 操作人員

deal with　phr. 應對；處理

- It seems that the girl is texting, and the man beside her is **dealing with** business.
  看起來女孩正在傳訊息，而她旁邊的男人正在處理生意。

  MORE　deal with 的後面會接要處理或應對的人事物，另一個意思相似的片語是 cope with。

senior citizen　[ˋsinjɚ]　[ˋsɪtəzn̩]　n. 長者

- However, the **senior citizen** beside the man seems confused about how to handle his cell phone properly.
  不過，男子身旁的長者則看起來對要如何正確使用他的手機感到困惑。

  MORE　senior citizen 是由 senior（資深的）與 citizen（公民）組合而成的字，用來委婉代稱 elder man（老人）。

Day17_085　使用自動販賣機

→ 把你知道的單字打勾！
- [ ] vending machine
- [ ] entrance
- [ ] complex
- [ ] meanwhile
- [ ] quench

→ 用 5 個字說出這張圖片的故事！

vending machine　[ˋvɛndɪŋ]　[məˋʃin]　n. 自動販賣機

- When Helen felt thirsty, she saw a **vending machine** inside a building.
  當海倫覺得口渴時，她看到大樓裡面有一台自動販賣機。

  MORE　vend 是「販賣」的意思，加上 -ing 字尾後就變成「販賣的」，這時在後面接上 machine（機器）就會變成「vending machine（販賣的機器＝自動販賣機）」，用這種方式來理解，就會更容易記住。

  關聯字　vendor n. 小販　　street vendor n. 地攤

162

entrance [`ɛntrəns]　n. 入口，門口

- She walked through the **entrance** to the vending machine.
  她走過了入口去找那台自動販賣機。

  反義字 exit
  關聯字 entry n. 進入；入口　　enter v. 進入；參加

complex [kəm`plɛks]　adj. 複雜難懂的

- However, the control panel was **complex** and Helen didn't know how to use it to buy a drink.
  然而，那個控制面板很複雜難懂，所以海倫不知道要怎麼用它來買飲料。

  同義字 complicated

meanwhile [`min͵waɪl]　adv. 在此同時

- Helen stood helplessly in front of it; **meanwhile**, a man came to her and offered to help.
  海倫無助地站在它的前方，就在這時，一個男人走向她並表示要幫忙。

  同義字 meantime

quench [kwɛntʃ]　v. 解渴

- Helen finally got a bottle of water to **quench** her thirst.
  海倫終於買到了一瓶水來解渴。

  quench one's thirst 解某人的渴

Day 17 日常生活 081-085

回復記憶 階段

◆ 請參考以下在 Day17 中出現過的圖片，在單字旁的空格寫下字義。

081 烤肉趣
- barbecue ....
- ingredient ....
- aluminum foil ....
- purchase ....
- cozy ....

082 來釣魚吧
- partner ....
- lively ....
- taste bud ....
- concerned ....
- perfectly ....

083 餐廳訂位
- candlelit ....
- beneath ....
- atmosphere ....
- uniformed ....
- disappointedly ....

084 手機不離身
- necessary ....
- impression ....
- operate ....
- deal with ....
- senior citizen ....

085 使用自動販賣機
- vending machine ....
- entrance ....
- complex ....
- meanwhile ....
- quench ....

加深記憶 階段

◆ 請依照提示的單字字首，在下列空格中填入適當的單字。

(1) 一台自動販賣機　　　　　a v_____ machine
(2) 一些複雜的數學題　　　　some c_____ math questions
(3) 應對客戶　　　　　　　　_____ clients
(4) 一個必要的條件　　　　　a n_____ condition
(5) 一位穿著制服的店員　　　an u_____ clerk

◆ 請參考下列方框中的單字，在下列空格中填入適當的單字。

> 參考 | atmosphere | purchase | impression | entrance |
> | concerned | operate | cozy | disappointedly |

(1) The _____ between the two parties is hostile.
兩方之間的氣氛是充滿敵意的。

(2) It's your turn to _____ our groceries.
輪到你去採購雜貨了。

(3) When you are in a job interview, you have to leave a good _____ to your interviewer.
當你在進行工作面試時，你必須給面試官一個好印象。

(4) My doctor is _____ about my health.
我的醫生擔心我的健康。

(5) Tell me how to _____ the machine.
告訴我如何操作這台機器。

(6) I like to stay in my _____ room.
我喜歡待在我舒適的房間。

(7) My mother looked at me _____.
我的母親失望地看著我。

(8) Where is the _____ of this building?
這棟大樓的入口在哪裡？

Answers:
1. (1) vending (2) complex (3) deal with (4) necessary (5) uniformed
2. (1) atmosphere (2) purchase (3) impression (4) concerned (5) operate (6) cozy
   (7) disappointedly (8) entrance

Day 18 日常生活 086-090

Day18_086 買新車囉！

→ 把你知道的單字打勾！
- [ ] belong to
- [ ] budget
- [ ] extend
- [ ] bargain
- [ ] precaution

→ 用 5 個字說出這張圖片的故事！

belong to　phr. 屬於

S Angus always wants a car that **belongs to** himself.
安格斯一直想要一輛屬於自己的車。

關聯字 belongings n. 財物；隨身物品（恆複數）

budget　[ˈbʌdʒɪt]　n. 預算

S He has been looking for an ideal one, but most of them are over his **budget**.
他一直在尋找一台理想的車，但大部分的車都超出他的預算。

- over **budget** 超出預算
- within **budget** 在預算內

extend　[ɪkˈstɛnd]　v. 提供；給予

S One day, Angus walked into a car dealer, and the agent **extended** a warm welcome to him.
有一天，安格斯走進了一間車行，而服務專員向他表示了熱烈歡迎。

- **extend** thanks 表示感謝
- **extend** money 提供金錢

MORE　extend 還有「延伸；擴展；延長」的意思。

166

bargain [ˋbɑrgɪn]　v. 討價還價

🅢 Angus **bargained** with the agent, and finally she agreed to a price within Angus' budget.
安格斯和服務專員討價還價，最後她終於願意用在安格斯預算內的價錢成交。

🅔 **bargain** with sb. 與某人討價還價

MORE　bargain 這個字當名詞時，意思是「特價商品」或是「划算的交易」，例如 It's a real bargain.（這真的是個很划算的交易／商品）。

precaution [prɪˋkɔʃən]　n. 預防措施

🅢 The agent explained some **precautions** he needed to follow, and gave Angus the car key.
服務專員說明了一些他必須遵守的預防措施，然後把車鑰匙交給了安格斯。

關聯字　caution n. 小心，謹慎　　cautious adj. 小心的，謹慎的

Day18_087　市場買菜去

→ 把你知道的單字打勾！
- [ ] explore
- [ ] hypermarket
- [ ] organic
- [ ] gossip
- [ ] butcher

→ 用 5 個字說出這張圖片的故事！

explore [ɪkˋsplor]　v. 探索

🅢 Mrs. Ho likes to **explore** new or different ingredients in traditional markets.
何太太喜歡在傳統市場裡探索新奇的食材。

MORE　explore 的字義用英文來說就是「search and discover」，也就是「透過搜尋來發現或找到」，中文可以簡單翻譯成「探索」。

Day 18 日常生活 086-090

167

hypermarket [ˌhaɪpɚˈmɑrkɪt]   n. 大型量販店

S She thinks traditional markets or farmers markets are better than supermarkets or **hypermarkets**.
她認為傳統市場或農夫市集比超市或大型量販店要更好。

> **MORE** 字首 hyper- 是「超出，過多」的意思，除了 hypermarket 之外，常見的單字還有 hypertension（高血壓）、hyperactive（過動的）。

organic [ɔrˈgænɪk]   adj. 有機的

S That's because she thinks the food and groceries there are far fresher, and she can buy **organic** food with better quality.
原因是因為她認為那裡的食物和雜貨會新鮮很多，而且她可以買到品質更好的有機食品。

> **MORE** food（食物，食品）若加上 s，指的是「多種類的食物或食品」，若只是要講單一類項，或沒有特別區分類別的食物，那就不可以加 s。

You have to eat wholesome **food** to keep you healthy.
你必須吃健康的食物來維持你的健康。
There are several special **foods** catered by a famous restaurant.
有幾種由知名餐廳所供應的特殊食物。

gossip [ˈgɑsəp]   v. 聊八卦

S She also likes to **gossip** with people in the markets.
她也喜歡和市場裡的人聊八卦。

butcher [ˈbʊtʃɚ]   n. 肉販

S The **butchers** and farmers in the markets are all her friends.
市場裡的肉販與農夫們都是她的朋友。

Day18_088 披薩全吃光

→ 把你知道的單字打勾！
- [ ] chubby
- [ ] junk
- [ ] imaginable
- [ ] control
- [ ] avail

→ 用 5 個字說出這張圖片的故事！

chubby [ˋtʃʌbɪ]　adj. 肉肉的

Tina is a **chubby** girl, and she likes to eat pizza very much.
蒂娜是個肉肉的女孩，而且她非常喜歡吃披薩。

> **MORE** chubby 指的是「有肉但不到胖，而是豐滿的程度」，heavy 則是「帶有過重沉重感的程度」，fat 則真的是指「肉很多的胖」，「病態性肥胖」則會使用 obese 這個字。

junk [dʒʌŋk]　n. 垃圾；無用的東西

Her parents always warn her not to eat too much **junk** food.
她的父母總是警告她不要吃太多垃圾食物。

> 同義字 trash、garbage

imaginable [ɪˋmædʒɪnəbl̩]　adj. 可以想像得到的

They think it's **imaginable** that Tina would be fat one day.
他們認為可以想像得到蒂娜有天會變得很胖。

> 關聯字 imaginary adj. 幻想的　imaginative adj. 富有想像力的

control [kənˋtrol]　v. 控制

Tina knows eating too much pizza is not healthy, but she just can't **control** herself.
蒂娜知道吃太多披薩不健康，但她就是無法控制自己。

avail [ə`vel]　n. 幫助；效用

- She has tried to quit eating pizza, but to no **avail**; and this time she even ate a whole pizza all by herself!
她試過要戒掉吃披薩這件事，但沒有用，而且這次她甚至自己吃掉了一整個披薩！

Day18_089 下公車掉錢包

→ 把你知道的單字打勾！
- [ ] commuter
- [ ] compliance
- [ ] press
- [ ] simultaneously
- [ ] leave

→ 用 5 個字說出這張圖片的故事！

commuter [kə`mjutɚ]　n. 通勤者

- Alan is a **commuter**, and he goes to work by bus every day.
亞倫是通勤族，而且他每天都搭公車上班。

　關聯字 commute v. 通勤

compliance [kəm`plaɪəns]　n. 遵守

- He is usually in **compliance** with the etiquette of taking buses.
他通常都會遵守搭公車的禮儀。

　E in **compliance** with 遵守～
　關聯字 comply v. 遵守

press [prɛs]　v. 按壓

- He always **presses** the bell before he gets off the bus.
他總是會在下車前按下車鈴。

　MORE get off 是下車、get on 則是上車。

simultaneously [saɪməl`tenɪəslɪ]　adv. 同時地

S But today, he was talking on his cell phone and **simultaneously** taking a note, so he missed the timing to ring the bell.
但今天，他在講電話時一邊同時在做筆記，所以他錯過了按鈴的時機。

同義字 at the same moment、at the same time

leave [liv]　v. 遺留；留下

S Alan got off the bus in a hurry and accidentally **left** his wallet on his seat.
艾倫急急忙忙地下車，結果不小心把他的皮夾留在了座位上。

> **MORE** leave 也有「離開」的意思，過去式形態的 left 則與形容詞「左邊的」同形，而 leaf（樹葉）的複數形是 leaves，要小心別搞混了，一定要利用上下文來判斷單字字義。

He **left** the building.（離開）
他離開了大樓。
The bank will be on your **left** side.（左邊的）
銀行會在你的左邊。
I cleaned the **leaves** on the ground.（樹葉）
我清理了地上的樹葉。
He usually **leaves** at 5 o'clock.（離開）
他通常 5 點離開。

Day18_090 看 3D 電影

→ 把你知道的單字打勾！
☐ pity
☐ science fiction
☐ skyscraper
☐ invasive
☐ popcorn

→ 用 5 個字說出這張圖片的故事！

pity [ˋpɪtɪ] n. 可惜的事情

🄢 It's a **pity** that our children don't like to see movies with us, so my husband and I always go by ourselves.
可惜我們的孩子不喜歡跟我們一起去看電影,所以我先生和我總是自己去看。

🄔 What a **pity**! 真是可惜!

science fiction [ˋsaɪəns] [ˋfɪkʃən] n. 科幻

🄢 We like **science fiction** movies very much.
我們非常喜歡科幻片。

> **MORE** fiction(小說)指的是「杜撰出來的內容」,而如果是「事實」,如傳記、歷史紀錄等,則會被分類為 nonfiction(紀實)。這裡一併補充一些常見的電影類型:
> comedy 喜劇　war 戰爭　fantasy 奇幻　adventure 冒險　animation 動畫
> detective 偵探　documentary 紀錄片　action 動作　horror 恐怖
> romance 浪漫愛情　thriller 驚悚　western 西部　drama 劇情

skyscraper [ˋskaɪˏskrepɚ] n. 摩天大樓

🄢 We usually go to a movie theater located in a **skyscraper**.
我們通常會去一家位在一棟摩天大樓裡頭的電影院。

invasive [ɪnˋvesɪv] adj. 入侵的

🄢 The movie we saw today was about **invasive** aliens.
我們今天看的是和入侵的外星人有關的電影。

關聯字 invade v. 入侵

popcorn [ˋpɑpˏkɔrn] n. 爆米花

🄢 We were seeing the movie with a large **popcorn** and 3D glasses, and the movie was really nice!
我們拿著大份爆米花、戴著 3D 眼鏡看電影,這部片真的很棒!

回復記憶 階段

◆ 請參考以下在 Day18 中出現過的圖片，在單字旁的空格寫下字義。

086 買新車囉！
- belong to _____
- budget _____
- extend _____
- bargain _____
- precaution _____

087 市場買菜去
- explore _____
- hypermarket _____
- organic _____
- gossip _____
- butcher _____

088 披薩全吃光
- chubby _____
- junk _____
- imaginable _____
- control _____
- avail _____

089 下公車掉錢包
- commuter _____
- compliance _____
- press _____
- simultaneously _____
- leave _____

090 看 3D 電影
- pity _____
- science fiction _____
- skyscraper _____
- invasive _____
- popcorn _____

Day 18 日常生活 086・090

173

加深記憶階段

◆ 請依照提示的單字字首，在下列空格中填入適當的單字。

(1) 一份小的爆米花　　　　　a small p_____
(2) 一棟高聳的摩天大樓　　　a tall s_____
(3) 一位忙碌的通勤者　　　　a busy c_____
(4) 一位市場的肉販　　　　　a market b_____
(5) 一間知名大型量販店　　　a famous h_____

◆ 請參考下列方框中的單字，在下列空格中填入適當的單字。

| 參考 | budget | organic | pity | control |
| | imaginable | gossip | belong to | precaution |

(1) The management wants to _____ their staff.
　　管理階層想要控制他們的員工

(2) Please read the _____ before you use the machine.
　　在你使用這機器之前，請先閱讀預防措施。

(3) This year we have no _____ for bonuses.
　　今年我們沒有獎金的預算。

(4) The old house _____ to my grandfather.
　　這間老房子是屬於我祖父的。

(5) My mother is _____ with our neighbors.
　　我的母親正在和我們的鄰居聊八卦。

(6) I only buy _____ vegetables.
　　我只買有機蔬菜。

(7) What a _____! My favorite team lost the game.
　　真是可惜啊！我最愛的隊伍輸了比賽。

(8) The result is _____.
　　這個結果是可以想像得到的。

Answers:
1. (1) popcorn (2) skyscraper (3) commuter (4) butcher (5) hypermarket
2. (1) control (2) precautions (3) budgets (4) belongs (5) gossiping (6) organic (7) pity
　　(8) imaginable

記單字必備！掌握常見字尾 02

★ 表示人含意的字尾

1. -er

employ（雇用）→ employ**er**（雇主）
lecture（演說）→ lectur**er**（演說者）
compose（創作詩／曲）→ compos**er**（作詩／曲者）
manage（管理）→ manag**er**（經理）
report（報導）→ report**er**（記者）

*例外

rule（統治）→ rul**er**（尺）
print（印刷）→ print**er**（印表機）
compute（以機器計算）→ comput**er**（電腦）

2. -or

advise（忠告）→ advis**or**（顧問）
edit（編輯）→ edit**or**（編輯人員）
audit（審計）→ audit**or**（稽核人員）
conduct（引導）→ conduct**or**（指揮）
operate（操作）→ operat**or**（操作人員）

*例外

refrigerate（在冰箱中冷藏）→ refrigerat**or**（冰箱）
escalate（上升；增強）→ escalat**or**（手扶梯）
elevate（提升）→ elevat**or**（電梯）

3. -ian

music（音樂）→ musici**an**（音樂家）
physical（肉體的）→ physici**an**（內科醫生）
history（歷史）→ histori**an**（歷史學家）
politics（政治學）→ politici**an**（政治家）

4. **-ist**
   novel（小説）→ novel**ist**（小説家）
   piano（鋼琴）→ pian**ist**（鋼琴家）
   art（藝術）→ art**ist**（藝術家）
   tour（遊覽）→ tour**ist**（觀光客）

5. **-ee**
   refuge（庇護；避難處）→ refug**ee**（難民）
   train（培訓）→ train**ee**（受訓者）
   commit（把～交託）→ committ**ee**（委員）
   employ（雇用）→ employ**ee**（員工）
   interview（面試）→ interview**ee**（接受面試者）

6. **-mate**
   room（房間）→ room**mate**（室友）
   team（團隊，隊伍）→ team**mate**（隊友）
   class（課堂）→ class**mate**（同學）
   work（工作）→ work**mate**（工作夥伴）

7. **-ant**
   account（帳戶）→ account**ant**（會計）
   assist（協助）→ assist**ant**（助理）
   occupy（占據）→ occup**ant**（占有者；居住者）
   serve（服務）→ serv**ant**（僕人）

8. **-ese**
   Taiwan（台灣）→ Taiwan**ese**（台灣人）
   Vietnam（越南）→ Vietnam**ese**（越南人）
   Japan（日本）→ Japan**ese**（日本人）
   Portugal（葡萄牙）→ Portugu**ese**（葡萄牙人）

Day 19 文化與健康 091-095

Day19_091 健身

→ 把你知道的單字打勾！
- [ ] work out
- [ ] currently
- [ ] training
- [ ] besides
- [ ] stationary

→ 用 5 個字說出這張圖片的故事！

work out　phr. 健身

Working out is very popular among modern people.
健身在現代人之間很流行。

> **MORE** work out 是指「強度較強」的運動，如果只是散步或健走等「強度較低」的運動，則可以用 exercise 來統稱，如果是「球類運動」，則可用 play sports 來表達。

currently　[ˈkɝəntlɪ]　adv. 現在

As a result, **currently** there are many health clubs and fitness centers in the city.
因此，現在城市裡有很多健身俱樂部及健身中心。

> **關聯字** current adj. 現在的　current n.（氣體或液體的）流　currency n. 貨幣
> **MORE** 健身房有很多種說法，最常見的有 health club、fitness centers、fitness club、gym。

training [ˈtrenɪŋ]　n. 訓練

🅢 **Albert is a muscular man, and he needs to do a lot of training to keep his figure.**
艾伯特是個肌肉男，而他必須做很多訓練來保持身形。

🅔 weight **training** 重量訓練
🅔 cardio **training** 有氧訓練（心肺訓練）

關聯字　train v. 訓練 n. 火車　　trainer n. 培訓人員　　trainee n. 受訓人員

besides [bɪˈsaɪdz]　prep. 除了～以外

🅢 **Besides doing weight training, he also uses treadmills and bikes in the gym.**
除了做重訓以外，他也會用健身房裡的跑步機與訓練車。

MORE　besides 是「除了～以外」，而 beside 則是「在～的旁邊」。
Besides punk, John likes jazz, too.
除了龐克以外，約翰也喜歡爵士。
The girl **beside** John is his sister.
在約翰旁邊的女孩是他的妹妹。

stationary [ˈsteʃənˌɛrɪ]　adj. 固定式的

🅢 **He usually rides stationary bikes to train his cardio.**
他通常會騎固定式訓練車來訓練他的心肺。

🅔 a **stationary** bike 一台固定式訓練車

Day19_092 研究時尚

→ 把你知道的單字打勾！
☐ roommate
☐ common
☐ fashion
☐ trendy
☐ culture

→ 用 5 個字說出這張圖片的故事！

roommate [ˋrumˌmet]　n. 室友

🔊 Ruby and Isabella are **roommates** in the school dorm.
露比與伊莎貝拉是學校宿舍的室友。

common [ˋkɑmən]　n. 共通點

🔊 They became good friends, and they have a lot in **common**.
她們變成了好友，而且她們有著很多共通點。

> **MORE** common 當名詞時，除了「共通點」外，也有「公有地」的意思，另外，common 的名詞和形容詞同形，當形容詞時是「一般的；共通的」意思，務必要透過上下文來判斷 common 的詞性與字義。

They set up a tent on the **commons**.（公有地）
他們在公有地上架了帳篷。
It's a **common** sense.（一般的）
這是個常識。

fashion [ˋfæʃən]　n. 時尚；時裝

🔊 For example, they both like reading **fashion** magazines to learn about the latest **fashions**.
舉例來說，她們兩個都喜歡看時尚雜誌來了解最新的時尚。

> 關聯字 fashionable adj. 時尚的

trendy [ˋtrɛndɪ]　adj. 流行的

🔊 They are fond of wearing **trendy** accessories.
她們很喜歡穿戴流行的配件。

> **MORE** trendy 這個字來自於 trend（趨勢），可以把 trendy 想成是「符合趨勢的＝流行的」。

culture [ˋkʌltʃɚ]　n. 文化

🔊 They think fashion is a kind of popular **culture**, and everyone should know more about it.
他們認為時尚是種大眾文化，而且所有人都應該多一些了解。

> 關聯字 subculture n. 次文化

Day19_093 生病就該看醫生

→ 把你知道的單字打勾！
- [ ] ill
- [ ] hence
- [ ] physician
- [ ] inflammation
- [ ] stethoscope

→ 用 5 個字說出這張圖片的故事！

ill [ɪl]　adj. 生病的；身體不舒服的

🅢 Jack felt **ill** when he woke up this morning.
傑克今天早上醒來的時候覺得身體不舒服。

> 同義字 sick
> MORE ill 也有「壞的；惡意的」的意思。

hence [hɛns]　adv. 因此

🅢 **Hence**, he decided to see a doctor in a clinic.
因此他決定去診所看醫生。

> MORE 除了 hence 以外，其他常用來表示「因此」的單字或片語還有：
> therefore、thus、as a result、consequently、as a consequence

physician [fɪˋzɪʃən]　n.（內科）醫師

🅢 Dr. Lin is his family doctor, and he is a reputable **physician**.
林醫生是他的家庭醫師，他是一位有名的內科醫師。

> MORE 這裡補充其他常見科別的醫師說法：
> surgeon 外科醫師　psychiatrist 精神科醫師　cardiologist 心臟科醫師
> pediatrician 小兒科醫師　therapist 治療師

inflammation [ˌɪnfləˋmeʃən]　n. 發炎

🅢 Dr. Lin checked his throat to see if he had a throat **inflammation**.
林醫師檢查了他的喉嚨，來看看他是否有喉嚨發炎。

> MORE 喉嚨發炎也可以說 sore throat（喉嚨痛）。

stethoscope [ˋstɛθəˏskop]　n. 聽診器

🅢 He also used a **stethoscope** to check Jack's lungs.
他也用了聽診器來檢查傑克的肺。

Day19_094 打桌球

→ 把你知道的單字打勾！
- ☐ sort
- ☐ table tennis
- ☐ gymnasium
- ☐ accurately
- ☐ concentrate

→ 用 5 個字說出這張圖片的故事！

sort [sɔrt]　n. 種類

🅢 I'm a sports fan, and I like to play all **sorts** of sports.
我是個球迷，而且我喜歡打各種球類運動。

同義字 type、kind

table tennis [ˋtebḷ] [ˋtɛnɪs]　n. 桌球

🅢 My brother and I like playing **table tennis** the most.
我哥哥和我最喜歡打桌球。

同義字 ping pong

gymnasium [dʒɪmˋnezɪəm]　n. 體育館

🅢 We go to our school **gymnasium** to play table tennis every weekend.
我們每個週末都會去學校體育館打桌球。

　🅔 a public **gymnasium** 一間公立體育館
　🅔 a comprehensive **gymnasium** 一間綜合體育館
　MORE gymnasium 所指的是「一整棟的體育館」，裡面多半會有室內籃球場、羽球場、桌球場、體操場地等各種運動設施，另一個很常見的體育館說法則是 stadium，stadium 指的通常會是以中間場地為中心、周圍環繞著觀眾席的那種體育館，中間的場地多半是足球場或棒球場。

Day 19 文化與健康 091-095

181

accurately [ˈækjərɪtlɪ]　adv. 精準地

S **People sometimes ask us how we can hit the ball so accurately.**
人們有時會問我們是怎麼能這麼精準地打到球。

關聯字 accurate adj. 精準的

concentrate [ˈkɑnsɛnˌtret]　v. 專注

S **I tell them, "You have to concentrate on the ball and move your body nimbly."**
我告訴他們：「你必須要專注在球上，並且靈活地移動你的身體」。

同義字 focus

Day19_095 減肥不可能

→ 把你知道的單字打勾！
- [ ] exercise
- [ ] dessert
- [ ] snack
- [ ] gain
- [ ] impossibility

→ 用 5 個字說出這張圖片的故事！

exercise [ˈɛksɚˌsaɪz]　n. 運動

S **Mike is a couch potato, and he never does any exercise.**
麥克是一個沙發馬鈴薯，而且他從不做任何運動。

> MORE　exercise 當名詞時也有「練習題」的意思，務必要從上下文來判斷字義。另外，exercise 多指一般的運動，而 sport 指的則是球類運動。
>
> I have a lot of math **exercises** to do today.（練習題）
> 我今天有很多數學練習題要做。
> Several **exercises** can help you build your muscle.（運動）
> 有幾種運動可以幫助你練肌肉。

182

dessert [dɪˋzɝt]   n. 甜點

🅢 What's more, he likes to eat **desserts**, like cheese cakes and chocolates.
而且，他喜歡吃甜點，像是起士蛋糕與巧克力。

　MORE　dessert 長的和 desert（沙漠）很像，小心別搞混了。

snack [snæk]   n. 點心

🅢 He cannot quit the habit of eating late-night **snacks**, either.
他也戒不掉吃宵夜的習慣。

gain [gen]   v. 得到

🅢 They are the reasons why he **gains** weight so quickly.
它們是他胖得這麼快的原因。

　🅔 **gain** weight 增重，變胖

impossibility [ɪmˌpɑsəˋbɪlətɪ]   n. 不可能的事

🅢 For Mike, losing weight is an **impossibility**.
對於麥克來說，減重是件不可能的事。

　關聯字　impossible adj. 不可能的

Day 19 文化與健康 091-095

183

回復記憶 階段

◆ 請參考以下在 Day19 中出現過的圖片，在單字旁的空格寫下字義。

091 健身
- work out
- currently
- training
- besides
- stationary

092 研究時尚
- roommate
- common
- fashion
- trendy
- culture

093 生病就該看醫生
- ill
- hence
- physician
- inflammation
- stethoscope

094 打桌球
- sort
- table tennis
- gymnasium
- accurately
- concentrate

095 減肥不可能
- exercise
- dessert
- snack
- gain
- impossibility

加深記憶 階段

Day 19 文化與健康 091-095

◆ 請依照提示的單字字首，在下列空格中填入適當的單字。

(1) 固定式的設備　　　　　s_____ equipment
(2) 一些好吃的甜點　　　　some delicious d_____
(3) 規律的運動　　　　　　regular e_____
(4) 一個大型體育館　　　　a big g_____
(5) 嚴重的發炎　　　　　　serious i_____

◆ 請參考下列方框中的單字，在下列空格中填入適當的單字。

| 參考 | besides | currently | hence | common |
| | trendy | training | accurately | roommate |

(1) I have a difficult _____.
   我有一個難搞的室友。

(2) _____ I'm inventing a new machine.
   現在我正在發明一個新機器。

(3) My brother and I only have one thing in _____.
   我弟和我只有一個共通點。

(4) My superior thinks I need more _____.
   我的上司認為我需要更多的訓練。

(5) All the _____ clothes I bought last year are outdated now.
   我去年買的流行衣物現在全都過時了。

(6) _____ history, I also like math and science.
   除了歷史以外，我也喜歡數學和科學。

(7) He is rich; _____, he doesn't need to work.
   他很有錢，因此，他不需要工作。

(8) They calculated the numbers _____.
   他們精確地計算這些數字。

Answers:
1. (1) stationary (2) desserts (3) exercises (4) gymnasium (5) inflammation
2. (1) roommate (2) Currently (3) common (4) training (5) trendy (6) Besides (7) hence
   (8) accurately

Day 20 文化與健康 096-100

Day20_096 勤洗手不生病

→ 把你知道的單字打勾！
- [ ] observe
- [ ] protect
- [ ] germ
- [ ] hygiene
- [ ] urge

→ 用 5 個字說出這張圖片的故事！

observe [əb`zɝv]　v. 遵守

S In order to avoid getting sick, there are some rules that should be **observed**.
為了避免生病，有一些規則應該要遵守。

> **MORE** observe 當動詞時也有「觀察；注意到」的意思。
> Lisa is **observing** her teacher's demonstration.（觀察）
> 麗莎正在觀察她老師的示範。
> The police officer **observed** a man carrying a gun.（注意到）
> 警察注意到一個男人拿著槍。

protect [prə`tɛkt]　v. 保護

S For example, I wash my hands before eating to **protect** myself.
例如，我會在吃東西前先洗手來保護我自己。

> 關聯字　protection n. 保護　　protective adj. 保護性的

germ [dʒɝm]　n. 病菌

There are a lot of viruses and **germs** on our hands.
我們的手上有很多病毒及病菌。

> **MORE** 常見的病原體（pathogen）除了 germ（病菌，複數形為 germs）之外，還有 bacterium（細菌，複數形為 bacteria）及 fungus（真菌，複數形為 fungi）。

hygiene [ˈhaɪdʒin]　n. 衛生

Good personal **hygiene** is one of the key elements of staying healthy.
良好的個人衛生是保持健康的關鍵要素之一。

- **hygiene** regulations 衛生法規
- personal **hygiene** 個人衛生
- public **hygiene** 公共衛生

urge [ɝdʒ]　v. 力勸；強烈要求

That's why I often **urge** my friends and family to keep good hygiene habits.
這就是為什麼我常會力勸我的朋友和家人要保持良好的衛生習慣。

Day20_097 踢足球

→ 把你知道的單字打勾！
- ☐ research
- ☐ celebrity
- ☐ match
- ☐ competitive
- ☐ aim at

→ 用 5 個字說出這張圖片的故事！

Day 20 文化與健康 096‧100

187

research [ˈrɪsɝtʃ]　　n. 研究，調查

🅢 According to some **research**, soccer is the most popular sport in the world.
根據一些調查，足球是世界上最受歡迎的運動。

MORE 足球在北美地區叫做 soccer，但在其他地區都是用 football 這個字。

celebrity [sɪˈlɛbrətɪ]　　n. 名人

🅢 Plenty of soccer players are not just athletes; instead, they are **celebrities**.
很多足球員不只是運動員而已，而是名人。

match [mætʃ]　　n. 比賽

🅢 Tom and Will are competing in a soccer **match** now.
湯姆與威爾現在正在比足球賽。

MORE 在英文裡「比賽」有很多種說法，會隨著比賽項目的不同而替換使用：
soccer/football match 足球賽　　baseball game 棒球賽　　car racing 賽車
golf tournament 高爾夫錦標賽　　speech contest 演講競賽

competitive [kəmˈpɛtətɪv]　　adj. 競爭激烈的

🅢 The match is very **competitive**, and both of the teams want to win.
這場比賽非常激烈，且這兩隊都想要贏。

關聯字 competition n. 比賽　　compete v. 競爭　　competitor n. 競爭對手

aim at　　phr. 瞄準～；以～為目標

🅢 For Tom and Will, winning the trophy is the only goal they **aim at**.
對於湯姆與威爾來說，贏得獎盃是他們瞄準的唯一目標。

MORE aim 在當動詞時是「瞄準」，當名詞時則是「瞄準的目標」。
Benny **aimed** at winning the championship.（瞄準）
班尼把目標瞄準了贏得冠軍。
Benny's **aim** is the championship.（瞄準的目標）
班尼的目標是冠軍。

Day20_098 是時候健康檢查了

→ 把你知道的單字打勾！
- [ ] checkup
- [ ] vessel
- [ ] abdomen
- [ ] consult
- [ ] detail

→ 用 5 個字說出這張圖片的故事！

checkup [ˋtʃɛk͵ʌp]　n. （健康）檢查

S I usually have a physical **checkup** every year.
我通常每年做一次身體健康檢查。

E physical **checkup** 身體健康檢查

MORE checkup 連在一起的時候是名詞，分開寫作 check up 時則是動詞，意思是「進行檢查」。

vessel [ˋvɛsl̩]　n. 血管

S I always have a blood test to see if there's anything causing a blocking of my **vessels**.
我總是會做血液檢查，看看是否有什麼東西會把我的血管堵住。

E blocked **vessels** 堵住的血管

MORE vessel 除了「血管」的意思之外，也是「船艦」和「容器」的意思，務必要透過上下文來理解單字字義。

Vessels are docked at the port.（船艦）
船艦停泊在碼頭。
I put all stuff in this **vessel**.（容器）
我把所有東西都放進這個容器裡。

abdomen [ˋæbdəmən]　n. 腹部

S The doctor checks my **abdomen** through an ultrasound scan.
醫生會透過照超音波來檢查我的腹部。

關聯字 abdominal adj. 腹部的

consult [kən`sʌlt]　v. 諮詢

🅢 I then **consult** my doctor about the results of the ultrasound image.
接著我會就超音波的成像來諮詢我的醫生。

關聯字 consultant n. 顧問

detail [`ditel]　n. 細節資訊

🅢 My doctor is very thorough, he tells me every **detail** of my problems and gives me suggestions every time.
我的醫生非常仔細,他每次都會告訴我所有問題的細節資訊,並提供我建議。

MORE　detail 當名詞時是「細節資訊」的意思,如果加上 -ed 字尾變成過去式形態 detailed,則會變成形容詞「詳細的」。

Day20_099 越算越嚇人

→ 把你知道的單字打勾!
☐ fortune teller
☐ whisper
☐ convince
☐ hesitantly
☐ liar

→ 用 5 個字說出這張圖片的故事!

fortune teller [`fɔrtʃən] [`tɛlɚ]　n. 算命師

🅢 Chris was walking down the street when he met a **fortune teller**.
克里斯在街上走的時候碰到了那位算命師。

MORE　fortune teller 的字面意義就是「告訴你命運的人」。

whisper [`hwɪspɚ]　v. 悄悄地說;耳語

🅢 The man leaned forward and **whispered** to Chris, "Young man, you'll be in trouble soon."
他往前傾身對克里斯悄聲說:「年輕人,你很快就會有麻煩了」。

190

convince [kənˋvɪns]　v. 使信服

Chris was not convinced, but he still followed the fortune teller to his booth.
雖然克里斯不信，但他還是跟著那位算命師去了他的攤位。

> **MORE** convince 是「使別人相信」或「說服別人」的意思，而 convinced 就是「被說服而相信」的意思，convincing 則是指「有說服力而值得相信的」，請一起記住。

hesitantly [ˋhɛzətəntlɪ]　adv. 猶豫地

After Chris hesitantly sat down before the booth, the fortune teller asked for one thousand dollars.
在克里斯猶豫地在攤位前坐下後，算命師要求要收 1000 元。

> 關聯字　hesitant adj. 猶豫的　hesitate v. 猶豫　hesitance n. 猶豫

liar [ˋlaɪɚ]　n. 騙子

At that moment, Chris knew the fortune teller was definitely a liar wanting to fool him.
在那一刻，克里斯知道這個算命師一定是個想要騙他的騙子。

Day20_100　減重有方法

→ 把你知道的單字打勾！
- [ ] search
- [ ] cause
- [ ] scrutinize
- [ ] calorie
- [ ] involve

→ 用 5 個字說出這張圖片的故事！

search [sɝtʃ]　v. 搜尋

🅢 Bob likes tasty food, and he loves **searching** for new restaurants.
鮑伯喜歡好吃的食物,而且他很愛搜尋新的餐廳。

> **MORE** search 和 find(找到)不同,search 是指搜尋的「動作」,find 則是搜尋的「成果」。
>
> We are **searching** the house.(重點在搜尋的動作)
> 我們正在搜尋這間屋子。
> We want to **find** a nanny.(重點在透過搜尋所得到的成果)
> 我們想要找到一個保姆。

cause [kɔz]　v. 造成

🅢 This hobby has **caused** him to become fatter and fatter.
這個嗜好造成他變得越來越胖。

> **MORE** cause 的名詞和動詞同形,當名詞時是「原因」的意思,例如 cause and effect(因果關係)。

scrutinize [ˈskrutn̩ˌaɪz]　v. 仔細檢視

🅢 His doctor urges him to lose weight and asks him to **scrutinize** what he eats every day.
他的醫生勸他減肥,並要求他仔細檢視自己每天吃了什麼。

calorie [ˈkælərɪ]　n. 卡路里,熱量

🅢 Trying to lose weight means he has to limit his daily **calorie** intake.
試圖減肥就意味著他必須限制每日的卡路里攝取量。

> 🅔 **calorie** deficit 熱量赤字

involve [ɪnˈvɑlv]　v. 包含,需要

🅢 His doctor also tells him that doing exercise should be **involved** in his plans for losing weight.
他的醫生也告訴他,他的減肥計畫裡應該要把運動包含在內。

回復記憶 階段

◆ 請參考以下在 Day20 中出現過的圖片，在單字旁的空格寫下字義。

096 勤洗手不生病
- observe _____
- protect _____
- germ _____
- hygiene _____
- urge _____

097 踢足球
- research _____
- celebrity _____
- match _____
- competitive _____
- aim at _____

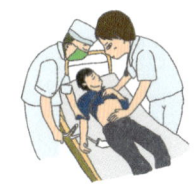

098 是時候健康檢查了
- checkup _____
- vessel _____
- abdomen _____
- consult _____
- detail _____

099 越算越嚇人
- fortune teller _____
- whisper _____
- convince _____
- hesitantly _____
- liar _____

100 減重有方法
- search _____
- cause _____
- scrutinize _____
- calorie _____
- involve _____

Day 20 文化與健康 096-100

193

加深記憶 階段

◆ 請依照提示的單字字首，在下列空格中填入適當的單字。

(1) 堵住的血管　　　　　　blocked v_____
(2) 說服我的客戶　　　　　c_____ my clients
(3) 一場競爭激烈的比賽　　a c_____ game
(4) 一份詳細的研究　　　　a detailed r_____
(5) 一個受歡迎的名人　　　a popular c_____

◆ 請參考下列方框中的單字，在下列空格中填入適當的單字。

> 參考 | germ | scrutinize | observe | urge | hesitantly | cause | consult | match

(1) Do you know how to kill _____?
   你知道要如何殺死病菌嗎？

(2) You have to _____ your operational process.
   你必須仔細檢視你的操作程序。

(3) Will you play in today's _____?
   你會打今天的比賽嗎？

(4) His boss _____ him to book a table first.
   他的老闆強烈要求他先去訂位。

(5) Traffic _____ air pollution.
   車流會造成空氣汙染。

(6) If you encounter difficulties, you can _____ your parents.
   假如你遇到困難，你可以諮詢你的父母。

(7) He told me the truth _____.
   他猶豫地告訴了我真相。

(8) Company's regulations should be _____.
   公司的規定應該被遵守。

Answers:
1. (1) vessels (2) convince (3) competitive (4) research (5) celebrity
2. (1) germs (2) scrutinize (3) match (4) urged (5) causes (6) consult (7) hesitantly (8) observed

Day 21 文化與健康 101-105

Day21_101 藥局拿藥

→ 把你知道的單字打勾！
- [ ] clinic
- [ ] prescribe
- [ ] fee
- [ ] receive
- [ ] pharmacist

→ 用 5 個字說出這張圖片的故事！

clinic [ˋklɪnɪk]　n. 診所

S Lisa went to a **clinic** because she had some skin problems.
麗莎因為有一些皮膚問題而去了一間診所。

> MORE 除了 clinic，常見的醫療院所還有 doctor's office（私人小診所）、hospital（醫院）、health center（衛生所）。

prescribe [prɪˋskraɪb]　v. 開處方

S After examining, the doctor **prescribed** some medicine for her.
在檢查之後，醫生開了一些藥給她。

> 關聯字 prescription n. 處方箋
> MORE 常見的藥物形式有 tablet（藥片）、pill（藥丸）、powder（藥粉）、capsule（膠囊）、potion（藥水）、gel（凝膠）、ointment（軟膏）。

fee [fi]　n. 費用

S After taking the prescription, she paid the **fee** at the registration desk, and got her receipt.
在拿了處方箋之後，她在櫃台付了費用並拿了她的收據。

> MORE fee 是付給醫師或律師等專業人士提供服務的費用。

receive [rɪˋsiv]　v. 收取

🅢 She held a number and waited for **receiving** her medicine.
她拿了一個號碼牌等著拿她的藥。

關聯字 receipt n. 收據　recipient n. 收受者

pharmacist [ˋfɑrməsɪst]　n. 藥師

🅢 The **pharmacist** gave her a tube of ointment and some capsules.
藥師給了她一管軟膏和一些膠囊。

同義字 dispenser

Day21_102 吃鮭魚很棒

→ 把你知道的單字打勾！
- [ ] diet
- [ ] fit
- [ ] cordially
- [ ] healthful
- [ ] salmon

→ 用 5 個字說出這張圖片的故事！

diet [ˋdaɪət]　n. 飲食；飲食法

🅢 Eason wants to go on a **diet**, so he asks his friend for some advice.
伊森想要節食，所以他向他的朋友尋求一些建議。

🅔 on a **diet** 節食

🅔 healthy **diet** 健康的飲食法

MORE diet 除了日常飲食的意思之外，也常會用來指「為達到特定目的而進行的特殊飲食法」，例如因為想減肥而進行的節食（**on a diet**），或是為了增肌而吃的高蛋白飲食（**high-protein diet**）等。

fit [fɪt]　adj. 健壯的

🅢 Eason also wants to keep **fit**, so it's important for him to eat right.
伊森也想要保持健壯的身材，所以對他來說吃對很重要。

> **MORE** fit 當形容詞也有「適合的；合身的」的字義，請一定要透過前後文來判斷單字字義。
>
> Does this pair of sneakers **fit**?（合身的）
> 這雙球鞋合腳嗎？
> I don't think it's **fit** for me to join the group.（適合的）
> 我不覺得我適合加入那個團體。

cordially [ˋkɔrdʒəlɪ]　adv. 熱情友好地

🅢 His friend answers **cordially**, "You should eat more foods with high-quality protein."
他的朋友熱情友好地回答：「你應該要多吃含有優質蛋白質的食物」。

healthful [ˋhɛlθfəl]　adj. 有助健康的

🅢 Eason asks him which foods are **healthful**.
伊森問他有哪些食物是對健康有幫助的。

> 關聯字　health n. 健康　　healthy adj. 健康的

salmon [ˋsæmən]　n. 鮭魚

🅢 "You can eat more fish, such as **salmon**!", his friend answers.
他的朋友回答：「你可以多吃魚，像是鮭魚！」

> **MORE** 其他常見的魚類還有：
> cod（鱈魚）、tuna（鮪魚）、marlin（旗魚）、perch（鱸魚）、tilapia（吳郭魚）。

> **Day21_103** 導盲犬幫忙

→ 把你知道的單字打勾！
- [ ] guide dog
- [ ] disabled
- [ ] order
- [ ] hazardous
- [ ] shun

→ 用 5 個字說出這張圖片的故事！

guide dog [gaɪd] [dɔg]　　n. 導盲犬

- **Lulu is a guide dog, and Jason is her owner.**
  露露是一隻導盲犬，而傑森是他的主人。

disabled [dɪsˋeblḍ]　　adj. 殘障的

- **Jason is disabled because he can't see things clearly.**
  傑森有殘疾，因為他無法清楚視物。

  > MORE 在 the 的後面加上形容詞，就會變成集體名詞，如 the blind（視障人士）、the deaf（聽障人士）、the dumb（聲障人士）。

order [ˋɔrdɚ]　　n. 命令

- **Although Jason can't see, he still can give Lulu orders accurately.**
  儘管傑森看不到，他還是可以準確地對露露下指令。

  > 同義字 command
  > MORE order 當名詞時還有「順序」及「訂單；訂購的品項」的意思。
  > Your job is to put the files in **order**.（順序）
  > 你的工作是把檔案照順序放好。
  > The **orders** need to be filled by noon.（訂單；訂購的品項）
  > 訂單必須在中午以前準備好。

hazardous [ˈhæzɚdəs]　adj. 有危險的

🅢 Lulu is a smart dog, so she can tell if a situation is **hazardous** or not.
露露是隻聰明的狗,所以她能分辨情況有沒有危險。

同義字 dangerous

shun [ʃʌn]　v. 避開

🅢 She can help Jason **shun** the dangers he encounters.
她可以幫助傑森避開他碰到的危險。

同義字 avoid

Day21_104　看牙醫

→ 把你知道的單字打勾!
☐ unwilling
☐ drill
☐ dental
☐ cavity
☐ correctly

→ 用 5 個字說出這張圖片的故事!

unwilling [ʌnˈwɪlɪŋ]　adj. 不情願的

🅢 Ivan is **unwilling** to see a dentist even though he has a toothache.
艾文即使牙痛也不情願去看牙醫。

反義字 willing adj. 有意願的,情願的

drill [drɪl]　n. 鑽頭;鑽機

🅢 He says that he can't stand the sound of the dental **drills**.
他說他無法忍受牙鑽的聲音。

> **MORE** drill 在當名詞的時候還有「演習」的意思,例如 fire drill（消防演習）、military drill（軍事演習）,都是很常見的用法。另外,drill 的名詞和動詞同形,當動詞時是「鑽孔」的意思。

dental [ˈdɛnt!]　adj. 牙齒的

S But today Ivan went to the dentist's office, because his **dental** problem worsened.
但今天艾文去了牙醫診所，因為他的牙齒問題惡化了。

> MORE　worsen 是由 bad 的比較級 worse 動詞化而來的。

cavity [ˈkævətɪ]　n. 蛀牙的洞

S After examination, the dentist cleaned his teeth and filled the **cavities** caused by tooth decay.
在檢查之後，牙醫清潔了他的牙齒，並填補了因為蛀牙而導致的孔洞。

correctly [kəˈrɛktlɪ]　adv. 正確地

S After the treatment, the dentist taught him how to brush his teeth **correctly**.
在治療之後，牙醫教了他要如何正確刷牙。

> 關聯字　correct adj. 正確的 v. 糾正

Day21_105 切洋蔥切到哭

→ 把你知道的單字打勾！
- [ ] benefit
- [ ] look through
- [ ] vegetarian
- [ ] kilogram
- [ ] chop

→ 用 5 個字說出這張圖片的故事！

---

benefit [ˈbɛnəfɪt]　v. 對～有益

S Steve cares about his health, so he wants to know what kind of food **benefits** him more.
史帝夫很在乎自己的健康，所以他很想知道什麼樣的食物會對他比較好。

> **MORE** benefit 除了當動詞之外，也可以當名詞，當名詞時的 benefit，意思是「福利；好處」。

The company provides lots of **benefits** for their employees.
這間公司提供很多福利給他們的員工。

look through　　phr. 瀏覽，快速看過

He **looks through** many books, trying to find the food he likes and that is also good for his health.
他瀏覽了很多書，試圖要找到他喜歡、對健康又好的食物。

> **MORE** look 後面接不同的介系詞，就會有不同的意思，這裡補充幾個特別常見的表達方式：

look after 照顧　　look up 查閱；向上看　　look into 調查
look for 尋找　　look up to 尊敬　　look down to 輕視

vegetarian [ˌvɛdʒəˈtɛrɪən]　　n. 素食者

He's not a **vegetarian**, but he finds that most vegetables are good for health.
他不是個素食者，但是他發現大部分的蔬菜都有益健康。

> **MORE** vegetarian 也可以當形容詞，表示「蔬菜的；素食的」。

I went to a **vegetarian** restaurant yesterday.
我昨天去了一間素食餐廳。

kilogram [ˈkɪləˌɡræm]　　n. 公斤

Steve bought one **kilogram** of onions, which was on sale, in a supermarket today.
今天史帝夫在一間超市買了一公斤的特價洋蔥。

關聯字　gram n. 公克

chop [tʃɑp]　　v. 切細，剁碎

When he was **chopping** the onions, the poignant smell stimulated his eyes and made him tear up.
當他在切洋蔥時，刺鼻的氣味刺激了他的眼睛並讓他流淚了。

回復記憶 階段

◆ 請參考以下在 Day21 中出現過的圖片，在單字旁的空格寫下字義。

101 藥局拿藥
- clinic _____
- prescribe _____
- fee _____
- receive _____
- pharmacist _____

102 吃鮭魚很棒
- diet _____
- fit _____
- cordially _____
- healthful _____
- salmon _____

103 導盲犬幫忙
- guide dog _____
- disabled _____
- order _____
- hazardous _____
- shun _____

104 看牙醫
- unwilling _____
- drill _____
- dental _____
- cavity _____
- correctly _____

105 切洋蔥切到哭
- benefit _____
- look through _____
- vegetarian _____
- kilogram _____
- chop _____

加深記憶 階段

◆ 請依照提示的單字字首，在下列空格中填入適當的單字。

(1) 一個牙齒問題　　　　　　a d_____ problem
(2) 五公斤　　　　　　　　　five k_____
(3) 一個會造成危險的情況　　a h_____ situation
(4) 一個直接的命令　　　　　an immediate o_____
(5) 一位努力的藥劑師　　　　a hardworking p_____

◆ 請參考下列方框中的單字，在下列空格中填入適當的單字。

| 參考 | prescribe | look through | receive | shun |
| vegetarian | cordially | unwilling | diet |

(1) Why do you need to go on a _____?
　　你為什麼需要節食？

(2) Dr. Wu _____ some pills for me.
　　吳醫生開了一些藥丸給我。

(3) I am _____ to change my job.
　　我不願意換工作。

(4) I'm trying to _____ all disturbing things.
　　我試圖避開所有令人煩心的事。

(5) Are you a _____?
　　你是素食者嗎？

(6) Did you _____ your report card?
　　你收到成績單了嗎？

(7) When I'm free, I like to _____ some magazines.
　　在我有空時，我喜歡瀏覽一些雜誌。

(8) He said he can help me _____.
　　他熱心地說他可以幫我。

Answers:
1. (1) dental (2) kilograms (3) hazardous (4) order (5) pharmacist
2. (1) diet (2) prescribed (3) unwilling (4) shun (5) vegetarian (6) receive (7) look through (8) cordially

記單字必備！掌握常見多義字 01

1. **live** [lɪv] **v.** 居住　[laɪv] **adj.** 現場的
   I **live** in the suburbs.
   我住在市郊。
   The **live** show is interesting.
   這場現場表演很有趣。

2. **present** [ˋprɛzn̩t] **adj.** 出席的　**n.** 禮物
   He was **present** in the meeting in the end.
   他最終出席了那場會議。
   I get a birthday **present** every year.
   我每年都會得到一個生日禮物。

3. **tear** [tɪr] **n.** 眼淚　[tɛr] **v.** 拆除
   She was moved to **tears**.
   她感動到流淚了。
   They try to **tear** down the building.
   他們試圖要把這棟建築物拆掉。

4. **desert** [ˋdɛzɚt] **n.** 沙漠　[dɪˋzɝt] **v.** 遺棄
   The dry land over there is a **desert**.
   在那裡的乾燥土地是一片沙漠。
   You are **deserted**.
   你被遺棄了。

5. **object** [əbˋdʒɛkt] **v.** 反對　[ˋabdʒɪkt] **n.** 物體
   We **objected** to this plan.
   我們反對這個計畫。
   That weird **object** is really an eyesore.
   那個奇怪的物體真是礙眼。

204

6. address [ˋædrɛs] **n.** 地址 [əˋdrɛs] **v.** 對～發言
Give me your **address**.
給我你的地址。
She is **addressing** a group of people.
她正在對一群人發言。

7. fine [faɪn] **adj.** 很好的 **n.** 罰款
My parents are **fine**.
我的父母很好。
The **fine** will be imposed soon.
很快就會收取罰金。

8. kind [kaɪnd] **adj.** 和善的 **n.** 種類
It's very **kind** of you to say that.
你這樣說人真的很好。
What **kind** of movies do you like?
你喜歡哪種電影？

9. contract [kənˋtrækt] **v.** 使縮小；使收縮 [ˋkɑntrækt] **n.** 契約
The two words can be **contracted**.
這兩個字可以縮寫。
We have to sign this **contract**.
我們必須簽這份契約。

10. record [ˋrɛkɚd] **n.** 紀錄 [rɪˋkɔrd] **v.** 錄音，錄影
He holds the **record** in the high jump.
他在跳高項目上保持紀錄。
They want to **record** a music show.
他們想要錄一個音樂節目。

Day 22 自然與環境 106-110

Day22.mp3

Day22_106 夕陽無限好

→ 把你知道的單字打勾！
- [ ] sunset
- [ ] catch sight of
- [ ] warmth
- [ ] savor
- [ ] like

→ 用 5 個字說出這張圖片的故事！

sunset [ˈsʌn,sɛt]　　n. 夕陽

Ⓢ **Jamie is sitting on the beach and watching the sunset.**
捷米正坐在海灘上看著夕陽。

> MORE　sunset 裡的 set 是「落下」的意思，而「日出」則是由「sun＋rise（升起）」組合而成的 sunrise。

catch sight of　　phr. 突然注意到；看見

Ⓢ **She was not meant to stop to see the sun setting, but she caught sight of the beautiful view in front of her.**
她本來沒打算停下來看日落的，但她突然注意到了眼前的美景。

> 同義字　have a glimpse of、suddenly notice

warmth [wɔrmθ]　　n. 溫暖

Ⓢ **The warmth and beauty of the sun were remarkable.**
太陽的溫暖和美麗是無與倫比的。

> MORE　warmth 是「溫暖」而不是熱，可以想成是冬天時的陽光，若是要講夏日的那種「炎熱」，則會使用 heat（高溫）或 hot（炎熱的）。

savor [ˋsevɚ]　　v. 欣賞；品味

S Now she is **savoring** the peace and the splendid view of the sunset.
現在她正在品味著安寧與夕陽的瑰麗景色。

關聯字　savory adj. 美味可口的；令人愉快的
　　　　savorless adj. 缺少風味的；無趣的

like [laɪk]　　prep. 像

S The sun is just **like** the origin of life, and its greatness makes her feel small.
太陽就像是生命的起源，而它的偉大讓她覺得自己很渺小。

MORE　like 這個字具有多種詞性，在當動詞時是「喜歡」、形容詞時是「相像的」，請務必要透過前後文來判斷字義。

Day22_107　美好的海洋

→ 把你知道的單字打勾！
- [ ] marine
- [ ] not to mention
- [ ] dig
- [ ] distraught
- [ ] evoke

→ 用 5 個字說出這張圖片的故事！

marine [məˋrin]　　adj. 海洋的

S My family and I sometimes go to the beach nearby to see **marine** animals.
我家人和我有時會去附近的沙灘看海洋生物。

關聯字　submarine n. 潛水艇

not to mention phr. 更不用說

- We can see sea turtles on the beach, **not to mention** crabs and starfish.
  我們可以在沙灘上看到海龜，更不用說螃蟹和海星了。

  > **MORE** not to mention 是用來強調後面所接內容的片語，表示「連前面提到的都可以／不行，更不用說～」。

dig [dɪg] v. 挖掘

- My kid likes to **dig** big holes on the beach, and then asks us to lie down in the holes.
  我的孩子喜歡在沙灘上挖大洞，然後要求我們躺在這些洞裡。

  > **MORE** dig 的動詞三態是不規則變化：dig-dug-dug。

distraught [dɪˋstrɔt] adj. 心煩意亂的

- Playing with my kid and viewing the sea can make me change my mood from **distraught** to calm and happy.
  和我的孩子一起玩和看海，可以讓我的心情從心煩意亂變成平靜和快樂。

evoke [ɪˋvok] v. 喚起

- Looking at the sea also **evokes** a lot of beautiful memories for me.
  看海也會喚起我很多美好的回憶。

Day22_108 璀璨星空

→ 把你知道的單字打勾！
- [ ] starry
- [ ] astronomical
- [ ] naked eye
- [ ] meteor
- [ ] kneel

→ 用 5 個字說出這張圖片的故事！

starry [ˋstɑrɪ]　adj. 星光閃耀的

S "The **Starry** Night" is a famous masterpiece created by Vincent van Gogh.
《星夜》是由梵谷創作的知名傑作。

關聯字 **starry-eyed** adj. 過於天真的；過分樂觀的
You are **starry-eyed** about flying in the sky.
你對在天上飛的這件事過於天真了。

astronomical [͵æstrəˋnɑmɪk!]　adj. 天文的

S In reality, stars are **astronomical** objects appearing in the sky as sparkling dots.
在現實之中，星星是會出現在天空中像小光點般的天體。

關聯字 **astronomy** n. 天文學　**astronomer** adj. 天文學家

naked eye [ˋnekɪd] [aɪ]　n. 肉眼

S There are countless stars in the sky, but most of them are invisible to the **naked eye**.
天空中有數不盡的星星，但大部分的星星是用肉眼看不見的。

同義字 **unaided eye**
MORE naked 是「赤裸的；無遮蓋的」的意思，所以 naked eye 就是「沒有戴眼鏡或使用其他輔助用具的眼睛」，也就是「肉眼」

meteor [ˋmitɪɚ]　n. 流星

S **Meteors**, also called shooting stars, are also attractive.
流星，也叫做掉落的星星，也很吸引人。

E a **meteor** shower 一場流星雨
同義字 **shooting star**

kneel [nil]　v. 跪下

S Seeing a shooting star, I **kneel** down to make a wish right away.
一看到流星，我就立刻跪下許願。

MORE kneel 的過去式和過去分詞，可以寫作 knelt 或 kneeled，因此三態變化是：kneel-knelt/kneeled-knelt/kneeled，使用時要特別注意。

Day22_109 種花很難

→ 把你知道的單字打勾！
- ☐ plant
- ☐ botanical
- ☐ balcony
- ☐ soil
- ☐ fragrance

→ 用 5 個字說出這張圖片的故事！

plant [plænt]　　n. 植物

S Different kinds of **plants** have different flowers.
不同種類的植物會有不同的花。

> **MORE** plant 除了「植物」的意思之外，當名詞時也有「工廠」的意思，且 plant 也能當動詞，這時是「種植」的意思，因此務必要透過前後文來判斷單字的字義。
> Many companies have **plants** in Vietnam.（工廠）
> 很多公司在越南有工廠。
> My father **plants** several trees in our back yard.（種植）
> 我父親在我們的後院裡種了幾棵樹。

botanical [bo`tænɪkl]　　adj. 植物的；植物學的

S Beautiful flowers are everywhere, but some of them are rare and can only be seen in a **botanical** garden.
漂亮的花到處都是，不過它們之中有些很罕見，而且只能在植物園裡看見。

> 關聯字 botanist n. 植物學家

balcony [`bælkənɪ]　　n. 陽台

S I once tried to grow rare flowers on my **balcony**, but they all died very soon.
我曾試圖在陽台上種稀有的花，但它們很快就全死了。

> **E** a **spacious** balcony 一個寬敞的陽台

210

soil [sɔɪl]　n. 土壤

🅢 Without the right **soil**, water and professional skills, it's really difficult to make them grow beautifully.
沒有正確的土壤、水和專業技巧，要讓它們長得漂亮很難。

fragrance [ˋfregrəns]　n. 香氣；香水

🅢 As a result, I sometimes go to a botanical garden to see the pretty flowers there and let myself indulge in the **fragrance**.
因此，我有時會去植物園看那裡漂亮的花，並讓自己沉浸在香氣之中。

| 同義字 | scent、aroma |
| 反義字 | odor、smell |

Day22_110 該重新粉刷了

→ 把你知道的單字打勾！
- ☐ surrounding
- ☐ responsible
- ☐ exterior
- ☐ painter
- ☐ be about to

→ 用 5 個字說出這張圖片的故事！

---

surrounding [səˋraʊndɪŋ]　n. 周遭環境

🅢 Making your **surroundings** clean and pleasing to the eye is everyone's responsibility.
讓你的周遭環境乾淨與美觀是每個人的責任。

> **MORE** surrounding 當名詞表示「周遭環境」時都必須加上 s 以複數形來使用，不過 surrounding 也可以當成形容詞，這時就不需要加 s 了，意思是「周圍的；附近的」。

Day 22 自然與環境 106・110

responsible [rɪˋspɑnsəb!]　adj. 負責的

⑤ The appearance of my house was very old and dull, so I was **responsible** for making a change.
我房子的外觀非常老舊又死氣沉沉，所以我有責任要做出改變。

關聯字 responsibility n. 責任　respond v. 回應
MORE responsible（負責的）和 responsive（回應的）長得很像，但意思完全不同，小心不要搞混了。

Parents should be **responsible** for their kids.
家長應該對他們的小孩負責。
The gadget is not **responsive**.
這個裝置沒有回應。

exterior [ɪkˋstɪrɪɚ]　adj. 外部的

⑤ The **exterior** paint of my house was peeling and faded.
我房子外面的油漆既剝落又褪色。

反義字 interior
MORE exterior 和 external（外部的）這個字長得很像，甚至字典上的字義也很像，但 external 指的是「來自外部的；外面的」，而 exterior 則是「某物的外面；外表的」，雖然有時可以通用，但還是有所不同，使用時必須特別注意。

I have to paint the **external** wall of my house.
我必須粉刷我房子的外牆。
The **exterior** of my house needs to be renovated.
我房子的外表需要整修。

painter [ˋpentɚ]　n. 油漆工

⑤ So I have hired a **painter** to repaint my house.
所以我雇了一位油漆工來重新粉刷我的房子。

MORE painter 也是「畫家」的意思。

be about to　phr. 馬上

⑤ The paint work is on schedule now and I think it**'s about to** finish.
油漆作業現在正按照計畫進行，而且我想就快要完成了。

回復記憶 階段

◆ 請參考以下在 Day22 中出現過的圖片，在單字旁的空格寫下字義。

106 夕陽無限好
- sunset _____
- catch sight of _____
- warmth _____
- savor _____
- like _____

107 美好的海洋
- marine _____
- not to mention _____
- dig _____
- distraught _____
- evoke _____

108 璀璨星空
- starry _____
- astronomical _____
- naked eye _____
- meteor _____
- kneel _____

109 種花很難
- plant _____
- botanical _____
- balcony _____
- soil _____
- fragrance _____

110 該重新粉刷了
- surrounding _____
- responsible _____
- exterior _____
- painter _____
- be about to _____

加深記憶 階段

◆ 請依照提示的單字字首，在下列空格中填入適當的單字。

(1) 一個植物園　　　　　　　a b_____ garden
(2) 一個負責的工人　　　　　a r_____ worker
(3) 一個乾淨的周遭環境　　　a clean s_____
(4) 一個寬敞的陽台　　　　　a spacious b_____
(5) 一個海洋生物　　　　　　a m_____ creature

◆ 請參考下列方框中的單字，在下列空格中填入適當的單字。

| 參考 | fragrance | kneel | like | savor |
| | catch sight of | let alone | evoke | dig |

(1) I am happy when I _____ the blue sky.
　　我在看到藍天時感到開心。

(2) Do you like the _____ of my new perfume?
　　你喜歡我新香水的味道嗎？

(3) These new dishes are worth _____.
　　這些新菜值得品嚐。

(4) The gardener is busy _____.
　　園丁正在忙著挖土。

(5) The sculpture is really _____ a real person.
　　這個雕像很像真人。

(6) My son is _____ to lift up the boxes.
　　我的兒子跪著要抬起那些箱子。

(7) Does this picture _____ something?
　　這張照片有喚起什麼嗎？

(8) This question is too difficult for adults, _____ children.
　　這個問題對於成人來說都太困難，更別說小孩了。

Answers:
1. (1) botanical (2) responsible (3) surroundings (4) balcony (5) marine
2. (1) catch sight of (2) fragrance (3) savoring (4) digging (5) like (6) kneeling (7) evoke
　　(8) not to mention

Day 23 自然與環境 111-115

Day23_111 天乾物燥小心火燭

→ 把你知道的單字打勾！
- [ ] average
- [ ] temperature
- [ ] firefighter
- [ ] massive
- [ ] put out

→ 用 5 個字說出這張圖片的故事！

average [ˈævərɪdʒ]　adj. 平均的

🅢 It's terribly hot recently, and the **average** temperature is higher than normal.
最近非常炎熱，且平均氣溫比正常要高。

> **MORE** average 也可以當名詞，表示「平均」。另外，「最大值」是 maximum，「最小值」則是 minimum。

temperature [ˈtɛmprətʃɚ]　n. 氣溫

🅢 If the **temperature** is high, and the air is dry, then it's easy for wooden houses to catch fire.
如果氣溫高，空氣又乾，那麼木造房屋就容易著火。

🄴 take the **temperature** 量體溫

firefighter [ˈfaɪrˌfaɪtɚ]　n. 消防員

🅢 A house is on fire now, and **firefighters** are on the scene.
現在有一間房子著火了，而消防員們正在現場。

關聯字 fire station n. 消防局

massive [ˋmæsɪv]　adj. 巨大的；大規模的

- It's truly horrifying to see the **massive** fire swallowing up the house.
  看到大火正在將房屋吞噬的樣子真的很嚇人。

put out　phr. 撲滅

- I hope the firefighters can **put out** the fire very soon, and no one is hurt by the fire.
  我希望消防員們可以很快把火滅了，且沒人因為這場火而受傷。

  > **MORE** put 後面接的介系詞不同，就會有不同的意義，常見的還有：put off（延後）、put on（穿上）、put up with（忍受）、put up（架設）、put in（提出；插話），請一併記住。

Day23_112　梅雨季節溼答答

→ 把你知道的單字打勾！
- [ ] season
- [ ] front
- [ ] torrential
- [ ] gear
- [ ] dry

→ 用 5 個字說出這張圖片的故事！

---

season [ˋsizn̩]　n. 季節

- In Taiwan, the "plum rain **season**" happens during May and June every year.
  在台灣，「梅雨季」發生在每年的五六月期間。

  > **關聯字** seasonal adj. 季節的　seasonable adj. 合於季節的
  > 　　　　　seasoned adj. 有經驗的
  > **MORE** 四個季節的英文分別是 spring（春）、summer（夏）、fall/autumn（秋）、winter（冬）。

front [frʌnt]　n. 鋒面

S During the plum rain season, stationary **fronts** cause extremely heavy rain.
在梅雨季期間，滯留鋒面會造成豪雨。

E cold **front** 冷鋒
E warm **front** 暖鋒

torrential [tɔˋrɛnʃəl]　adj. 滂沱的

S Sometimes **torrential** rains make many areas flood.
有時滂沱大雨會使很多地方淹水。

E a **torrential** downpour 滂沱的傾盆大雨

gear [gɪr]　n. 器具，裝備

S Today John got totally wet on his way to school, even though he carried his rain **gear**.
今天約翰在去上學的路上完全濕透了，即使他有帶著他的雨具。

MORE gear 也有「汽車排檔」的意思。

dry [draɪ]　v. 弄乾

S Now he is trying to **dry** his bag and books.
現在他正在試圖弄乾他的包包和書。

MORE dry 也可以當作形容詞，表示「乾燥的」。

Day23_113 垃圾分類保護地球

→ 把你知道的單字打勾！
☐ recycle
☐ bin
☐ generally
☐ combustible
☐ wanton

可燃垃圾
Combustible

21 星期三

→ 用 5 個字說出這張圖片的故事！

recycle [rɪˋsaɪkl]　v. 回收再利用

S In order to protect our earth, **recycling** is important.
為了保護我們的地球，回收再利用很重要。

- **E** trash **recycling** 垃圾回收
- **E** a **recycling** bin 一個回收箱

bin [bɪn]　n. 箱子，容器

S To recycle, you have to sort out the recyclables, and put them into separate **bins**.
要做回收，你必須把可回收的東西分類出來並放進獨立的容器裡。

> **MORE** 垃圾桶有很多種說法，最常見的是 trash/garbage can/bin，如果是字紙簍那種的，則是 wastebasket，回收桶則是 recycling bin。

generally [ˋdʒɛnərəlɪ]　adv. 一般，通常

S **Generally** speaking, most of the recyclable stuff can be sorted into kitchen waste, plastic and paper.
一般來說，大部分可回收的東西可以被分類成廚餘、塑膠與紙類。

> **MORE** generally speaking（一般來說）很常用來發表意見，其他常用的片語還有 roughly speaking（大致上來說）、strictly speaking（嚴格來說）、frankly speaking（坦白說）、honestly speaking（老實說）、sincerely speaking（真心說），請一併記下來。

combustible [kəmˋbʌstəbl]　adj. 可燃的

S But some people sort them into **combustibles** and non-combustibles.
不過有些人們會把它們分類成可燃物與不可燃物。

wanton [ˋwɑntən]　adj. 輕率隨便的；不負責任的

S In short, people shouldn't throw away their trash in a **wanton** way; otherwise the planet suffers.
總之，人們不該用不負責任的方式丟垃圾，不然地球就會受苦了。

- **E** a **wanton** attitude 輕率隨便的態度

Day23_114 過敏超難過

→ 把你知道的單字打勾！
- [ ] allergic
- [ ] symptom
- [ ] sneeze
- [ ] allergen
- [ ] dust mite

→ 用 5 個字說出這張圖片的故事！

allergic [əˋlɝdʒɪk]　adj. 過敏的

S I'm **allergic** to many things; having allergies is a part of my daily life.
我對很多東西都過敏，過敏已經是我日常生活的一部分了。

關聯字 allergy n. 過敏

symptom [ˋsɪmptəm]　n. 症狀

S Do you know the **symptoms** of being allergic?
你知道過敏的症狀是什麼嗎？

關聯字 syndrome n. 症候群

sneeze [sniz]　v. 打噴嚏

S **Sneezing**, coughing, and itchy eyes or skin are all the common symptoms of allergies.
打噴嚏、咳嗽以及發癢的眼睛或皮膚，都是常見的過敏症狀。

MORE 這裡補充一些常見的生病症狀：
sneeze（打噴嚏）、cough（咳嗽）、running nose（流鼻水）、fever（發燒）、headache（頭痛）、sore throat（喉嚨痛）、muscle ache（肌肉痠痛）

allergen [ˋælɚ͵dʒɛn]　n. 過敏原

S To get rid of allergies, you need to know your **allergens**.
為了擺脫過敏，你必須了解你的過敏原。

E common **allergens** 常見的過敏原

dust mite [dʌst] [maɪt]　n. 塵蟎

S The clothes I am wearing today were on a shelf for a long time, and the **dust mites** on them are making me sneeze nonstop.
我今天穿的衣服放了很久，而上面的塵蟎讓我噴嚏打個不停。

關聯字 mite n. 蟎蟲　termite n. 白蟻

Day23_115　下雪好麻煩

→ 把你知道的單字打勾！
- [ ] panic
- [ ] slippery
- [ ] providing that
- [ ] blizzard
- [ ] climate

→ 用 5 個字說出這張圖片的故事！

panic [`pænɪk]　v. 驚慌

S The sudden snow makes Amanda **panic**.
突如其來的雪讓艾曼達驚慌。

> **MORE** panic 這個字不只可以當動詞，也能當作形容詞和名詞，請透過 panic 出現在句子中的位置來判斷它的詞性。

Don't **panic**! Stay calm.（動詞）
不要驚慌！保持冷靜。
The **panic** caused by the earthquake made me shiver.（名詞）
地震造成的驚慌讓我發抖。
The **panic** woman rushed out right away.（形容詞）
那個驚慌的女人立刻衝了出去。

slippery [`slɪpərɪ]　adj. 很滑的

S That's because she is very bad at walking on **slippery** streets covered by snow.
這是因為她非常不擅長在被雪覆蓋又很滑的街道上走路。

關聯字 slip v. 滑動　slipper n. 拖鞋

providing that　phr. 假如

- Plus, **providing that** it snows continually, it will be difficult for her to go out to buy groceries.
  而且，假如雪一直下，去外面採買雜貨對她來說就變得很困難。

  同義字 provided that、on condition that

blizzard　[ˋblɪzɚd]　n. 暴風雪

- Last time, a horrible **blizzard** even got her stuck at home for several days!
  上次，一場可怕的暴風雪甚至讓她被困在了家裡好幾天！

  同義字 snowstorm

climate　[ˋklaɪmɪt]　n. 氣候

- That's why Amanda likes warmer **climates** more, and she even considered moving to a warmer place.
  這就是為什麼艾曼達比較喜歡溫暖一點的氣候，而且她甚至考慮要搬去比較溫暖的地方。

回復記憶 階段

◆ 請參考以下在 Day23 中出現過的圖片，在單字旁的空格寫下字義。

111 天乾物燥小心火燭
average .... massive ....
temperature .... put out ....
firefighter ....

112 梅雨季節溼答答
season .... gear ....
front .... dry ....
torrential ....

113 垃圾分類保護地球
recycle .... combustible ....
bin .... wanton ....
generally ....

114 過敏超難過
allergic .... allergen ....
symptom .... dust mite ....
sneeze ....

115 下雪好麻煩
panic .... blizzard ....
slippery .... climate ....
providing that ....

222

加深記憶 階段

◆ 請依照提示的單字字首，在下列空格中填入適當的單字。

(1) 不要驚慌　　　　　Don't p_____
(2) 一件雨具　　　　　a rain g_____
(3) 滂沱大雨　　　　　t_____ rain
(4) 常見過敏原　　　　common a_____
(5) 一道冷鋒　　　　　a cold f_____

◆ 請參考下列方框中的單字，在下列空格中填入適當的單字。

> 參考 | temperature | generally | providing that | dust mite |
> | put out | combustible | dry | firefighter |

(1) Being a _____ is a dangerous job.
當消防員是份危險的工作。

(2) What is today's _____?
今天幾度？

(3) Be careful with these _____ things.
小心這些可燃物。

(4) _____ can cause allergies
塵蟎可能會造成過敏。

(5) Don't _____ the campfire.
不要撲滅營火。

(6) Where will you go _____ you have some free time?
假如你有一些空閒時間，你會去哪裡？

(7) I need to _____ my hair.
我必須把我的頭髮弄乾。

(8) _____ speaking, most of my students are hardworking.
一般來說，我的學生大部分都很認真。

Answers:
1. (1) panic (2) gear (3) torrential (4) allergens (5) front
2. (1) firefighter (2) temperature (3) combustible (4) dust mites (5) put out (6) providing that (7) dry
    (8) Generally

Day 24 自然與環境 116-120

Day24_116 龍捲風

→ 把你知道的單字打勾！
- [ ] tornado
- [ ] take place
- [ ] continent
- [ ] violently
- [ ] devastating

→ 用 5 個字說出這張圖片的故事！

tornado [tɔr`nedo]　　n. 龍捲風

S A **tornado**, also known as a twister, is widely considered to be a kind of natural disaster.
龍捲風，也稱為捲風，被普遍認為是一種天然災害。

MORE tornado 的複數形可以加 s 或 es，不過 tornado**es** 比較常用。

take place　　phr. 發生

S Tornadoes often **take place** in the middle states of America.
龍捲風常會發生在美國中部的州裡。

同義字 happen

MORE 除了 take place 之外，take 後面還可以加上其他單字，組成其他常用的片語，例如 take turns（輪流）、take on（承接）、take in（消化；攝取）、take after（與～相像）、take off（脫掉；起飛）等等。

continent [ˈkɑntənənt]　n. 大陸；洲

- Of course, they can also happen on any other **continent**.
  當然，它們也可能會發生在其他的任何大陸之上。

  關聯字　continental adj. 大陸的　continental breakfast n. 歐陸式早餐

violently [ˈvaɪələntlɪ]　adv. 猛烈地，劇烈地

- Tornadoes form when cold and warm air currents interact **violently**.
  龍捲風會在冷熱氣流劇烈交互作用時形成。

devastating [ˈdɛvəsˌtetɪŋ]　adj. 毀滅性的

- When tornadoes happen in populous areas, they often cause **devastating** damage.
  當龍捲風發生在人口稠密地區時，它們常常會造成毀滅性的損害。

  - a **devastating** disaster　一個毀滅性的災難
  - a **devastating** plan　一個毀滅性的計畫

Day24_117　水資源的重要

→ 把你知道的單字打勾！
- [ ] imperative
- [ ] be short of
- [ ] drought
- [ ] rationing
- [ ] suspend

→ 用 5 個字說出這張圖片的故事！

imperative [ɪmˈpɛrətɪv]　adj. 極為重要的

🅢 Water resources management is **imperative** to people all over the world.
水資源管理對於全世界的人而言都是極為重要的。

> 同義字 critical、crucial、vital
> MORE resource 在指「資源」時都是複數形，前面可以加上各種單字組成複合名詞，例如 oil resources（石油資源）、natural resources（自然資源）、human resources（人力資源）等等。

be short of　phr. 缺少～

🅢 However, there **are** many places in the world still **short of** water.
然而，世界上還是有很多地方都缺水。

> MORE short of 的後面會接缺少的東西，如 short of money（缺錢）。

drought [draʊt]　n. 乾旱

🅢 **Drought** is one of the reasons for the lack of water.
發生乾旱是缺水的其中一個原因。

🅔 a long-term **drought** 一次長期性的乾旱

> 反義字 flood

rationing [ˈræʃənɪŋ]　n. 定量配給

🅢 In the case of water shortage, water **rationing** measures should be put in place.
萬一發生缺水，就應該執行限水措施。

> MORE rationing 指的是「用來限制每個人可以擁有某物數量的機制」，因此中文可以翻譯成「限～」或「～配給」，例如 power rationing（限電）、fuel rationing（燃料配給）。

suspend [səˈspɛnd]　v. 暫緩進行；中止

🅢 The restrictions will be **suspended** after there's enough rainfall.
在有足夠的降雨之後，這種限制就會中止。

> 關聯字 suspension n. 暫緩；中止；停職

Day24_118 颱風

→ 把你知道的單字打勾！
- ☐ recurrent
- ☐ preparation
- ☐ gust
- ☐ blow away
- ☐ instant noodles

→ 用 5 個字說出這張圖片的故事！

---

recurrent [rɪ`kɝənt]　adj. 一再發生的；經常性的

Ⓢ **Incidents of a typhoon hitting Taiwan are recurrent during summertime.**
颱風在夏季期間經常襲擊台灣。

preparation [ˏprɛpə`reʃən]　n. 準備

Ⓢ **That's why we have to make preparations before the typhoon season.**
這就是為什麼我們必須在颱風季節來臨前做好準備。

> MORE　preparation 是指「做準備的時間」或是「為做準備而做的事項」，準備的動詞則是 prepare。

gust [gʌst]　n. 一陣強風

Ⓢ **Typhoons will bring pouring rains and strong gusts of wind to us.**
颱風會帶給我們傾盆大雨和強勁的陣風。

> 反義字　breeze
>
> MORE　typhoon（颱風）和 hurricane（颶風）都是熱帶氣旋，只是因生成的位置不同而有著不同的名稱，在太平洋生成的叫「颱風」，在大西洋生成的則是「颶風」。

blow away   phr. 吹走

- Therefore, don't go out when there is a typhoon striking, or you may be **blown away**.
  因此，颳颱風的時候不要出去，否則你可能會被吹走。

  > MORE   blow（吹；颳）的後面加上不同的介系詞，就會有不同的意思，常見的有 blow out（吹熄）、blow up（爆炸）等等。

instant noodles   [`ɪnstənt] [`nudḷs]   n. 泡麵

- Just stay at home, and make sure your flashlights and **instant noodles** are on hand, then you'll be safe.
  只要待在家裡，確保你的手邊有手電筒和泡麵，那麼你就會是安全的。

  > MORE   instant 是「立即的」，所以 instant noodles 就是「立即可以吃的麵」，也就是「泡麵」。

Day24_119   淹大水

→ 把你知道的單字打勾！
- ☐ tropical
- ☐ exceed
- ☐ sewage
- ☐ inundate
- ☐ break down

→ 用 5 個字說出這張圖片的故事！

tropical   [`trɑpɪkḷ]   adj. 熱帶的

- The **tropical** storm has brought heavy rainfall to Taiwan today.
  今天熱帶氣旋為台灣帶來了大雨。

  > MORE   這裡補充一些與其他氣候帶相關的單字：
  > subtropical adj. 亞熱帶的   temperate adj. 溫帶的
  > polar adj. 極地的   frigid adj. 寒冷的

exceed [ɪk`sid]　v. 超過

- In only one day, the rainfall has **exceeded** 500 millimeters.
  才一天的時間，降雨量已經超過了 500 毫米。

  關聯字 exceeding adj. 超越的

  MORE　exceed 是由「ex-（超出）＋-ceed（行走）」組合而成的，而 proceed（前進；進行）則是由「pro-（向前）＋-ceed（行走）」組合而成的，可以透過字首及字根把這兩個單字一併記起來。

sewage [`sjuɪdʒ]　n. 汙水

- Because of the heavy rains, the **sewage** systems aren't working properly.
  因為雨下的很大，所有的汙水系統都無法正常運作。

inundate [`ɪnʌn͵det]　v. 淹沒

- Thus, some of the areas in Taipei have been **inundated** by floods.
  因此，台北的有些區域都已經被洪水淹沒了。

  關聯字 inundation n. 泛濫；洪水

break down　phr. 拋錨；故障

- Furthermore, many cars and motorcycles have been **breaking down** on the roads.
  而且，已經有很多汽車和摩托車都在路上拋錨了。

Day24_120　害蟲

→ 把你知道的單字打勾！
- [ ] pest
- [ ] mosquito
- [ ] loathe
- [ ] pesticide
- [ ] at any rate

→ 用 5 個字說出這張圖片的故事！

Day 24 自然與環境 116–120

pest [pɛst]　n. 害蟲

- There are various **pests** living with us every day.
  我們的身邊每天都有著各種害蟲。

  關聯字 pester v. 糾纏

mosquito [məsˋkito]　n. 蚊子

- Flies, **mosquitoes**, cockroaches and termites are all common pests.
  蒼蠅、蚊子、蟑螂與白蟻都是常見的害蟲。

loathe [loð]　v. 厭惡

- Most people **loathe** cockroaches most.
  大部分的人都最厭惡蟑螂。

  同義字 hate、dislike、abhor

pesticide [ˋpɛstɪ͵saɪd]　n. 殺蟲劑

- When they see cockroaches, they'll kill them with **pesticides** immediately.
  當他們看到蟑螂，他們就會立刻用殺蟲劑把牠們殺掉。

  MORE 字根 -icide 有「殺」的意思，所以 pesticide 其實就是「殺害蟲」的意思。

at any rate　phr. 無論如何

- **At any rate**, pesticides are harmful, so we had better keep our household environment clean to make pests go away.
  無論如何，殺蟲劑會造成傷害，因此我們最好讓我們的居家環境保持乾淨，來讓害蟲遠離。

  同義字 at all events、in any case、in any event

回復記憶 階段

◆ 請參考以下在 Day24 中出現過的圖片,在單字旁的空格寫下字義。

116 龍捲風
tornado .... violently ....
take place .... devastating ....
continent ....

117 水資源的重要
imperative .... rationing ....
be short of .... suspend ....
drought ....

118 颱風
recurrent .... blow away ....
preparation .... instant noodles ....
gust ....

119 淹大水
tropical .... inundate ....
exceed .... break down ....
sewage ....

120 害蟲
pest .... pesticide ....
mosquito .... at any rate ....
loathe ....

Day 24 自然與環境 116-120

231

加深記憶階段

◆ 請依照提示的單字字首，在下列空格中填入適當的單字。

(1) 一隻討人厭的蚊子　　　　an annoying m_____
(2) 一碗泡麵　　　　　　　　a bowl of i_____
(3) 一個熱帶地區　　　　　　a t_____ area
(4) 一場糟糕的乾旱　　　　　a horrible d_____
(5) 汙水系統　　　　　　　　s_____ systems

◆ 請參考下列方框中的單字，在下列空格中填入適當的單字。

| 參考 | recurrently | take place | break down | imperative |
| tornado | preparation | be short of | loathe |

(1) I _____ his arrogant attitude
　　我厭惡他的傲慢態度。

(2) Are you _____ money?
　　你缺錢嗎？

(3) Keeping a healthy lifestyle is _____ to be a successful person.
　　保持健康的生活方式對成為成功人士來說是極為重要的。

(4) The game _____ every other week.
　　這個比賽隔周舉行一次。

(5) The _____ caused a lot of damages.
　　這個龍捲風造成了很多損害。

(6) After making some _____, I did my presentation.
　　在做了一些準備之後，我進行了我的簡報。

(7) Did your car _____ on the highway?
　　你的車在公路上拋錨了嗎？

(8) Buying flowers is a _____ job for me.
　　買花對我來說是一件經常性的工作。

Answers:
1. (1) mosquito (2) instant noodles (3) tropical (4) drought (5) sewage
2. (1) loathe (2) short of (3) imperative (4) takes place (5) tornado (6) preparations (7) break down (8) recurrent

記單字必備！掌握常見多義字 02

◆ 請選出正確的中文字義。

1. appear v. 似乎；出現

As soon as the shower passed, a rainbow **appeared** in the sky.
陣雨一停，一道彩虹便（☐似乎 ☐出現）在天空之中。

He **appears** to be unhappy.
他（☐似乎 ☐出現）不開心。

2. book v. 預訂 n. 書

Put those **books** on the shelf.
把那些（☐書 ☐預訂）放在架上。

Our hotel is fully **booked**.
我們的旅館全（☐書 ☐預訂）滿了。

3. change v. 改變 n. 零錢

I need to **change** my diet.
我需要（☐零錢 ☐改變）我的飲食。

Here is your **change**, $2.07.
這是你的（☐零錢 ☐改變）2.07 元。

4. company n. 公司；同伴

ACME is a foreign **company**.
ACME 是一間外國（☐公司 ☐同伴）。

When I need a **company**, she is always my first choice.
當我需要（☐公司 ☐同伴）時，她總是我的第一選擇。

5. check v. 檢查 n. 支票

All passengers' luggage needs to be **checked**.
所有乘客的行李都必須被（☐檢查 ☐支票）。

I'd like to pay my tuition by **check**.
我想用（☐檢查 ☐支票）來付我的學費。

6. **date** n. 日期；約會對象

   What is your birthday **date**?
   你生日的（☐日期 ☐約會對象）是什麼？

   She is my **date**.
   她是我的（☐日期 ☐約會對象）。

7. **light** adj. 輕的 n. 燈

   The tennis racket is **light**.
   這個網球拍很（☐輕 ☐燈）。

   Turn on the **light**. It's dark inside.
   把（☐輕 ☐燈）打開。這裡頭很暗。

8. **train** v. 訓練 n. 火車

   The swimmers are in **training**.
   泳者正在（☐火車 ☐訓練）中。

   The **train** is approaching quickly.
   這列（☐火車 ☐訓練）正在快速接近。

9. **bright** adj. 明亮的；聰明的

   Always look at the **bright** side.
   總是要看（☐明亮 ☐聰明）的那面。

   She is a **bright** girl.
   她是一個（☐明亮 ☐聰明）的女孩。

10. **match** n. 火柴；比賽

    Never play with a **match**.
    絕對不要玩（☐火柴 ☐比賽）。

    The tennis **match** took place yesterday.
    網球（☐火柴 ☐比賽）昨天舉行了。

Answer:
1. 出現／似乎　2. 書／預訂　3. 改變／零錢　4. 公司／同伴　5. 檢查／支票
6. 日期／約會對象　7. 輕／燈　8. 訓練／火車　9. 明亮／聰明　10. 火柴／比賽

Day 25 經濟生活 121-125

Day25.mp3

Day25_121 好老闆

→ 把你知道的單字打勾！
- ☐ specialist
- ☐ advertising
- ☐ mask
- ☐ kindly
- ☐ thoughtful

→ 用 5 個字說出這張圖片的故事！

---

specialist [ˈspɛʃəlɪst]　n. 專家

S Linda is a marketing **specialist** working in a local company.
琳達是一位在一家本地公司裡工作的行銷專家。

關聯字　special adj. 特別的　specialize v. 專門做～
This company **specializes** in manufacturing toys.
這間公司專門製造玩具。
The food provided in this restaurant is **special**.
這間餐廳提供的食物很特別。

advertising [ˈædvɚˌtaɪzɪŋ]　n. 打廣告的行為；（總稱）廣告

S She has to deal with **advertising** campaigns every day.
她每天都必須處理廣告活動的事。

MORE　advertising 是由動詞 advertise（打廣告）而來的，在英文裡，單一廣告會用 advertisement 這個字，不過因為這個字比較長，所以常會以縮寫 ad 來表示。advertisement 的前面也可加上各種單字，用來說明廣告類型，例如 commercial ad（電視上的商業廣告）、spot radio ad（廣播插播廣告）、online ad（網路廣告）、classified ad（分類廣告）。

mask [mæsk]　n. 口罩

- She caught a cold today, but she still worked at her desk with a **mask** on her face.
  她今天感冒了，但她仍然臉上戴著口罩地在桌前工作。

kindly [ˋkaɪndlɪ]　adv. 親切地；和藹地

- Her boss was worried about her sickness and **kindly** told her to go home and get some rest.
  她的老闆擔心她的病情，並親切地要她回家休息一下。

  同義字 nicely

thoughtful [ˋθɔtfəl]　adj. 體貼的；設想周到的

- Linda thought her boss was **thoughtful** and really cared about his staff.
  琳達認為她的老闆很體貼又真的很關心員工。

  同義字 considerate
  反義字 indifferent

Day25_122　技術好才能留住客人

→ 把你知道的單字打勾！
- [ ] attribute
- [ ] disagree
- [ ] hairdressing
- [ ] hairstylist
- [ ] loyalty

→ 用 5 個字說出這張圖片的故事！

attribute [ə`trɪbjʊt]　v. 把～歸因於

I **attribute** the reason a hair salon has good business to its staff.
我會把一間髮廊生意好的原因歸因於他們的員工。

> MORE　attribute 的用法是 attribute sth to sb/sth，可以用來表達「認為～是因為～；把～歸因於～」。

The man **attributed** his mistakes **to** his assistant.
這個男人把他的錯歸咎到他的助理身上。

disagree [ˌdɪsə`gri]　v. 不同意

Perhaps you would **disagree** with my opinion.
也許你會不同意我的看法。

反義字　agree

hairdressing [`hɛrˌdrɛsɪŋ]　n. 美髮

But in the **hairdressing** industry, customers do change their hair salons if their hairdressers quit.
但在美髮業，顧客的確會因為他們的美髮師不做了而換髮廊。

關聯字　hairdresser n. 美髮師
> MORE　提供美髮及造型服務的「髮廊」是 hair salon，而 barber shop 則是會提供男士理髮及修鬍服務的「理髮院」。

hairstylist [`hɛrˌstaɪlɪst]　n. 髮型設計師

Although most of the **hairstylists** working in hair salons are well-trained, their capabilities and styles vary.
儘管大部分在髮廊裡工作的髮型設計師都受過良好的訓練，但他們的能力和風格還是會不同。

同義字　hairdresser

loyalty [`lɔɪəltɪ]　n. 忠誠度

That's why hiring good hairstylists is the key to building customer **loyalty**.
這就是為什麼雇用好的髮型設計師是建立顧客忠誠度的關鍵。

關聯字　loyal adj. 忠誠的

Day25_123 換份工作吧

→ 把你知道的單字打勾！
- [ ] prospect
- [ ] counsel
- [ ] job-hop
- [ ] candidate
- [ ] certificate

→ 用 5 個字說出這張圖片的故事！

prospect [ˋprɑspɛkt]　n. 前景，前途

S I always want to find a job with better **prospects**.
我一直都想要找一個更有前途的工作。

E career **prospects** 職涯前景

MORE prospect 當「前景，前途」時，都要加 s 用複數形，另外，prospect 也有「景色」的意思，這時就可視需求使用複數形。特別要注意的是，若 prospect 指的是「預期」，則是不可數名詞，不可以加 s。請務必透過上下文來判斷單字字義。

The **prospect** of the valley is spectacular.（景色）
這個山谷的景色很壯觀。
There's no **prospect** that he'll achieve the sales goal.（預期）
沒有預期他會達成銷售目標。

counsel [ˋkaʊnsl]　n. 建議，忠告

S My parents sometimes give me **counsel**, saying that changing jobs is a good way to get a higher pay.
我的父母有時會給我建議，說換工作是一個拿到更多薪水的好方法。

[同義字] advice、suggestion

job-hop [ˋdʒɑb͵hɑp]　v. 跳槽

S I do think that **job-hopping** is a nice way to get a better position with higher pay, so I started to look for another job.
我確實認為跳槽是獲得更好職位和更高薪水的一個好方法，所以我開始尋找其他工作。

[關聯字] job-hopper n. 跳槽者　job-seeker n. 求職者

candidate [ˋkændədet]　n. 人選，應徵者

- As a successful **candidate**, I'm answering the interviewer's questions now.
  做為一位符合資格的應徵者，我現在正在回答面試官的問題。

  - a qualified **candidate** 一個適任的人選

  同義字 applicant

certificate [səˋtɪfəkɪt]　n. 證照

- The interviewer is interested in my work experience and the **certificates** I have.
  面試官對於我的工作經驗及我擁有的證照很感興趣。

  - an official **certificate** 一張官方證照

Day25_124　網路購物

→ 把你知道的單字打勾！
- [ ] retail
- [ ] gradual
- [ ] consensus
- [ ] exist
- [ ] contact

→ 用 5 個字說出這張圖片的故事！

retail [ˋritel]　adj. 零售的

- More and more **retail** shops provide online shopping services.
  越來越多的零售商店提供線上購物服務了。

  MORE retail 是指販售的商品可以少量購買或是小包裝販售，如果一次必須購買的量比較大，則會說是 wholesale（量販的）。

gradual [ˋgrædʒʊəl]　adj. 漸進的

- It has been a **gradual** process where people are getting used to ordering online.
  人們越來越習慣在網路上下單的這件事是一個漸進的過程。

  關聯字 gradually adv. 逐漸地

consensus [kənˈsɛnsəs]　n. 共識

S Besides, most people have grown a **consensus** that home delivery is really convenient.
此外，大部分的人都逐漸取得共識，認為宅配非常方便。

- **E** broad **consensus** 廣泛共識
- **E** grow **consensus** 逐漸取得共識

exist [ɪgˈzɪst]　v. 存在

S However, some problems of ordering online still **exist**, such as wrong deliveries.
然而，線上訂購仍有一些問題依舊存在，像是送錯商品。

contact [kənˈtækt]　v. 聯絡

S People have to **contact** the online seller to get what they ordered, which is much more inconvenient than buying in stores directly.
人們必須和網路賣家聯絡來拿到他們訂購的東西，這樣就比在店裡直接買要不方便得多了。

> **MORE** contact 也能夠當名詞，意思是「聯絡；接觸；聯絡窗口」。
> There is no **contact** from the manager.（聯絡）
> 那個經理沒有來聯絡。
> Physical **contact** is a common way to spread the virus.（接觸）
> 物理接觸是病毒傳播的常見途徑。
> I have to send a mail to my **contact** in the marketing department.（聯絡窗口）
> 我必須寄一封信給我在行銷部裡的聯絡窗口。

Day25_125　用電腦打字好難

→ 把你知道的單字打勾！
- [ ] middle-aged
- [ ] utilize
- [ ] instance
- [ ] browse
- [ ] intensively

→ 用 5 個字說出這張圖片的故事！

middle-aged [ˈmɪdl̩ˌedʒd]　adj. 中年的

- I am already a **middle-aged** man, and learning how to use computers to type is difficult for me.
  我已經是個中年男子了，而學習要如何使用電腦打字對我來說很難。

utilize [ˈjutl̩ˌaɪz]　v. 利用

- However, recently I have a new job that needs to **utilize** computers to do a lot of typing.
  但是，最近我有了一項新工作，這項新工作需要用電腦大量打字。

  關聯字　utility n. 效用；公用事業（水電瓦斯等）

instance [ˈɪnstəns]　n. 實例

- I have encountered many problems, for **instance**, I can't find the right characters.
  我遇到了很多問題，舉例來說，我找不到正確的字。

  同義字　example

browse [braʊz]　v. 瀏覽

- To improve my typing skills, I have **browsed** many tutorial materials online.
  為了改善我的打字技巧，我在網路上瀏覽了很多教學資料。

  關聯字　browser n. 瀏覽器

intensively [ɪnˈtɛnsɪvlɪ]　adv. 密集地；強烈地

- In addition, I have also practiced **intensively** to improve faster.
  此外，我也為了要快點進步而進行了密集練習。

  關聯字　intensive adj. 密集的；強烈的

回復記憶 階段

◆ 請參考以下在 Day25 中出現過的圖片，在單字旁的空格寫下字義。

121 好老闆
specialist _____ kindly _____
advertising _____ thoughtful _____
mask _____

122 技術好才能留住客人
attribute _____ hairstylist _____
disagree _____ loyalty _____
hairdressing _____

123 換份工作吧
prospect _____ candidate _____
counsel _____ certificate _____
job-hop _____

124 網路購物
retail _____ exist _____
gradual _____ contact _____
consensus _____

125 用電腦打字好難
middle-aged _____ browse _____
utilize _____ intensively _____
instance _____

242

加深記憶階段

Day 25 經濟生活 121-125

◆ 請依照提示的單字字首，在下列空格中填入適當的單字。

(1) 一位行銷專家　　　　　　a marketing s＿＿＿＿＿
(2) 一張有用的證照　　　　　a useful c＿＿＿＿＿
(3) 聯絡製造商　　　　　　　c＿＿＿＿＿ the manufacturer
(4) 一項逐漸的成長　　　　　a g＿＿＿＿＿ growth
(5) 令人印象深刻的忠誠　　　impressive l＿＿＿＿＿

◆ 請參考下列方框中的單字，在下列空格中填入適當的單字。

參考	mask	exist	disagree	attribute
	candidate	thoughtful	instance	utilize

(1) It is ＿＿＿＿＿ of you to do that for me.
你幫我做那件事真是體貼。

(2) Do you ＿＿＿＿＿ with my opinion?
你不同意我的意見嗎？

(3) I ＿＿＿＿＿ my good health to daily exercises.
我把我很健康歸因於每天運動。

(4) We should ＿＿＿＿＿ time well.
我們應該善用時間。

(5) Don't forget to wear a ＿＿＿＿＿ when you get sick.
當你生病時別忘了戴口罩。

(6) I like many kinds of music, for ＿＿＿＿＿, I like jazz and country.
我喜歡很多種音樂，舉例來說，我喜歡爵士與鄉村樂。

(7) Which ＿＿＿＿＿ did you choose?
你的人選是誰？

(8) Some of the problems still ＿＿＿＿＿.
有些問題依舊存在。

Answers:
1. (1) specialist (2) certificate (3) contact (4) gradual (5) loyalty
2. (1) thoughtful (2) disagree (3) attribute (4) utilize (5) mask
   (6) instance (7) candidate (8) exist

Day 26 經濟生活 126-130

Day26_126 做一位演員

→ 把你知道的單字打勾！
- ☐ interpret
- ☐ extraordinary
- ☐ alter
- ☐ sophisticated
- ☐ elaborate

→ 用 5 個字說出這張圖片的故事！

interpret [ɪnˋtɝprɪt] v. 詮釋；口譯

S I think every actor has their own angle to **interpret** a script.
我認為每個演員都有他們自己詮釋腳本的角度。

> 關聯字 interpreter n. 口譯人員
> MORE 如果只看中文，會覺得 interpret 和 translate 很相似，但其實 interpret 只表示「口語上的翻譯」，而 translate 則是「書面文字上的翻譯」，使用時須特別注意。

extraordinary [ɪkˋstrɔrdnˌɛrɪ] adj. 令人驚奇的；出色的

S Some people may think that doing acting is boring, but I think it's **extraordinary**.
有些人可能會覺得表演很無聊，但我認為表演是很令人驚奇的。

> **E** an **extraordinary** great man 一個出色的偉人
> 同義字 outstanding、exceptional
> 反義字 ordinary、bland

alter [`ɔltɚ]　v. 修改

- To improve, I have spent plenty of time **altering** the way I perform.
  為了進步，我花了很多時間修改我表演的方法。

sophisticated [sə`fıstı‚ketıd]　adj. 老練的

- Now I become a **sophisticated** actor.
  現在我成為了一個老練的演員。

elaborate [ə`læbərɪt]　adj. 精心計劃（或製作）的

- Besides that, thanks to those **elaborate** scripts, I have won several awards.
  而且，多虧了那些精心設計的腳本，我已經贏得了幾個獎。

  - an **elaborate** lie 一個精心設計的謊言

Day26_127　什麼都要排

→ 把你知道的單字打勾！
- [ ] community
- [ ] novelty
- [ ] excite
- [ ] distinct
- [ ] gulp

→ 用 5 個字說出這張圖片的故事！

community [kə`mjunətɪ]　n. 社區；社群

- It's easy to get new information through online news or Internet **communities** now.
  現在透過線上新聞或網路社群可以輕鬆取得新資訊。

  - **community** center 社區中心

novelty [ˈnɑvḷtɪ]　n. 新奇；新穎的事物

S **Novelties**, like newly released sneakers or new restaurants, always attract people to stand in line.
新穎的事物，像是新發表的球鞋或新餐廳，總是會吸引人們去排隊。

關聯字 novel adj. 新奇的；新穎的 n. 小說
The **novel** ideas he came up with were interesting.（新奇的）
他提出來的新奇想法很有趣。
JK Rowling's **novel** series "Harry Patter" are good.（小說）
JK 羅琳的小說《哈利波特》系列很棒。

excite [ɪkˈsaɪt]　v. 引起，激起

S A new pizza house opened nearby, and it **excited** me to stand in line for a taste.
一間新的披薩店在附近開了，它讓我想要去排隊吃吃看。

關聯字 exciting adj. 令人興奮的　excited adj. 覺得興奮的　excitement n. 興奮

distinct [dɪˈstɪŋkt]　adj. 與其他不同的

S The pizzas there were worth the wait because they were really **distinct** and tasty.
等待是值得的，因為那裡的披薩真的很不一樣又好吃。

E **distinct** from others 與眾不同

同義字 special
關聯字 distinctive adj. 特殊而具鑑別度的　distinction n. 不同點；區別

gulp [gʌlp]　v. 狼吞虎嚥

S After standing in line for a long time, I was so hungry that I **gulped** down ten pieces of the pizza.
在排了很久的隊之後，我餓到狼吞虎嚥了十片披薩。

同義字 devour

Day26_128 實驗人生

→ 把你知道的單字打勾！
- [ ] laboratory
- [ ] experiment
- [ ] tablet
- [ ] hurdle
- [ ] race

→ 用 5 個字說出這張圖片的故事！

laboratory [ˈlæbrəˌtorɪ]　n. 實驗室

S I am a technician working in a **laboratory**.
我是一個在實驗室裡工作的技術人員。

> MORE　laboratory 常會在口語上簡化成 lab。technician 指的是「擁有專業技術／技巧（technique）的人」

experiment [ɪkˈspɛrəmənt]　n. 實驗

S At work, I have to do a lot of different **experiments** to find the best formula.
工作的時候，我必須做很多不同的實驗來找出最佳的配方。

> 關聯字　experimental adj. 實驗性的

tablet [ˈtæblɪt]　n. 藥片

S My job is to make new medicines, such as **tablets** for relieving headaches.
我的工作是製作新的藥物，例如緩解頭痛的藥片。

> MORE　除了「藥片」之外，tablet 現在也是「平板電腦」的意思。

hurdle [ˈhɝdl̩]　n. 障礙，困難

S It's a difficult job because we have to overcome so many **hurdles** before inventing a new medicine.
這份工作很難，因為我們在發明出新藥之前必須克服的困難非常多。

> **E** knock down various **hurdles** 克服各種難關
> 同義字　difficulty、obstacle

race [res]　n. 賽跑；比賽

🅢 **Furthermore, we are always having a race against time to develop life-saving medicines.**
此外，我們總是在與時間賽跑，以開發出可以救人性命的藥物。

🅔 a **race** against time 與時間賽跑

🅔 a car **racing** 賽車

> MORE　race 當名詞時還有「種族」的意思，另外，race 是名詞和動詞同形的單字，當動詞時是「比賽跑；競速」的意思。

People from different **races** should be treated with the same attitude.（種族）
應該要以相同的態度來對待不同種族的人。
Alan will **race** against Justin on Friday.（比賽跑；競速）
艾倫會在星期五和賈斯汀比賽跑。

Day26_129　同事之間的禮數

→ 把你知道的單字打勾！
- [ ] corporation
- [ ] chief
- [ ] hospitable
- [ ] extravagance
- [ ] accede

→ 用 5 個字說出這張圖片的故事！

---

corporation [ˌkɔrpəˋreʃən]　n. 公司；企業

🅢 **Neil and Jeff work in the same corporation.**
尼爾與傑夫在同一間公司工作。

> 同義字　large company/firm
>
> MORE　英文裡的「公司」有很多種說法，最常見的就是 **company** 和 **firm**，**corporation** 則是「大公司」或「集團公司」，**conglomerate** 也是「集團」，但這種集團內會有各式各樣的產業類別，而不是集中在單一產業之內，**venture** 則是「帶有風險的公司」或「投機事業」，**start-up** 則是年輕的小公司，一般可以理解成「新創公司」。

chief [tʃif]　adj. 等級最高的

- Their **chief** financial officer's newborn is one month old, so they are discussing what gifts they should give.
  他們財務長的新生兒滿月了，所以他們正在討論該送什麼禮物。

  MORE 大公司內不同業務會有各自的最高負責人，常見的有 chief financial officer（CFO，財務長）、chief executive officer（CEO，執行長）、chief operating officer（COO，營運長）等等。

hospitable [ˋhɑspɪtəb!]　adj. 好客的

- To protect the baby, though their CFO is usually **hospitable**, it's not suitable for them to pay him a visit.
  為了保護孩子，儘管他們的財務長通常很好客，但他們不適合去拜訪他。

  關聯字 hospitality n. 殷勤款待

extravagance [ɪkˋstrævəgəns]　n. 鋪張浪費

- On the other hand, the CFO doesn't like **extravagances**, so it will be better to give him useful things.
  另一方面，財務長不喜歡奢侈品，所以送有用的東西給他會比較好。

accede [əkˋsid]　v. 同意

- Neil insists they should give gifts together, so Jeff **accedes** to sharing the cost with him.
  尼爾堅持他們應該要一起送禮物，所以傑夫同意和他一起分擔費用。

Day26_130　服務生不好當

→ 把你知道的單字打勾！
- [ ] tolerant
- [ ] captious
- [ ] arrogant
- [ ] weird
- [ ] peer

→ 用 5 個字說出這張圖片的故事！

249

tolerant [ˈtɑlərənt]　adj. 容忍的

- Molly is a waitress, and she is always **tolerant** to bad customers.
  茉莉是一個女服務生,而她總是對不好的客人很容忍。

  關聯字 tolerate v. 容忍　tolerance n. 容忍

captious [ˈkæpʃəs]　adj. 吹毛求疵的

- Some of the customers are very **captious**, and they complain about everything.
  有些顧客非常吹毛求疵,而且什麼都要抱怨。

  同義字 picky

arrogant [ˈærəgənt]　adj. 傲慢的

- And some of the customers are **arrogant**, they even see servers as their own maids.
  還有一些客人很傲慢,他們甚至會把服務人員當成他們自己的女傭。

  關聯字 arrogance n. 傲慢
  MORE arrogant 是「輕視他人,認為自己高人一等」的傲慢,和因為自己達成某項目標或成就而自豪(proud)是不同的。

weird [wɪrd]　adj. 怪異的

- There's a **weird** man sitting at the table, pretending he's reading the menu.
  有一個怪異的男子坐在桌前假裝他正在看菜單。

  關聯字 weirdo n. 怪胎

peer [pɪr]　v. 盯著看

- The man is **peering** at Molly, and Molly is disgusted by his behavior.
  這個男子盯著茉莉看,而茉莉覺得他的行為很噁心。

  MORE peer 當名詞時是「同儕」的意思,**peer pressure** 就是「同儕壓力」。

回復記憶 階段

◆ 請參考以下在 Day26 中出現過的圖片,在單字旁的空格寫下字義。

126 做一位演員
interpret _____　　sophisticated _____
extraordinary _____　　elaborate _____
alter _____

127 什麼都要排
community _____　　distinct _____
novelty _____　　gulp _____
excite _____

128 實驗人生
laboratory _____　　hurdle _____
experiment _____　　race _____
tablet _____

129 同事之間的禮數
corporation _____　　extravagance _____
chief _____　　accede _____
hospitable _____

130 服務生不好當
tolerant _____　　weird _____
captious _____　　peer _____
arrogant _____

加深記憶 階段

◆ 請依照提示的單字字首，在下列空格中填入適當的單字。

(1) 一個老練的表演者　　　　a s_____ performer
(2) 一位傲慢的學者　　　　　an a_____ scholar
(3) 很多的困難　　　　　　　many h_____
(4) 一位主廚　　　　　　　　a c_____ chef
(5) 一位吹毛求疵的顧客　　　a c_____ customer

◆ 請參考下列方框中的單字，在下列空格中填入適當的單字。

參考 | gulp | extraordinary | elaborate | experiment |
     | accede | alter | tolerant | distinct |

(1) I met an _____ businessman.
    我見到了一位非凡的商人。

(2) Don't _____! Eat slowly!
    不要狼吞虎嚥！慢慢吃！

(3) I hate your _____ lies.
    我討厭你精心設計的謊言。

(4) This is a _____ design.
    這是一個不一樣的設計。

(5) Don't _____ to this unfair agreement.
    不要同意這個不公平的協議。

(6) I did a lot of _____ in the laboratory.
    我在實驗室裡做了很多實驗。

(7) Did you _____ your pants?
    你修改了你的長褲嗎？

(8) Meg is _____ to her noisy neighbors.
    梅格對她吵鬧的鄰居很容忍。

Answers:
1. (1) sophisticated (2) arrogant (3) hurdles (4) chief (5) captious
2. (1) extraordinary (2) gulp (3) elaborate (4) distinct (5) accede
   (6) experiments (7) alter (8) tolerant

Day 27 經濟生活 131-135

Day27_131 在便利商店工作

→ 把你知道的單字打勾！
- [ ] convenience store
- [ ] workload
- [ ] cash register
- [ ] affluent
- [ ] promising

→ 用 5 個字說出這張圖片的故事！

convenience store [kən`vinjəns] [stor]　n. 便利商店

S Angela works at a **convenience store**.
安琪拉在一間便利商店裡工作。

> **MORE** 其他類型的商店的英文說法：
> warehouse store 大型量販店　supermarket 超市
> hypermarket 大型超市　boutique 精品店　grocery store 雜貨店
> shopping mall 購物中心　outlet 暢貨中心　department store 百貨公司

workload [`wɝk͵lod]　n. 工作量

S The **workload** is heavy, but she enjoys interacting with her customers.
雖然工作量很大，但她很喜歡和客人互動。

> **MORE** load 本身是「裝載量」的意思，因此 workload 就是「工作的裝載量」，也就是「工作量」的意思。

cash register [kæʃ] [`rɛdʒɪstɚ]　n. 收銀機

S She uses a **cash register** to do the transactions, and she bags the items for her customers.
她會用收銀機來進行交易，然後她會替她的客人們將商品裝袋。

affluent [ˈæfluənt]　adj. 富裕的

Angela was not born to an affluent family, so she knows she has to work hard.
安琪拉的出身並不富裕,因此她知道她必須認真工作。

[同義字] wealthy、well-off

promising [ˈprɑmɪsɪŋ]　adj. 大有可為的

She thinks working hard is the only way that she can have a promising future.
她認為努力是她可以擁有大有可為的未來的唯一方法。

Day27_132 包包維修店

→ 把你知道的單字打勾!
- [ ] repair
- [ ] pocketbook
- [ ] ingenious
- [ ] liability
- [ ] foreseeable

→ 用 5 個字說出這張圖片的故事!

repair [rɪˈpɛr]　v. 修理

Alex has a good hand at repairing bags.
艾力克斯對修理包包很在行。

[同義字] fix

[MORE] have a good/great hand at 照字面翻譯就是「在~上面有很好/很棒的手」,其實就是「擅長」的意思,另外一個很常用的表達方式就是 be good at。如果要表示「不擅長」,則可以用 be not good at 或 be poor at,這些都是很常用的表達方式,請一起記下來。

Gina **is good at** making cookies.
吉娜非常擅長做餅乾。

Spencer **is not good at** convincing people.
史賓瑟不擅長說服人。

Joel **is poor at** swimming.
喬不擅長游泳。

pocketbook [ˈpɑkɪtˌbʊk]　n. 隨身包，錢包

He can repair wallets, handbags, **pocketbooks** and so on.
他會修皮夾、手提包及隨身包等等。

> **MORE** and so on 就是中文裡舉例時會說的「～等等」，前面至少要舉出三個例子，例子之間以「逗號」隔開，不能使用 and。

ingenious [ɪnˈdʒinjəs]　adj. 心靈手巧的

He's also an **ingenious** man that can make his own bags for sale.
他也是一個心靈手巧的人，所以他也能自己做包包來賣。

an **ingenious** gadget 一個別出心裁的裝置

> **MORE** ingenious 用來形容人的話是指這個人「聰明、有創意，又有發明能力」，用來形容構想或用具時，則表示「設計得很聰明又具創意，且非常符合用途」的意思。

liability [ˌlaɪəˈbɪlətɪ]　n. 負債

In order to buy a workshop for himself, he has borrowed money from banks and had some **liabilities**.
為了為他自己買一間工作室，他已經向銀行借了錢且有了一些負債。

have all **liabilities** liquidated 清償了所有的債務

同義字 debt

foreseeable [forˈsiəbl̩]　adj. 可以預見的

With his hard work, he definitely can settle all the liabilities and has his own workshop in the **foreseeable** future.
在他的努力之下，他一定可以在可預見的未來清償他的所有債務並擁有他自己的工作室。

同義字 predictable
關聯字 foresee v. 預期　forecast v. 預測　foretell v. 預言　predict v. 預期

Day27_133 午餐踩到雷

→ 把你知道的單字打勾！
- [ ] troublesome
- [ ] optional
- [ ] canteen
- [ ] disgusting
- [ ] credulous

→ 用 5 個字說出這張圖片的故事！

troublesome [ˈtrʌbl̩səm]　adj. 麻煩的；令人煩惱的

🅢 As an office worker, deciding what to eat at lunchtime is truly **troublesome**.
身為上班族，決定中午要吃什麼真的很麻煩。

同義字 bothersome adj. 麻煩的

optional [ˈɑpʃən̩l]　adj. 可以選擇的

🅢 There are so many **optional** places near my company.
我公司附近有非常多可以選擇的地方。

關聯字 option n. 選擇　opt v. 選擇
MORE optional 是指「可以選擇，但非強制」，例如「選擇方案」的英文就是 optional package。

canteen [kænˈtin]　n. 員工餐廳；學生餐廳

🅢 I usually choose from the **canteen**, cafeterias, and the food stands nearby.
我通常會從員工餐廳、自助餐廳和附近的小吃攤裡做選擇。

MORE food stand（小吃攤）也可以叫做 food stall。

disgusting [dɪsˈɡʌstɪŋ]　adj. 噁心的

🅢 However, I went to a new restaurant for a change today, but the food there was really **disgusting**.
不過，我今天因為想要改變一下而去了一間新餐廳，但那裡的食物真的很噁心。

credulous [ˈkrɛdʒʊləs]　　**adj.** 輕信的；好騙的

🅢 I think I was too **credulous** that I believed the restaurant's sales pitch.
我想我是太好騙了，才會相信了餐廳的銷售話術。

　🅔 a **credulous** consumer 一個好騙的消費者

Day27_134　老闆愛監視

→ 把你知道的單字打勾！
- ☐ oversee
- ☐ monitor
- ☐ pretend
- ☐ dreadful
- ☐ exaggerate

→ 用 5 個字說出這張圖片的故事！

---

oversee [ˈovɚˈsi]　　**v.** 監視

🅢 Darla's boss likes to **oversee** his employees working in the office.
達拉的老闆喜歡在辦公室裡監視他的員工工作。

　同義字 supervise、inspect

---

monitor [ˈmɑnətɚ]　　**n.** 監視器

🅢 He is just like a human **monitor**.
他就像是個人肉監視器一樣。

　🅔 a **monitor** mounting on the wall 一個裝在牆壁上的監視器
　關聯字 baby monitor n. 嬰兒監視器　security camera n. 安全監視器

---

pretend [prɪˈtɛnd]　　**v.** 假裝

🅢 Darla knows her boss likes to watch everyone, so she sometimes **pretends** that she's very busy.
達拉知道她老闆喜歡監視所有人，所以她有時候會假裝她非常忙碌。

257

關聯字 **pretender** n. 冒充者　**pretentious** adj. 做作的
She is a **pretentious pretender, pretending** she is very rich.
她是一位做作的冒充者，假裝她非常有錢。

dreadful [ˋdrɛdfəl]　adj. 非常糟糕的；可怕的

🅢 It's really a **dreadful** experience for Darla to have her boss standing by and staring at her.
對達拉來說，這種老闆站在一旁盯著她看的經驗，真是非常糟糕。

同義字 terrible、awful

exaggerate [ɪgˋzædʒəˌret]　v. 誇大

🅢 She is not **exaggerating** when she says her boss is an annoying man.
當她說她老闆是個討人厭的人時，她沒在誇大。

關聯字 **exaggeration** n. 誇張

Day27_135　做房仲就是要會說話

→ 把你知道的單字打勾！
- [ ] real estate
- [ ] realtor
- [ ] open house
- [ ] description
- [ ] out of question

→ 用 5 個字說出這張圖片的故事！

real estate [ˋriəl] [əsˋtet]　n. 不動產

🅢 Natalia is a successful **real estate** agent.
娜塔莉亞是一位成功的不動產仲介。

> **MORE** real estate 是指「房屋、土地等不動產」，意思相似的還有 property（房地產），如果是現金等動產，則可以用 asset（資產）這個字，belongings（財物）則是可以帶在身上的財物，像是錢包、珠寶等等。

realtor [ˈriəltɚ]　n. 房地產仲介

🅢 Actually, she won the Best **Realtor** of the Year last month.
其實,她在上個月贏得了年度最佳房仲獎。

同義字 real estate agent

open house [ˈopən] [haʊs]　n. 開放看屋時間

🅢 Now she is having an **open house** with the potential buyers.
現在她正在和潛在買家們進行開放看屋。

MORE open house 指的是如學校、私人住宅、工廠等這些平常不會開放的地方,開放一般大眾入內參觀的日子,用在房屋買賣上時,指的就是房仲帶可能的買家看房子的時間。

description [dɪˈskrɪpʃən]　n. 描述

🅢 Her glowing **descriptions** of the house make all the potential buyers interested.
她熱情讚美這間房子的描述,讓所有潛在買家都產生了興趣。

關聯字 describe v. 描述
MORE glowing description 直翻是「像會發光般的描述」,意思就是「帶有熱情地表達讚美,而讓某事物像會發光般的描述」。

out of question　phr. 毫無疑問

🅢 It's **out of question**, she's a great realtor.
毫無疑問她是個很棒的房仲。

MORE out of question 是「毫無疑問」的意思,而 out of **the** question 則是「不可能」的意思,要特別注意兩者間的差異,小心不要搞混了。

回復記憶 階段

◆ 請參考以下在 Day27 中出現過的圖片，在單字旁的空格寫下字義。

131 在便利商店工作
convenience store .... affluent ....
workload .... promising ....
cash register ....

132 包包維修店
repair .... liability ....
pocketbook .... foreseeable ....
ingenious ....

133 午餐踩到雷
troublesome .... disgusting ....
optional .... credulous ....
canteen ....

134 老闆愛監視
oversee .... dreadful ....
monitor .... exaggerate ....
pretend ....

135 做房仲就是要會說話
real estate .... description ....
realtor .... out of question ....
open house ....

加深記憶階段

◆ 請依照提示的單字字首，在下列空格中填入適當的單字。

(1) 一台壞掉的監視器　　　　a broken m_____
(2) 一個成功的房仲　　　　　a successful r_____
(3) 一個非常糟糕的經驗　　　a d_____ experience
(4) 一個選擇性的計畫　　　　an o_____ plan
(5) 一個容易上當的人　　　　a c_____ man

◆ 請參考下列方框中的單字，在下列空格中填入適當的單字。

| 參考 | pretend | affluent | description | ingenious |
| convenience store | oversee | repair | load |

(1) I was born to an _____ family.
　　我出生在一個富裕的家庭。

(2) Does your boss like to _____ your moves?
　　你的老闆喜歡監視你的一舉一動嗎？

(3) The student has a part-time job at the _____ .
　　這個學生在這間便利商店裡兼職。

(4) The _____ was too heavy, so he quit.
　　因為工作量太大，所以他辭職了。

(5) Don't _____ you are a victim.
　　不要假裝你是個受害者。

(6) Please _____ the machine for me.
　　請幫我修理這個機器。

(7) Can you give me the job_____?
　　你可以給我職務描述嗎？

(8) The _____ artist is making her exhibit.
　　這個心靈手巧的藝術家正在製作她的展品。

Answers:
1. (1) monitor (2) realtor (3) dreadful (4) optional (5) credulous
2. (1) affluent (2) oversee (3) convenience store (4) workload (5) pretend
　　(6) repair (7) description (8) ingenious

記單字必備！掌握常見易混淆字 01

★ 常見的易混淆字

1. **adapt** v. 適應
   You must have the ability to **adapt** if you want to live in a foreign country.
   如果你想要住在國外，你必須要有適應能力。

   adopt v. 採用
   My boss **adopted** my ideas.
   我的老闆採用了我的想法。

   adept adj. 熟練的
   She is an **adept** cook.
   她是個熟練的廚子。

2. **assay** v. 化驗
   The medicine should be **assayed** first.
   必須先化驗這個藥物。

   essay n. 論文，文章
   Sheila has to complete her term **essay**.
   席拉必須完成她的學期論文。

3. **addition** n. 增加的人事物
   The hat is the **addition** of the summer collection.
   這個帽子是夏裝新增的。

   edition n. 版本
   The old **edition** needs to be revised.
   這個舊版本需要修改。

★ 常見的易混淆片語

1. **break down** phr. 拋錨；故障
   Your car **broke down** on the street.
   你的車在街上拋錨了。

   break away phr. 逃脫
   The robber **broke away** from the police.
   搶匪從警方那裡逃脫了。

   break up phr. 分手
   Anna **broke up** with her boyfriend without any reasons.
   安娜毫無緣由的和男友分手了。

2. **act on** phr. 對～產生作用
   The drug doesn't **act on** your liver.
   這藥不會對你的肝臟產生作用

   act up phr. 出問題
   My computer has been **acting up** for a month.
   我的電腦已經一直出問題出一個月了。

   act out phr. 執行
   You should **act out** your plans.
   你應該要執行你的計畫。

3. **drop out** phr. 退出
   You shouldn't **drop out** the game.
   你不應該退出比賽。

   drop by phr. 順道拜訪
   I'll **drop by** to give you the gift.
   我會順道去給你禮物。

   drop off phr. 下車
   Please let me **drop off** at the next stop.
   請讓我在下一站下車。

Day 28 國家與社會 136-140

Day28_136 關心新聞

→ 把你知道的單字打勾！
- [ ] modern
- [ ] latest
- [ ] journalist
- [ ] anchor
- [ ] keep abreast of

→ 用 5 個字說出這張圖片的故事！

modern [ˋmɑdɚn]　adj. 現代的

S **Modern** people often watch TV to get new information and knowledge.
現代人常會看電視來獲得新的資訊與知識。

MORE 這裡補充一些與「現代化」有關的字，可以一起記下來。
contemporary adj. 當代的　**state-of-the-art** adj. 最先進的
cutting-edge adj. 最尖端　**up to date** phr. 最新的

latest [ˋletɪst]　adj. 最新的

S Furthermore, we can learn the **latest** news by watching news shows.
此外，我們可以藉由看新聞節目來知道最新的新聞。

MORE late 的比較級和最高級各有兩種，意思也不同，下面透過表格整理，請務必透過前後文來判斷該用哪一種形態。

詞性	比較級	最高級
形容詞	latter 後者的	latest/last 最新的；最晚的／最後的
副詞	later 較遲地	latest/last 最新地；最晚地／最後地

journalist [ˋdʒɝnəlɪst]　n. 記者

Journalists report the news by observing, investigating and doing interviews.
記者會藉由觀察、調查與進行採訪來報導新聞。

同義字 reporter
關聯字 journal n. 報章雜誌；期刊

anchor [ˋæŋkɚ]　n. 新聞主播

My family and I often sit on the couch, watching news shows reported by professional **anchors** after dinner.
我的家人和我經常在晚餐後坐在沙發上看由專業主播們報導的新聞節目。

keep abreast of　phr. 了解～的最新情況

We want to **keep abreast of** trends by watching news shows.
我們想要透過看新聞節目來了解最新的潮流。

Day28_137　最喜歡周年慶了

→ 把你知道的單字打勾！
☐ boutique
☐ department
☐ merchandise
☐ anniversary
☐ food court

→ 用 5 個字說出這張圖片的故事！

boutique [buˋtik]　n. 小店，精品店

I know some people like to shop at **boutiques**.
我知道有些人喜歡在小店裡購物。

MORE boutique 和 bouquet（花束）乍看之下滿像的，使用的時候要小心別搞混了。另外，**boutique** 指的是販售流行服飾、配件、鞋包等商品的小店或精品店，而不一定是指販售名牌精品的店家。

Day 28 國家與社會 136-140

department [dɪˋpɑrtmənt]　n. 部門

⑤ However, I prefer shopping at the **department** stores, because there are chances that I can get great deals.
不過，我比較喜歡在百貨公司裡購物，因為我會有機會可以買到很划算的東西。

> **MORE** department store（百貨公司）可以理解成是「一間由各部門所組成的店」，這邊的「各部門」也就是百貨公司裡的分區櫃位。

merchandise [ˋmɝtʃənˏdaɪz]　v. 推銷

⑤ Some of the famous brands in the department stores, like MAC or Dior, will **merchandise** their products when there's a sale.
一些百貨公司裡的知名品牌，像 MAC 或 Dior，會在打折時推銷他們的產品。

> **MORE** merchandise 也可以當名詞，這時是「商品」的意思。

anniversary [ˏænəˋvɝsərɪ]　adj. 周年的

⑤ They even offer deep discounts during the **anniversary** sales season.
他們甚至會在周年慶期間提供很好的折扣。

food court [fud] [kort]　n. 美食街

⑤ Besides, if I'm hungry, I can conveniently go to the **food court** for tasty food.
此外，如果我餓了，我可以很方便地去美食街吃好吃的東西。

Day28_138　發生車禍了

→ 把你知道的單字打勾！
- [ ] collision
- [ ] veer
- [ ] react
- [ ] ambulance
- [ ] congest

→ 用 5 個字說出這張圖片的故事！

collision [kəˋlɪʒən]　n. 碰撞

⑤ A car **collision** happened at the intersection of Park Road and First Street this morning.
今天早上在公園路與第一街的交叉口發生了車輛碰撞。

> 關聯字 collide v. 碰撞
> MORE car collision（車輛碰撞）也可以說是 car accident（車禍）或 vehicle collision（車輛碰撞）。

veer [vɪr]　v. 改變方向，轉向

⑤ The car on the westbound lane lost control, and **veered** into the eastbound lane.
西向道的車失控而改變了方向朝東向道而去。

> MORE -bound 本身是「往～方向的」的意思，因此前面加上「方向」，如 westbound、eastbound，就會變成「西向的」、「東向的」。

react [rɪˋækt]　v. 反應

⑤ The car on the eastbound lane couldn't **react** in time, so the two cars collided directly.
在東向道的車無法及時做出反應，所以兩輛車直接撞上了。

> 關聯字 reaction n. 反應　　reactive adj. 容易起反應的　　reactant n. 反應物
> reactionary adj. 反對改革的；極端保守的

ambulance [ˋæmbjələns]　n. 救護車

⑤ The police and the **ambulance** arrived at the scene immediately.
警方與救護車立即到達了現場。

congest [kənˋdʒɛst]　v. 堵塞

⑤ The roads were **congested** after the accident because they had to seal off the intersection for accident investigation.
馬路在車禍後就塞住了，因為他們必須封鎖交叉口進行事故調查。

> Ⓔ congested traffic 交通堵塞（＝traffic congestion＝traffic jam）
> 關聯字 congestion n. 堵塞

Day28_139 銀行搶案

→ 把你知道的單字打勾！
- [ ] sensational
- [ ] gangster
- [ ] tactic
- [ ] lethal
- [ ] calm

→ 用 5 個字說出這張圖片的故事！

sensational [sɛn`seʃənəl]　adj. 轟動的

S A piece of **sensational** news was on TV today.
今天在電視上出現了一則轟動的消息。

E a sensational murder 一個轟動的謀殺案

關聯字 sense n. 感官　sensation n. 轟動；轟動的人事物
　　　sensationalize v. 以造成轟動的方式處理

gangster [`gæŋstɚ]　n.（結夥的）歹徒

S A group of **gangsters** robbed a bank in the afternoon.
一群歹徒在今天下午搶了一家銀行。

E a dangerous **gangster** 一個危險的歹徒

MORE gangster 是結夥犯案的歹徒，如果是指「犯罪的個人」，
則要用 criminal（罪犯）這個字。

tactic [`tæktɪk]　n. 戰術

S According to the report, the criminals adopted aggressive **tactics** in the robbery.
根據報導，這些罪犯在這次搶案中採用了攻擊性的戰術。

關聯字 tact n. 處事技巧　tactful adj. 手段圓融的
　　　tactical adj. 戰術性的　tactician n. 戰術家

lethal [ˋliθəl]　　adj. 致命的

S **They were carrying and wielding lethal weapons to threaten people in the bank.**
他們那時拿著且揮舞著致命的武器來威脅銀行裡的人們。

E **lethal** weapons 致命武器
E **lethal** drugs 致命藥物
關聯字 **lethally** adv. 致命地　**lethality** n. 致死率

---

calm [kɑm]　　adj. 冷靜的

S **Fortunately, the bank tellers stayed calm, and no one was hurt during the robbery.**
幸運的是，銀行櫃員們保持了冷靜，所以沒人在搶案中受傷。

E stay **calm** 保持冷靜

Day28_140 解決停車問題

→ 把你知道的單字打勾！
☐ unresolved
☐ available
☐ lot
☐ vehicle
☐ raise

→ 用 5 個字說出這張圖片的故事！

---

unresolved [ˌʌnrɪˋzɑlvd]　　adj. 未解決的

S **The lack of parking spaces has always been an unresolved problem in our society.**
缺乏停車位一直是我們社會中的一個未解決的問題。

反義字 **resolved** adj. 已解決的
MORE un- 是表示「否定」的字首，resolved 則是「解決的」，因此 unresolved 就是「未解決的」。

Day 28 國家與社會 136-140

269

available [əˋvelǝbl]   adj. 可使用的；可得的

🅢 **The average time for a driver to find an available parking space is twenty minutes at the minimum.**
駕駛人平均至少要花上二十分鐘才能找到一個可使用的停車位。

關聯字 availability n. 可利用性
反義字 unavailable

lot [lɑt]   n.（具特定用途的）地

🅢 **Indeed, we don't have enough parking garages or parking lots.**
的確，我們沒有足夠的停車塔或停車場。

MORE parking garage 是指有獨立建物的停車場，也就是停車塔或立體停車場，而 parking lot 則是平面的一塊用來停車的土地，使用時請小心不要混淆了。

vehicle [ˋviɪkl]   n. 車輛

🅢 **What we should do is reduce the amount of vehicles.**
我們應該做的是要減少車子的數量。

🅔 a recreation **vehicle** 一台露營車（RV）
🅔 a sport utility **vehicle** 一台休旅車（SUV）

MORE vehicle 除了車輛的意思之外，能夠用來泛指所有具有「載運功能」的工具，如太空船、直升機等，也都可以用 vehicle 來代稱，另外，vehicle 也有「媒介」的意思，在看到 vehicle 這個字時請務必要透過前後文來判斷字義。

My dream is to ride a space **vehicle** one day.（搭載工具）
我的夢想是有一天能搭上太空船。
Telephone is not an ideal **vehicle** for communication anymore.（媒介）
電話不再是溝通的一個理想媒介了。

raise [rez]   v. 提升

🅢 **Maybe we can do this by raising taxation on cars.**
也許我們可以藉由增加汽車的賦稅來做到這件事。

回復記憶 階段

◆ 請參考以下在 Day28 中出現過的圖片，在單字旁的空格寫下字義。

136 關心新聞
modern .... anchor ....
latest .... keep abreast of ....
journalist ....

137 最喜歡周年慶了
boutique .... anniversary ....
department .... food court ....
merchandise ....

138 發生車禍了
collision .... ambulance ....
veer .... congest ....
react ....

139 銀行搶案
sensational .... lethal ....
gangster .... calm ....
tactic ....

140 解決停車問題
unresolved .... vehicle ....
available .... raise ....
lot ....

加深記憶 階段

◆ 請依照提示的單字字首，在下列空格中填入適當的單字。

(1) 一個停車場　　　　　　a parking l_____
(2) 保持冷靜　　　　　　　keep c_____
(3) 一次意外的碰撞　　　　an accidental c_____
(4) 一次周年慶　　　　　　an a_____ sale
(5) 一台聲音很大的救護車　a loud a_____

◆ 請參考下列方框中的單字，在下列空格中填入適當的單字。

> 參考 | sensational | boutique | react | keep abreast of |
> | vehicle | unresolved | food court | anchor |

(1) Too many _____ are on the road now.
　　現在馬路上有太多車了。

(2) Did you shop in the _____ yesterday?
　　你昨天有在精品店裡購物嗎？

(3) The _____ is broadcasting news.
　　這位主播正在播報新聞。

(4) He has to _____ our work schedule.
　　他必須要跟上我們的工作進度。

(5) Listen to this _____ news.
　　聽聽這個轟動的消息。

(6) Please don't let this problem _____.
　　請別讓這個問題得不到解決。

(7) Why did you _____ so strongly?
　　為何你反應如此激烈？

(8) We are going to eat in the _____.
　　我們打算去美食街吃飯。

Answers:
1. (1) lot (2) calm (3) collision (4) anniversary (5) ambulance
2. (1) vehicles (2) boutique (3) anchor (4) keep abreast of
　　(5) sensational (6) unresolved (7) react (8) food court

Day 29 國家與社會 141-145

Day29_141 抽菸有害健康

→ 把你知道的單字打勾！
- [ ] indulge
- [ ] bronchitis
- [ ] yearn
- [ ] sheer
- [ ] restrain

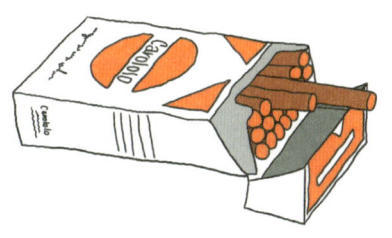

→ 用 5 個字說出這張圖片的故事！

---

indulge [ɪn`dʌldʒ]　v. 沉迷於；放縱自己

S I used to **indulge** in smoking, but now I quit it for my health.
我以前曾沉迷於抽菸，但是我現在為了健康而戒掉了。

關聯字　indulgence n. 沉迷；放縱　indulgent adj. 放縱的；縱容的
His **indulgence** in alcohol slowly kills himself.
他對酒精的沉迷在緩慢地殺死他自己。
He is **indulgent** to his children.
他對於他的孩子很縱容。

bronchitis [brɑn`kaɪtɪs]　n. 支氣管炎

S My doctor told me that I may have **bronchitis**, even lung cancer, if I don't quit it.
我的醫生告訴我，假如我不戒的話，我也許會得到支氣管炎，甚至是肺癌。

MORE　bronchitis 是很常見的疾病名稱，這裡補充一些常見的疾病名稱，一起記下來吧！
pneumonia 肺炎　appendicitis 盲腸炎　arthritis 關節炎　inflammation 發炎
conjunctivitis 結膜炎（＝red eye）　asthma 氣喘　diabetes 糖尿病

yearn [jɝn]　　**v.** 渴望

🅢 But to be frank, sometimes I still **yearn** for the taste of tobacco.
但是坦白說，我有時仍然會渴望菸草的味道。

🅔 **yearn** for the embrace of fame 渴望獲得名聲

sheer [ʃɪr]　　**adj.** 全然的；純粹的

🅢 I miss the **sheer** pleasure of smoking after meals.
我會想念飯後抽菸的那種全然的快樂。

🅔 a **sheer** fraud 全然的騙局

restrain [rɪˋstren]　　**v.** 克制

🅢 However, I know smoking is really bad for my health, so I do my best to **restrain** myself and completely quit it.
不過，我知道抽菸對我的健康真的很不好，所以我盡我所能地克制自己，並完全把菸戒掉了。

同義字 control

Day29_142　疫情衝擊

→ 把你知道的單字打勾！
☐ pandemic
☐ communicable
☐ mandatory
☐ fine
☐ vaccine

→ 用 5 個字說出這張圖片的故事！

pandemic [pænˋdɛmɪk]　　**n.** 流行病；疫情

🅢 Now the **pandemic** has changed our daily lives.
現在這場疫情已經改變了我們的日常生活。

MORE　pandemic 和另一個字 endemic 都是「流行病」的意思，但 endemic 所指的是「僅在部分地區內」流行的傳染疾病，而 pandemic 所指的則是「跨越疆界限制、四處傳染」的流行病。

274

communicable [kə`mjunəkəbl]　adj. 傳染性的

S The **communicable** viruses have made a huge impact on our behavior.
這些傳染性的病毒對我們的行為已經造成了巨大的影響。

關聯字 communicate v. 溝通；傳染　communication n. 溝通；傳染

mandatory [`mændə,tɔrɪ]　adj. 強制的；義務的

S For example, wearing masks is **mandatory** when taking mass transportation.
舉例來說，在搭乘大眾運輸工具時必須戴口罩。

關聯字 mandate n. 命令，指令
MORE mandatory 是指透過命令而「具有強制力的」，因此像是政府的規定、合約條文或是老闆的命令，都可以說是 mandatory。

My boss told us that the attendance of the meeting next week is **mandatory**.
我的老闆告訴我們下周的會議是強制出席的。

fine [faɪn]　v. 罰款

S Besides, people will be **fined** if they don't wear masks.
此外，人們如果不戴口罩就會被罰款。

MORE fine 當形容詞時是「很好的；優質的」的意思。

vaccine [`væksin]　n. 疫苗

S Even though most people have already gotten their **vaccines**, wearing masks is still necessary.
儘管大部分人都已經打過疫苗了，但戴口罩仍然是必要的。

MORE 這裡補充一些和疫情有關的字彙，可以一併記下來：
apex 高峰　asymptomatic 無症狀的　community spread 社區傳播
contact tracing 接觸者追蹤　coronavirus 冠狀病毒　herd immunity 群體免疫
rapid test 快篩　antibody 抗體　virus strain 病毒株

Day29_143 排擠

→ 把你知道的單字打勾！
- [ ] social
- [ ] consolation
- [ ] adverse
- [ ] freeze out
- [ ] avert

→ 用 5 個字說出這張圖片的故事！

social [`soʃəl]　　adj. 社交的

S Human beings are **social** animals, and we like to stay in groups.
人類是社交動物，而且我們喜歡成群結隊。

關聯字 sociable adj. 善於交際的　society n. 社會

consolation [ˌkɑnsə`leʃən]　　n. 慰藉

S In groups, people can get support and **consolation** from each other.
在團體中，人們可以從彼此身上獲得支持與慰藉。

同義字 comfort
關聯字 console v. 慰藉　consolation prize n. 安慰獎

adverse [æd`vɝs]　　adj. 不利的

S However, if there are too many groups in one organization, it will have an **adverse** effect on management.
然而，假如一個組織裡的團體太多，將會對管理產生不利的影響。

freeze out　　phr. 排擠

S For example, if a person doesn't belong to the group he/she is working with, then he/she might be **frozen out**.
舉例來說，假如一個人不屬於正與他／她一同工作的團體，那麼他／她就可能會被排擠。

MORE freeze out 就是「把他人冰凍在外、不理他」的意思。

276

avert [əˋvɝt]　v. 避免

S In order to **avert** the awkward situation, the management should do team building activities to keep the organization healthy.
為了避免這種尷尬的狀況，管理階層應該進行團隊建立的活動來讓組織保持健康。

Day29_144 線上教學

→ 把你知道的單字打勾！
- [ ] conduct
- [ ] accustomed
- [ ] laptop
- [ ] material
- [ ] remind

→ 用 5 個字說出這張圖片的故事！

conduct [kənˋdʌkt]　v. 實施；帶領；指揮

S Due to the pandemic, many schools have started to **conduct** online courses.
由於疫情，很多學校已經開始進行線上課程了。

E **conduct** a project 進行一個專案
E **conduct** an orchestra 指揮一個管絃樂團

關聯字　conductor n. 指揮家；列車長　conduction n. 傳導；輸送

accustomed [əˋkʌstəmd]　adj. 習慣的

S For teachers who are **accustomed** to teach in real classrooms, it's not easy to prepare for online courses.
對於習慣課堂教學的老師而言，要為線上課程做準備並不容易。

MORE be accustomed to 是「習慣於～」的意思，後面要接名詞或動名詞，與 be used to 的意思相近。另外，get accustomed to 則是「漸漸習慣於～」的意思，這些表達方式在意義上都很相近，使用的時候要小心別搞混了。

I **am accustomed to** sitting in the front row of the classroom.
我習慣坐在教室的前排。

I **am used to** the cold weather.
我習慣了寒冷的天氣。
I **get accustomed to** living in this new neighborhood.
我漸漸習慣住在這個新社區了。

laptop [ˈlæptɑp]　n. 筆記型電腦

🅢 First, teachers must have a **laptop** equipped with a high resolution webcam and a good microphone.
首先，老師們必須要有一台備有高畫質鏡頭和高品質麥克風的筆記型電腦。

material [məˈtɪrɪəl]　n. 資料；用具

🅢 Then, they have to share their teaching **material** with the students online.
再來，他們必須在線上和學生分享他們的教學資料。

🅔 teaching **material** 教學資料
🅔 teaching **materials** 教學用具

> MORE　material 當作「用具；工具」的意思時，必須恆用複數形，如果是「資料；素材」的意思，則和 information 一樣都是不可屬名詞。

remind [rɪˈmaɪnd]　v. 提醒

🅢 But most important of all, teachers have to **remind** their students to show up on time for the class.
但最重要的是，老師們必須要提醒學生們準時出現上課。

Day29_145　月光族

→ 把你知道的單字打勾！
☐ graduate
☐ salary
☐ per
☐ paycheck
☐ income

→ 用 5 個字說出這張圖片的故事！

graduate [ˈgrædʒʊˌet]　v. 畢業

I just graduated from school, and I am trying to find a good job.
我剛從學校畢業，正試圖要找到一份好工作。

salary [ˈsælərɪ]　n. 月薪

Some of the interviewers asked me about the salary I had expected.
一些面試官問了我的期望月薪。

> 同義字 monthly pay
> MORE 在英文裡「薪水」有很多種講法，最常見的有 salary、wage 和 pay。salary 指的是「每年固定獲得的薪資」，這種薪水通常會每月匯進戶頭，wage 和 salary 不同，通常是「每週支付的特定數額」，且多是付出勞力的工作內容。pay 則是「完成工作後拿到的錢」，不管做的是什麼樣的工作、什麼時候支付的薪資，都可以用 pay 這個字，下面補充一些與薪水有關的字彙，一起記下來吧！
>
> hourly pay 時薪　weekly pay 週薪　annual salary 年薪
> minimum wage 最低工資　pension 退休金　bonus 獎金
> benefit package 福利方案　incentive payment 激勵獎金

per [ˈpɝ]　prep. 每一～

I told them honestly that if the salary was less than 30,000NTD per month, then I couldn't live.
我老實告訴他們，如果月薪少於三萬新台幣，那我就活不下去了。

paycheck [ˈpeˌtʃɛk]　n. 薪資支票

I don't want to live from paycheck to paycheck, but it's risky to ask for a higher pay.
我不想當月光族，不過要求較高的薪水會有風險。

> MORE live from paycheck to paycheck 是指「過著月光族的生活」。在國外常會用支票來發薪，而「靠著一張接一張的薪資支票來過日子」，便是月光族的意思。

income [ˈɪnˌkʌm]　phr. 收入

Frankly speaking, an income like this is just barely enough for living!
坦白說，這樣的收入只是勉強夠生活而已！

回復記憶 階段

◆ 請參考以下在 Day29 中出現過的圖片，在單字旁的空格寫下字義。

141 抽菸有害健康
indulge .... sheer ....
bronchitis .... restrain ....
yearn ....

142 疫情衝擊
pandemic .... fine ....
communicable .... vaccine ....
mandatory ....

143 排擠
social .... freeze out ....
consolation .... avert ....
adverse ....

144 線上教學
conduct .... material ....
accustomed .... remind ....
laptop ....

145 月光族
graduate .... paycheck ....
salary .... income ....
per ....

加深記憶 階段

◆ 請依照提示的單字字首，在下列空格中填入適當的單字。

(1) 有支氣管炎　　　　　　　have b_____
(2) 一張薪資支票　　　　　　a p_____
(3) 期待的薪資　　　　　　　expected s_____
(4) 一台昂貴的筆記型電腦　　an expensive l_____
(5) 尋求慰藉　　　　　　　　seek for c_____

◆ 請參考下列方框中的單字，在下列空格中填入適當的單字。

參考 | accustomed | graduate | per | fine |
　　 | conduct | avert | restraint | material |

(1) I am _____ to getting up late.
我習慣晚起。

(2) Did you bring all the _____ I need?
你帶了所有我需要的資料嗎？

(3) The worker is _____ a new case.
這個員工正在進行一個新案子。

(4) He has to _____ himself from smoking.
他必須克制他自己不要抽菸。

(5) I go to the library twice _____ week.
我每周去圖書館兩次。

(6) Don't park here, or you'll be _____.
不要在這裡停車，否則你會被罰款。

(7) Can you _____ this year?
你今年可以畢業嗎？

(8) They _____ mentioning the incident.
他們避免提到這件事。

Answers:
1. (1) bronchitis (2) paycheck (3) salary (4) laptop (5) consolation
2. (1) accustomed (2) material (3) conducting (4) restrain (5) per (6) fined (7) graduate (8) avert

Day 30 國家與社會 146-150

Day30_146 在意的是品質！

→ 把你知道的單字打勾！
- ☐ magnate
- ☐ flaunt
- ☐ despise
- ☐ kind-hearted
- ☐ foremost

→ 用 5 個字說出這張圖片的故事！

magnate [ˋmæɡnet]　n. 權貴，鉅子

S I have happened to meet some **magnates**' wives.
我碰巧遇見了一些權貴的太太。

flaunt [flɔnt]　v. 炫耀

S Indeed, some of the rich people like to **flaunt** their wealth.
的確，有些有錢人喜歡炫耀他們的財富。

同義字 show off

despise [dɪˋspaɪz]　v. 看不起

S Due to the gaps between the haves and have-nots in the society, some rich people might **despise** the poor.
由於社會上的貧富差距，有些有錢人可能會看不起窮人。

同義字 look down on
反義字 respect、look up to
MORE haves and have-nots 照字面翻譯就是「擁有的人與沒有擁有的人」，也就是「有錢人與窮人」，因此「貧富差距」就可以說成 the gaps between the haves and have-nots。

kind-hearted [ˌkaɪndˋhɑrtɪd]　adj. 熱心的

But most of the wealthy people I know are kind-hearted and willing to share their wealth with people in need.
但大部分我認識的有錢人都很熱心，且願意和需要的人分享自己的財富。

> **MORE** -hearted 用來表示「擁有～心腸的」，通常前面會加形容詞來組成複合形容詞，就像這裡的 kind-hearted 一樣。

foremost [ˋforˌmost]　adj. 最重要的

However, they do like expensive things, but what is foremost to them is the quality, not the brand.
不過，他們的確喜歡昂貴的東西，但對他們來說，最重要的是品質，而不是品牌。

Day30_147　別隨意穿越馬路

→ 把你知道的單字打勾！
- [ ] jaywalk
- [ ] crosswalk
- [ ] coarse
- [ ] reciprocate
- [ ] posterity

→ 用 5 個字說出這張圖片的故事！

jaywalk [ˋdʒeˌwɔk]　v. 隨意穿越馬路

Jaywalking is an illegal and dangerous behavior.
隨意穿越馬路是一種違法又危險的行為。

> **MORE** behavior 這個字一般是「某人行為舉止所呈現出來的樣子」的意思，而不是指特定的動作，因此會是不可數名詞，但當 behavior 當作「某情境下的特定行為」時，則是可數名詞。

Leon's **behavior** is always unpredictable.
里昂的行為總是難以預測。
Smoking indoors is not **a** good **behavior**.
在室內抽菸不是個好的行為。

crosswalk [ˈkrɔsˌwɔk]　　n. 行人穿越道

🅢 Although Rocco had known that, he still ignored the **crosswalk** a few blocks away, and jaywalked for convenience.
儘管洛可知道這件事，但他還是無視了距離幾個街區遠的行人穿越道，且為了方便而隨意穿越馬路。

同義字 zebra crossing n. 斑馬線，行人穿越道（英式英文）

coarse [kors]　　adj. 粗俗的

🅢 A taxi almost hit Rocco, and the driver was so angry that he yelled at Rocco with **coarse** language.
一輛計程車差點撞到洛可，駕駛氣到用粗話對著洛可大吼。

🅔 a **coarse** joke 一個粗俗的笑話
同義字 vulgar、rude

reciprocate [rɪˈsɪprəˌket]　　v. 互相回報

🅢 I think being respectful to each other is something that drivers and pedestrians should **reciprocate**.
我認為對彼此保持尊重這件事是駕駛和行人都要互相做到的。

posterity [pɑsˈtɛrətɪ]　　n. 後代子孫

🅢 In short, for our **posterity**, we should respect each other and establish a safer environment.
簡而言之，為了我們的後代子孫，我們應該彼此尊重並建立更安全的環境。

Day30_148 貧窮問題

→ 把你知道的單字打勾！
☐ hatred
☐ shabby
☐ malnourished
☐ famished
☐ custodian

→ 用 5 個字說出這張圖片的故事！

hatred [ˋhetrɪd]　n. 仇恨

- Poverty in society is a big problem which may lead to crimes and **hatred**.
社會中的貧窮是一個大問題，它可能會導致犯罪與仇恨。

shabby [ˋʃæbɪ]　adj. 破爛的；衣衫襤褸的

- Take Gary as an example, he comes from a poor family and lives in a **shabby** house.
就拿蓋瑞為例，他來自一個貧窮的家庭，且住在一個破爛的房子裡。

關聯字 shabbily adv. 破爛地；衣衫襤褸地
The poor guy **shabbily** dressed in an old coat.
這個可憐的人衣衫襤褸地穿著舊大衣。

malnourished [mælˋnɝɪʃt]　adj. 營養不良的

- He is even a bit **malnourished** because he has little money to buy food.
他甚至有點營養不良，因為他沒什麼錢可以買食物。

- a **malnourished** kid 一個營養不良的小孩

反義字 well-nourished
關聯字 malnourishment n. 營養不良
MORE malnourished 是把用來構成複合形容詞的 -nourished（營養～的）前面，加上表示「不好的；壞地」的字首 mal- 所形成的字。
若在 -nourished 的前面加上表示「好地」的 well-，就會變成反義字 well-nourished。

famished [ˋfæmɪʃt]　adj. 非常飢餓的

- Sometimes he feels dizzy because he is totally **famished**.
有時候他會覺得暈眩，因為他實在太餓了。

同義字 starving

custodian [kʌsˋtodɪən]　n.（建築物的）守衛

- In order to make more money, besides his daytime job, Gary also works as a **custodian** at night.
為了賺更多的錢，除了白天的工作之外，蓋瑞也在晚上做守衛的工作。

關聯字 **custodial** adj. 監管的；具有監護權的
MORE **custodian** 是被雇來維護像是學校或大樓等大型建築物的人，除了巡守之外，也會負責清潔或維修等工作，和單純的 security（保全）略有不同，但和 janitor（管理員）的職責相同。

Day30_149 藥物濫用很嚴重

→ 把你知道的單字打勾！
- [ ] rampant
- [ ] dropout
- [ ] harm
- [ ] drastic
- [ ] eradicate

→ 用 5 個字說出這張圖片的故事！

rampant [ˈræmpənt]　adj. 猖獗的；蔓延的

S Drug abuse is a **rampant** problem in our society.
藥物濫用是我們社會中一個猖獗的問題。

E **rampant** corruption 猖獗的腐敗
E **rampant** inflation 蔓延的通貨膨脹
關聯字 **rampantly** adv. 猖獗地；蔓延地
MORE **drug** 在英文裡除了「藥物」之外，也有著「毒品」的含意，這是因為很多藥物雖可治療疾病，卻也有著成癮性或做為興奮劑的效果，例如近年來猖獗的止痛藥成癮問題，因此這些藥物雖然不是傳統意義上的毒品，但仍會在特定情況下被視為是毒品的一種。

dropout [ˈdrɑp,aʊt]　n. 中輟生

S Some **dropouts** are easily influenced by drugs from bad guys.
一些中輟生會很容易被從壞人那裡得來的藥物所影響。

關聯字 **drop out** phr. 輟學

harm [hɑrm]　v. 傷害

They think they can get happiness through using drugs, but they are actually harmed by the drugs very much.
他們認為他們可以透過使用藥物得到快樂，但其實他們深受這些藥物的傷害。

關聯字 **harmful** adj. 有害的
Staying up late is **harmful** to your health.
熬夜到很晚對你的健康有害。

drastic [`dræstɪk]　adj. 嚴厲的

I think our government should take drastic measures to stop drug abuse.
我認為我們的政府應該採取嚴厲的措施來阻止藥物濫用。

關聯字 **drastically** adv. 激烈地

eradicate [ɪ`rædə͵ket]　v. 根除

However, it's not possible for us to eradicate the problem very soon.
不過，我們不可能可以在短時間內根除這個問題的。

Day30_150　華人的新年

→ 把你知道的單字打勾！
- [ ] kinship
- [ ] polyglot
- [ ] lunar
- [ ] spring couplet
- [ ] supersede

→ 用 5 個字說出這張圖片的故事！

kinship [ˈkɪnʃɪp]　n. 親戚關係

🅢 Nina and I have **kinship**, though I don't know much about her.
妮娜和我有著親戚關係，不過我和她不是很熟。

> **MORE** 這裡補充一些以 -ship 結尾的單字，這些字多與「特質、狀態、關係、行為」等意義有關：
> membership 會員身分　sportsmanship 運動家精神　friendship 友誼關係
> championship 冠軍身分　relationship 關係　dictatorship 獨裁者的地位

polyglot [ˈpɑlɪˌɡlɑt]　n. 精通多國語言的人

🅢 Nina lives in a Chinatown, and she is a **polyglot**, who speaks English, Mandarin, Cantonese and Spanish.
妮娜住在中國城裡，而且她會說多國語言，她會說英文、中文、廣東話和西班牙文。

> **關聯字** bilingual adj. 雙語的　multilingual adj. 多國語的

lunar [ˈlunɚ]　adj. 農曆的

🅢 Once she told me how they celebrate **Lunar** Chinese New Year in Chinatown.
她曾有一次告訴我，他們在中國城裡是如何慶祝農曆年的。

spring couplet [sprɪŋ] [ˈkʌplɪt]　n. 春聯

🅢 Just like us, they also have dragon and lion dances, family reunion dinners and **spring couplets** pasted on their doors.
就像我們一樣，他們也有舞龍舞獅、團圓飯以及貼在門上的春聯。

supersede [ˌsupɚˈsid]　v. 取代

🅢 However, setting off real firecrackers has been **superseded** by playing firecracker sound effects in some places.
然而，放真的鞭炮的這件事在一些地方已經被放鞭炮音效取代了。

回復記憶 階段

◆ 請參考以下在 Day30 中出現過的圖片，在單字旁的空格寫下字義。

146 在意的是品質！

magnate _____ kind-hearted _____
flaunt _____ foremost _____
despise _____

147 別隨意穿越馬路

jaywalk _____ reciprocate _____
crosswalk _____ posterity _____
coarse _____

148 貧窮問題

hatred _____ famished _____
shabby _____ custodian _____
malnourished _____

149 藥物濫用很嚴重

rampant _____ drastic _____
dropout _____ eradicate _____
harm _____

150 華人的新年

kinship _____ spring couplet _____
polyglot _____ supersede _____
lunar _____

加深記憶 階段

◆ 請依照提示的單字字首，在下列空格中填入適當的單字。

(1) 一個猖獗的問題　　　　a r_____ problem
(2) 在農曆七月　　　　　　in l_____ July
(3) 一位中輟生　　　　　　a d_____
(4) 被深深傷害　　　　　　be h_____ deeply
(5) 一間破爛的房子　　　　a s_____ house

◆ 請參考下列方框中的單字，在下列空格中填入適當的單字。

參考 | jaywalk | posterity | despise | custodian |
　　 | famished | drastic | magnate | coarse |

(1) _____ is against traffic rules.
　　隨意穿越馬路違反交通規則。

(2) William is a _____ in financial business.
　　威廉是位金融業鉅子。

(3) They took _____ measures.
　　他們採取了嚴厲的措施。

(4) For our _____, we should protect our environment.
　　為了我們的後代子孫，我們應該保護我們的環境。

(5) Don't say _____ languages.
　　不要說粗俗的話。

(6) Please tell the _____ to post the notice.
　　請告知守衛來張貼公告。

(7) Do you _____ the poor?
　　你會看不起窮人嗎？

(8) If you are _____, you should eat more.
　　如果你很餓，你應該吃多一點。

Answers:
1. (1) rampant (2) lunar (3) dropout (4) harmed (5) shabby
2. (1) Jaywalking (2) magnate (3) drastic (4) posterity (5) coarse
   (6) custodian (7) despise (8) famished

記單字必備！掌握常見易混淆字 02

★ 常見的易混淆形容詞

1. **alternate** 輪流的 — **alternative** 選擇的
2. **regretful** 遺憾的（人） — **regrettable** 遺憾的（事物）
3. **likely** 很可能的 — **likable** 可愛的
4. **sensible** 明智的 — **sensitive** 敏感的
5. **continual** 一再的，頻頻的 — **continuous** 連續不斷的
6. **intense** 強烈的 — **intensive** 集中的；密集的
7. **confident** 有自信的 — **confidential** 機密的
8. **memorable** 難忘的 — **memorial** 紀念的
9. **social** 社會的；社交的 — **sociable** 善於交際的
10. **childish** 幼稚的 — **childlike** 孩子般的
11. **distinct** 明顯的 — **distinctive** 獨特的
12. **economic** 經濟的 — **economical** 節約的
13. **industrial** 工業的 — **industrious** 勤勉的
14. **considerate** 體貼的 — **considerable** 相當大量的
15. **effective** 有效的 — **efficient** 有效率的
16. **historic** 有歷史價值的 — **historical** 與歷史有關的
17. **respectable** 值得尊敬的 — **respective** 個別的
18. **imaginable** 想像得到的 — **imaginative** 有想像力的
19. **classic** 經典的 — **classical** 古典的
20. **comprehensible** 可以理解的 — **comprehensive** 全面的

★ 選出正確的常見易混淆字彙

① **access**（進入權；使用權）/ **assess**（評估）

(1) Students don't have the _____ to the limited area.
學生沒有可以進入限制區域的權利。

(2) They _____ the house at one million US dollars.
他們評估這房子值美金一百萬元。

② beside（在～的旁邊）/ besides（除此之外）

(1) There are a lot of people at the party _____ us.
除了我們還有很多人來派對。

(2) I am sitting _____ my friend, Charles.
我坐在我朋友查爾斯的旁邊。

③ aboard（登上～）/ abroad（到海外）

(1) He decides to study _____.
他決定到海外念書。

(2) They went _____ the ship.
他們上船了。

④ desert（v. 拋棄 n. 沙漠）/ dessert（甜點）

(1) What would you like for your _____?
你甜點想吃什麼？

(2) He _____ his family and left for the USA.
他拋棄了家人並前往美國。

(3) Land without water is _____.
沒有水的土地是沙漠。

⑤ confident（有自信的）/ confidential（機密的）

(1) The _____ document should be kept in the safe.
這個機密文件應該要被放在保險箱裡。

(2) I am _____ that I'll win the competition.
我有自信我會贏得比賽。

Answers:
①access / assess ② besides / beside ③ abroad / aboard
④ dessert / deserted / desert ⑤ confidential / confident

附錄

◆ 一起看圖開口說說看吧！

001 值得稱讚的優秀學生

▶ Mary is so hardworking at school that she always gets good grades.
▶ She is good at almost every subject, especially English and math.
▶ Mary's teacher always praises her for her good grades.
▶ A lot of Mary's classmates are jealous of her being praised.
▶ Regardless of the ill words from her classmates, she still works diligently at school.

Day01.mp3

002 作弊抓包

▶ Yesterday, our science teacher gave us a pop quiz.
▶ Most of the students in my class were anxious about the quiz.
▶ Some of the students decided to cheat, because they didn't prepare for this at all.
▶ They tried to pass notes to each other secretly.
▶ When our science teacher found they were cheating, he was furious and shouted at us angrily.

003 大學新生活！

▶ When John was notified that he had been accepted by a renowned university, he was proud of himself.
▶ Being a university freshman has always been John's dream.
▶ "It's a whole new start!", said John excitedly.
▶ John has been thinking about how to have an ideal university life.
▶ On his first day in the university, he immediately took some elective courses he liked very much.

004 校園遊

▶ One day, I happened to walk into an elementary school.
▶ The campus is spacious, and there were energetic students everywhere.
▶ I saw some of the students doing exercises in their PE class.
▶ Two girls were sitting on the bench chatting.
▶ What's more, I also saw a boy jogging on the track.

293

005 知名教授來了！

- Mr. Wang is a reputable and very well respected professor.
- He is not only knowledgeable but also nice to his students.
- He will give a speech on economy in the seminar next month.
- The seminar will be held in the school auditorium.
- It is expected that this seminar will be well-attended.

006 我的好朋友

- Tom and I are good friends, and he always gives me a hand when I encounter difficulties.
- The friendship between us makes a lot of people impressed.
- Last week he came all the way just to give me a birthday present, and I really appreciated what he did for me.
- I gave him a firm hug and thanked him sincerely.
- I will definitely cherish the precious friendship forever.

Day02.mp3

007 暗戀一個人

- Tina wants to be Charles' girlfriend, but she is not a proactive person.
- Many of Tina's friends encourage her to express herself directly to Charles.
- One time she saw Charles chatting with a gorgeous girl; she felt a little depressed.
- In spite of all the hurt feelings she had, she still decided to just be a silent admirer.
- Hopefully, he would understand her mind sometime in the future.

008 患難見真情

- Eric and I grew up together in the suburbs.
- Just as a saying goes, "A friend in need is a friend indeed."
- Whenever I need him, he just shows up immediately.
- Yesterday I was frustrated about work; he came to accompany me and drank with me.
- Moreover, he always gives me solid suggestions, so I won't be indecisive when I have to make a decision.

009 這種朋友不交也罷！

- Last night, May invited Jessie over for a party, but she said she had to work overtime.
- It was May's birthday yesterday, so she really wanted to celebrate with her best friend.
- After the party, some of May's friends felt like singing at a karaoke bar.
- Shortly after they arrived, May saw Jessie was in the lobby too, and she's with a handsome boy!
- May was filled with dismay and said she would never want to see Jessie again.

010 從小認識的朋友
▶ Jason and Jimmy have known each other since childhood.
▶ They used to live in the same neighborhood; however, Jason moved out last year.
▶ Now they connect with each other via messaging apps.
▶ They also write to each other, from paper to electronic, the only thing unchanged is their friendship.
▶ They will cherish each other's company forever.

011 學校社團展
▶ Anna went to the school club fair a few days ago.
▶ Many booths were set up on campus to show the students all the benefits they would get if they join a club.
▶ She was particularly interested in the debate club a the chess club.
▶ After she was introduced to a variety of clubs, Anna decided to sign up for the debate club.
▶ She has always hoped that she could express herself better, so she joined the club to practice more.

Day03.mp3

012 學語言不容易
▶ Ed is always interested in language learning.
▶ He hopes he can speak English fluently one day.
▶ Consequently, he has tried to find the best way to learn English, but he still barely can talk in English.
▶ Some people advise him to enroll in a language learning program.
▶ Besides English, he also wants to learn other languages, such as French and German; and with proper training methods, he may be multilingual one day.

013 網友
▶ I have a net friend named Jane, who is a really lovely girl.
▶ We often chat in a forum on the Internet, but we never meet face-to-face.
▶ We usually talk about fashion and share the latest information with each other.
▶ Although we are not the typical type of friends, we still care about each other.
▶ It's truly fortunate that I could meet Jane on the Internet and befriend her!

014 好朋友帶你飛！

▶ Lillian is one of my best friends, and she is accommodating and considerate.
▶ When I was facing financial problems, she was the one who volunteered to help.
▶ She is the kind of friend who is full of wisdom.
▶ She often tells me how to manage my money for better use.
▶ The relationship between us is very special and close, and I'm lucky to have her as my friend.

015 閨密奪愛

▶ Holly used to be my close friend, and she was a cheerful person to me.
▶ One day, I introduced my beloved boyfriend to her, and we had an awesome dinner together that night.
▶ However, yesterday I found my boyfriend talking to someone suspiciously on the phone and he went out right away.
▶ I followed him and caught him kissing Holly on her lips.
▶ What a shocking sight! My best friend and my dear boyfriend betrayed me!

016 英倫之旅

▶ As a backpacker, traveling to foreign countries is my hobby.
▶ When I go abroad traveling, I always carry a camera with me.
▶ For me, taking pictures is the best way to preserve those memorable experiences.
▶ I will never forget the joy of seeing Big Ben, which is a famous landmark in England, for the first time.
▶ I can just pull up the pictures whenever I want to recall those precious memories.

Day04.mp3

017 令人毛骨悚然的景點

▶ Last summer, our family had a trip to Europe, and we were interested in seeing ancient architecture.
▶ Following the recommendation of the guidebooks, we went to an old castle in central Europe.
▶ According to the guidebooks, it's a beautiful and well-known scenic spot.
▶ However, when we finally arrived there, we were all shocked by its creepy appearance and weird atmosphere.
▶ Apart from that, the weather that day was really terrible, and it made us feel even more uncomfortable.

018 旅途中看音樂表演

- When I was traveling in New York, I went to a wonderful outdoor concert.
- There were many spectators in front of the stage, and they really enjoyed the show very much, just like me.
- On the stage, a total of three musicians were playing their instruments beautifully.
- Among all the musicians, I especially liked the double bass player; the tones he played were truly a pleasure to hear.
- Even better, the music he played was all original!

019 巴黎之旅

- This was the first time that I had been abroad.
- European countries have been always the dream destinations for me, especially France.
- France is notable for its long history, beautiful scenery, and romantic atmosphere.
- The most attractive tourist spot in Paris is the Eiffel Tower.
- See, I was in front of the Eiffel Tower to have my photograph taken.

020 日本神社之旅

- When it comes to traveling abroad, Japan is my first choice.
- Every time I travel to Japan, I always behave myself and try to act like a Japanese person.
- Last year I went to a Japanese traditional temple in Japan.
- Many people there were following a unique procedure for worshipping and praying.
- I imitated the people beside me and prayed for gaining good luck in my future career and love life.

021 難得的露營之旅

- Jason and I had been looking forward to this camping trip since last month.
- We had planned it for a while, and we'd prepared a lot of stuff before we set off.
- At the campsite, we put up the tent quickly and without any problem.
- At night, we set up the campfire to warm us, and we chatted happily all night.
- We had a superb time together, so we immediately decided to start planning for the next camping trip.

Day05.mp3

022 我是背包客
- Lisa has always wanted to be a backpacker.
- She is brave and has a good sense of direction.
- Every time she plans to travel, she puts a lot of effort into doing the research.
- Lisa tells me that she likes to be prepared in advance.
- To save money, she chooses to book hostels instead of fancy hotels.

023 坐錯位子啦！
- Instead of taking a train, I always choose to travel by HSR.
- Today, I went to Tainan to visit historic buildings and have great food.
- After I found my seat and sat down, the conductor came to me and asked me to show my ticket.
- After checking my ticket, he politely said, "Miss., your seat is 26A, not 28A".
- I thanked him and stood up right away to move to the correct seat.

024 可怕的搭機經驗
- I was flying from Taipei to New York, and it's the bumpiest flying experience ever.
- The turbulence made me sick and very uncomfortable.
- The headache and dizziness also made me feel like vomiting.
- I asked a flight attendant to give me an extra blanket to keep myself warm.
- I have truly wished I had never been on this awful flight.

025 一個人看恐怖片
- Let me tell you a secret, I'm a timid person and I'm really afraid of ghosts and darkness.
- One day, my best friend recommended a horror movie to me.
- My friend said it was a popular movie, and the leading actress was nominated for the Oscar for best actress.
- I was persuaded to watch the film alone on Saturday night.
- I really regret I made this decision, because I was almost frightened to death.

026 好玩的節慶活動
- Have you ever been to a festival held abroad?
- My classmate and I attended a festival when we were studying abroad.
- There were many different exhibitions and interesting shows held there.
- The festival was about agriculture, so we saw a lot of unique vegetables and fruits.
- Although the venue was really large, we still felt energetic and not tired at all.

Day06.mp3

027 老鼠的復仇

- In a little wooden cabin, there is a cat, a mouse and their owner.
- The cat likes to chase the mouse for fun, which irritates the mouse very much.
- The mouse wants to seek revenge on the cat.
- It is difficult for a mouse to fight back facing a cat, so he decides to ambush the cat.
- One day, the mouse jumps out of nowhere and bites the cat's tail really hard.

028 滑雪之旅

- Both Stephanie and Oliver have a great passion for skiing.
- They have continued strengthening their skills for a skiing trip in the future.
- People sometimes ask them how they can ski so well, and they always say the key is being attentive.
- Finally, they have left for a ski resort to fulfill their dream of going on a ski trip.
- Their skiing skills were highly acclaimed by people around them.

029 健行很棒！

- I had been living overseas before I changed my job.
- The humid climate in Taiwan makes me suffer from allergies all the time.
- I often go hiking on weekends, hoping the fresh air can relieve my allergies.
- The views in the mountains are so marvelous that I even exclaim with joy sometimes.
- Every time when I am strolling along the trails, I feel the joy of being surrounded by nature.

030 在飛機上

- I had been waiting at the airport for quite a while before I could board the plane.
- With my passport and boarding pass, I finally stepped onto the plane.
- I was standing in the aisle, trying to put my baggage into the overhead compartment, but I was too short to do it.
- "Could you help me put my baggage up there?" I asked a pretty flight attendant.
- She replied to me gently, "No problem, let's do it together."

031 老公來做飯

- Henry's wife, Emma, sometimes **complains** that he never cooks for the family.
- In order to make his wife feel **contented**, Henry decided to cook a meal for her.
- Henry didn't know how to use the gas stove, so he chose to use the **microwave**.
- Just as Henry was microwaving some food, the food he put inside suddenly **exploded** and made a mess.
- Henry felt really **embarrassed** and he ended up calling for food delivery instead.

Day07.mp3

032 哥哥捉弄弟弟

- Edison and Edward are **siblings**, and their parents want Edison, the older one, to take care of Edward.
- **Nevertheless**, naughty Edison always does the opposite.
- What's more, Edison likes to **tease** Edward, and he often tries to scare him.
- He even spooked his younger brother with a **fake** snake yesterday.
- Although Edison knows he is supposed to take care of Edward, he just **can't help but** keep making fun of him.

033 全家去動物園

- What kind of **leisure** activities does your family do on weekends?
- One of our **preferable** choices is to go to the City Zoo.
- There are many kinds of animals **alive** in the zoo.
- Giraffes and zebras are **tame** animals, and they are well-liked by people.
- Every time we go to the zoo, we always **spend** a whole day browsing thoroughly.

034 在遊樂園約會

- Alan and I had a date at an **amusement** park last weekend.
- Alan is a **considerate** boyfriend.
- After I told him that I'd want to go to an amusement park, he **promptly** bought the tickets.
- We bought some snacks from the **vendors** in the park.
- It was an amazing date, and no one else could be **comparable** to Alan in my mind.

035 家庭主婦忙忙忙

- Being a full-time housewife is an **exhausting** job.
- After years, my **multitasking** skills have been polished.
- Cleaning the house, preparing meals and taking care of my kids are my basic **daily** jobs.

- My schedule is so tight that there's no flexibility to make time for myself.
- To organize a family and make it work smoothly is really difficult!

036 全家來野餐

- Every weekend, the Chen family always goes on a picnic in a neighborhood park.
- Today is a sunny day, so they sit on the grass and enjoy the food Mrs. Chen prepared.
- Mr. and Mrs. Chen value the time that the whole family gets together very much.
- With the nice weather and the awesome food, everyone enjoys the atmosphere and chats with each other.
- The kids are discussing what they want to bring for their next picnic enthusiastically.

037 媽媽的早晨

- Being a homemaker is a tough job for every mother in the world.
- I have two kids, so I have to do various things every morning.
- My kids have to go to school today, so I dress them up.
- After my kids leave for school, I start to sweep and clean the house all by myself.
- Cleaning house is always tiring, but it's worthwhile when I see my floors are shiny.

038 我想買鋼琴！

- When Kelly was a kid, she dreamed of becoming a musician in the future.
- One day, Kelly and her daughter were walking down the street and there was something shiny that caught her daughter's eye.
- An enormous but beautiful piano was displayed inside a store.
- Kelly's daughter liked the instrument very much and asked her to buy the piano.
- Kelly was full of surprise when her daughter told her that she also has wanted to be a musician in the future.

039 倒數計時做功課

- I was born in a single-parent family, and I have a strict mother.
- As a career woman, she is very good at striking a balance between family and work.
- She is a senior executive in her company, so she is used to giving orders.
- She asks me to finish all my school assignments before she comes back from work.
- I always do my best to be obedient to her orders.

040 有人求婚好幸福
- Lisa and her boyfriend have been dating for years.
- They are serious to each other; in addition, their family members get along with one another.
- On a beautiful Sunday, Lisa's boyfriend proposed to her, and gave her a big diamond ring.
- Lisa was deeply touched, and she exclaimed, "Yes, I do!"
- She felt she was the most blessed woman in the world.

041 什麼是幸福
- Have you ever asked yourself what's the definition of happiness?
- People say that being rich or having their own business is happiness.
- However, true happiness for me is to gather my family and have some quality time together.
- In short, no matter what we do, as long as I stay with my family, I am happy.
- Life with them is never tedious but marvelous.

Day09.mp3

042 好孕到
- Allison has been pregnant for eight months.
- This is her first baby, so everything for her is new and unpredictable.
- Now Allison is meeting with her supervisor and talking about her maternity leave.
- Her supervisor is nice and approves her leave request at once.
- Allison is uncertain what her life will be in the future, but she's certain that she won't regret having a baby.

043 一家人的週末
- Every Saturday is vital to the Wang family.
- On Saturday mornings, they usually trim the bushes and take care of their beautiful garden.
- On Saturday afternoons, they go to the supermarket to buy groceries together.
- A Saturday night feast is also the Wang family's ritual.
- To sum up, Saturdays are their family day and they all enjoy each other's company.

044 雙胞胎不一樣
- Vic and Nick are twins.
- Though they look alike, they act very differently.
- They have different personalities; Vic is shy, and Nick is outgoing.
- People sometimes ask them whether they have the so-called "twin telepathy".

▶ They say; they don't know if it's telepathy or not, but if one is uncomfortable, the other sometimes will feel nauseous, too.

045 懷念阿嬤

▶ Tim remembers his grandmother took care of him carefully when he was little.
▶ Tim also remembers that his grandmother was adept at painting.
▶ She created many masterpieces, and she was well-known for her talent.
▶ A few years ago, Tim's grandmother passed away peacefully one night.
▶ For Tim, his grandmother is a legend and always lives in his mind.

046 抓到小偷了！

▶ Michael is a righteous policeman and he is respected by everyone.
▶ The core of police work is to protect people.
▶ He does his best to put burglars, thieves, and con artists behind bars.
▶ These bad guys are not allowed for the sake of safety.
▶ Michael caught a thief today, who had once broken into someone's house; he's happy to keep him off the streets.

Day10.mp3

047 手機不見去報案

▶ Jenny bought a new cell phone, which she has longed for for months.
▶ In fact, the new mobile phone cost her an arm and a leg.
▶ Although she was really careful, her phone went missing today!
▶ She believed her phone was definitely stolen, so she went to the police to report the crime.
▶ The police officer assured her that he would try his best to find it.

048 視而不見沒禮貌

▶ As a saying goes, "Courtesy costs nothing."
▶ However, there are no standard norms about courtesy.
▶ People can only follow those unwritten rules of courtesy to act.
▶ For example, nodding one's head when a person sees another is a common way to say hi.
▶ But some of my classmates don't think so, in fact, they don't even greet me.

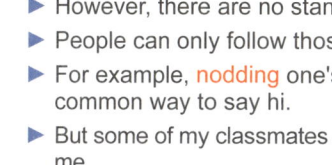

303

049 別遲到了
- An office is like a small society, and some regulations mustn't be ignored.
- Rule number one, "Don't be late for meetings."
- If you're late, the agenda will be delayed.
- Moreover, you should also avoid absence without any notice.
- Otherwise, your coworkers will think you're difficult to collaborate with.

050 餐桌禮儀
- Table manners are important and should be followed.
- For example, we should know how to use tableware orderly.
- When eating soup, be certain that you use the right spoon.
- When spreading butter onto bread, use the butter knife instead of your spoon.
- After having your meal, don't use a napkin to wipe your mouth, just blot it.

051 霸凌就不對
- Bullying is wrong, but unfortunately it's common in today's society.
- Some students like to tease or harass their classmates at school.
- At work, senior workers like to give impossible tasks to rookies.
- Bullying exists in families too, physical or mental abuse happens all the time.
- As a result, we should take measures to stop people threatening others.

Day11.mp3

052 遲到非好事
- Being late is not a good behavior when you're meeting someone.
- Take my boyfriend as an example, he is often late for our date, and I sometimes wonder if he's "crawling" to see me.
- Every time he is late, he always makes up ridiculous excuses.
- Today he made me wait for half an hour, and I was kind of getting used to it.
- I just took a deep breath, watching as he ran to me and said sorry.

053 騎車記得戴安全帽
- In accordance with traffic rules, we should wear a helmet when riding a motorcycle.
- In Taiwan, people living in urban areas tend to follow this regulation.
- However, people living in rural areas often ignore it.
- In fact, I think the police should force them to put on their helmets.
- After all, observing traffic rules can not merely protect yourself but also ensure others' safety.

054 騙子房東

- There are many bad landlords in the rental market.
- These deceitful landlords rent out their houses with false descriptions.
- Peter was a new tenant moving into an apartment.
- The landlord had told Peter that the apartment was just renovated, so the rent would be more expensive.
- Peter rented it anyway, but he soon found the ceiling was leaking!

055 收件人百百種

- After years of delivering packages, Johnny perceives that calling recipients is just like rolling dice.
- One day, he recounted what he had observed to his friends.
- Out of apprehension for no one being home, he would make a call before he delivered the packages.
- Sometimes he was lucky, the recipients were gentle, and they would thank him for checking in advance.
- On the other hand, some of the recipients would treat him with contempt or be impolite.

056 買花送人

- Hank is a sweet person, and he never hesitates to show his care for others.
- He remembers everyone's birthday and the special days worth celebrating.
- He thinks giving flowers is a kind of proper social etiquette for celebrating special moments.
- His care let him build harmonious relationships with people around him.
- His zeal for helping others also makes him well-liked.

Day12.mp3

057 醫院禁止吸菸

- Some behavior must be forbidden strictly.
- For example, smoking in the hospital is one of the big taboos.
- Nobody wants to inhale secondhand smoke, and the smoke may cause lung cancer.
- A man is smoking in the ward, and the nurse doesn't want to tolerate his behavior.
- The embarrassment swells in the man's mind, so he puts out his cigarette right away.

058 別打擾別人

- One of the basic elements of keeping good relationships is not to disturb others when they're busy.
- This principle can be applied to almost every circumstance.

- ▶ If you often disturb others for trivial things, your personal relationships will be frayed easily.
- ▶ Take diligent Eden as an example, his classmate Tom often disturbs him no matter how busy he is.
- ▶ If the situation keeps on like this, no matter how intimate they are now, their relationship won't keep long.

059 接待客人很難

- ▶ I am a receptionist at the information desk of a department store.
- ▶ This is a generic job, but I have to meet different customers every day.
- ▶ Sometimes I even quiver with anger when I encounter unreasonable customers.
- ▶ Those nuisances make me want to quit sometimes, but nice customers are the reason for me to stay on the job.
- ▶ Like the lady in front of me, she graciously asked me where the restrooms were, and her politeness makes me happy to help her.

060 不接受陌生人的食物

- ▶ Children should beware of certain kinds of crimes.
- ▶ Some bad guys would pretend they are acquainted with your parents, and provide snacks to lure you.
- ▶ They may take you in their car and kidnap you for ransom.
- ▶ To avoid something disastrous happening, you should say no to strangers, no matter how you want to eat the snacks they offer.
- ▶ Otherwise, the outcome will be unbearable.

061 所謂的能動能靜

- ▶ Jim has an adorable beagle.
- ▶ His beagle is different, instead of being feisty, he's rather even-tempered.
- ▶ They even can rest or sleep on the same bed without any mess.
- ▶ Today, Jim and his dog are playing fetch on the patio.
- ▶ He is really vigorous and excited during their play time.

Day13.mp3

062 就是喜歡狗！

- ▶ Last time when I went to a dog park, I saw a variety of dogs.
- ▶ Altogether I saw beagles, Labradors, poodles and bulldogs.
- ▶ Unlike wild animals, dogs are domesticated animals and it is difficult for them to survive without human beings.
- ▶ People like dogs because they are friendly and loyal.
- ▶ Dogs also perform different functions in human society, such as hunting, investigating and leading the blind.

063 我的膽小貓
- I have a kitten, and her name is "Tiger".
- Tiger is nothing like a real tiger, on the contrary, she is very timid.
- The weather today is terrible, because there is a hurricane striking.
- Thunder and lightning make Tiger scared.
- She is so scared that she hides herself under an armchair.

064 寵物看醫生
- If people are sick, they will seek a doctor's help.
- On the other hand, animals do need doctors too, their doctors are called "veterinarians".
- My dog vomited last night, and I thought he might be infected by a flu virus.
- The vet gave him a thorough checkup and decided to give him an injection.
- After the injection, he barked at the vet for a while like he was complaining.

065 青蛙真有趣
- I have been so interested in frogs since I heard the fairy tale, "The Frog Prince".
- In the story, a prince was turned into a frog by an evil fairy.
- In reality, frogs are rather fascinating and interesting.
- Adult frogs can live in fresh water or on dry land, and some species can even live underground.
- Based on where they live, they also lay eggs in different places.

066 我的好夥伴
- Mimi and Fufu were originally stray dogs before I adopted them.
- The adoption process was long and complicated, but it was necessary to make sure the adopter was a suitable one.
- Since they came, I have fed and played with them every day to establish the bond between us.
- They bring joy to my life and it's refreshing to be with them.
- Their company is no doubt the best gift of my life.

Day14.mp3

067 獅子生病了
- My kids begged me to take them to the zoo last weekend.
- As we were walking in the zoo, one of my kids shouted, "Look at that lion!"
- The lion was surprisingly thin as well as spiritless.
- "He is sick," a zookeeper passing by explained to us.
- "In fact, lions are normally strong and muscular," he continued.

068 猴子掉下來了！

- Most people think monkeys are naughty animals.
- Their bright minds and interesting behaviors make them special.
- It is said that monkeys and human beings evolved from the same ancestors.
- Looking at them, it's hard to imagine that we were once monkeys.
- Just when I was staring at them, there was a monkey that accidentally fell from a tree!

069 鄰居的狗

- My neighbor has a mixed-breed dog, which was given to him by his friend.
- He is an emotional dog, and he gets really excited when seeing food.
- He likes to dig a hole and bury his bones under the ground.
- However, now and then he buries bones in my yard, which upsets me every time.
- My neighbor apologizes and compensates me by giving me some gifts.

070 貓狗不合

- Are dogs and cats necessarily hostile to each other?
- If you ask me, I would say cats see dogs as real foes.
- I know people would question my opinion, but my cats reject my dog all the time.
- I remember I once watched a documentary about the relationships between dogs and cats.
- In the documentary, the hostile interactions between them are mostly started by the hissing cats.

071 被狗追超可怕

- Ben has been afraid of dogs since he was chased by a barking dog.
- He said what he had encountered then was not a dog but a fierce monster.
- Now, every time he comes across a dog, he always walks away quickly.
- Sometimes Ben's friends laugh at his cowardice.
- Ben always stammers, "I'm not afraid of them. I just don't like dogs!"

Day15.mp3

072 好命的貓

- My cat is my treasure, and she is spoiled by the whole family.
- She often strides about our house with a proud look on her face.
- She seems to know everyone in my family loves her, and she is proud of herself.
- She has sleek and soft fur.

▶ Every time I pet her, I can feel the rather comforting feeling filling my mind.

073 逝去的狗
▶ Karen's dog died of cancer last month.
▶ After her dog died, Karen lived in sorrow.
▶ She would sometimes dream about petting her dog.
▶ Sometimes she would feel miserable, and have a sleepless night.
▶ Karen declined her parents' offer to have another dog, because she didn't think she was ready for that.

074 恐龍時代
▶ Dinosaurs appeared during the Triassic period.
▶ Most of them belong to a group of diverse reptiles.
▶ It's impossible for us to see real dinosaurs, and most people have only seen them in the best-selling Jurassic Park movies.
▶ Scientists have learnt about dinosaurs through studying fossils.
▶ But until now, dinosaurs were still rather mysterious due to the lack of study materials.

075 人類常吃的動物
▶ The cattle farming business provides beef and dairy products for us.
▶ Bacon and pork chops are from pigs; eggs and chicken are from chickens.
▶ Among all the eatable animals, I like chickens best.
▶ Because I like chicken nuggets and fried chicken very much.
▶ Every time I go to a bar, I would definitely order chicken nuggets and fried chicken with a cold beer, what a life!

076 來不及追劇
▶ Joyce is a bank teller working in a bank nearby.
▶ Just like her colleagues, she likes to watch Korean soap operas.
▶ Believe it or not, she can watch them continuously for ten hours without a break.
▶ The romantic plots always drive Joyce crazy; she even watches every episode over and over.
▶ Joyce went back home late today, and she was really upset that she missed the finale.

Day16.mp3

077 做不完的功課
- Being a primary school student is not easy now.
- I have to get up very early in the morning to catch my school bus punctually.
- What's more, I have to earn good grades in numerous quizzes and tests.
- That is to say, I have to stay up late to burn the midnight oil.
- It's cruel for a kid like me to have so much work to do every day!

078 來電傳情
- Bill and Dora fell in love at first sight.
- They were seeing each other before Bill was transferred to the branch in Australia.
- Since then, they have had long distance calls every day.
- Although the distance between them is remote, it cannot stop their love.
- Bill is trying to get the opportunity to transfer, hoping he can be back home soon.

079 花錢如流水
- Peter and Amy are newlyweds.
- Peter always tells his friends and relatives that they live in happiness.
- But the truth is, Peter is kind of unsettled by Amy's desire for eating delicacies.
- Amy can't stand average foods and asks to go to expensive restaurants very frequently.
- Peter is worried that he will go broke and will not be able to afford the restaurants one day.

080 我愛打電動
- Speaking of interests, playing online games is my number-one choice.
- Playing online games is not easy, you need to acquire every skill to make clever moves.
- Sometimes you have to predict what your opponents will do next.
- But my mother always blames me for spending too much time playing online games.
- She says I waste too much time playing them, but I think the opposite.

081 烤肉趣
- Kevin likes to have a barbecue in his front yard every weekend.
- He likes to make his own barbecue sauce with the ingredients and tools he bought before.
- He usually prepares coal, grill racks, aluminum foil and tongs.
- He also goes to the supermarket nearby to purchase some chicken wings, sausages, meat and seafood.

Day17.mp3

▶ The cozy atmosphere of having a barbecue always makes him relaxed and happy.

082 來釣魚吧

▶ Ed often goes fishing with his fishing partner David.
▶ Today was a lucky day for them; they caught two lively fish in only ten minutes.
▶ The grilled fish they made by themselves really blew away their taste buds.
▶ When they went fishing together the first time, they were concerned about how to deal with the fish they caught.
▶ Gladly, they could always cook it quite perfectly.

083 餐廳訂位

▶ One day, William made a phone call to a restaurant to reserve a candlelit dinner.
▶ William liked the restaurant very much because it had a patio, and customers could have meals beneath the stars.
▶ The atmosphere there was romantic, so William thought it was a good place to have a candlelit dinner.
▶ The uniformed staff answered the phone and told William that all their tables were booked.
▶ William disappointedly hung up and started to think which restaurant he should call next.

084 手機不離身

▶ In terms of convenience, smartphones are necessary for modern people.
▶ I have a strong impression that people nowadays are using their cellphones anytime and anywhere.
▶ Now, there are three people in front of me, and they are all operating their cell phones.
▶ It seems that the girl is texting, and the man beside her is dealing with business.
▶ However, the senior citizen beside the man seems confused about how to handle his cell phone properly.

085 使用自動販賣機

▶ When Helen felt thirsty, she saw a vending machine inside a building.
▶ She walked through the entrance to the vending machine.
▶ However, the control panel was complex and Helen didn't know how to use it to buy a drink.
▶ Helen stood helplessly in front of it; meanwhile, a man came to her and offered to help.
▶ Helen finally got a bottle of water to quench her thirst.

311

086 買新車囉！
- Angus always wants a car that *belongs to* himself.
- He has been looking for an ideal one, but most of them are over his *budget*.
- One day, Angus walked into a car dealer, and the agent *extended* a warm welcome to him.
- Angus *bargained* with the agent, and finally she agreed to a price within Angus' budget.
- The agent explained some *precautions* he needed to follow, and gave Angus the car key.

087 市場買菜去
- Mrs. Ho likes to *explore* new or different ingredients in traditional markets.
- She thinks traditional markets or farmers markets are better than supermarkets or *hypermarkets*.
- That's because she thinks the food and groceries there are far fresher, and she can buy *organic* food with better quality.
- She also likes to *gossip* with people in the markets.
- The *butchers* and farmers in the markets are all her friends.

088 披薩全吃光
- Tina is a *chubby* girl, and she likes to eat pizza very much.
- Her parents always warn her not to eat too much *junk* food.
- They think it's *imaginable* that Tina would be fat one day.
- Tina knows eating too much pizza is not healthy, but she just can't *control* herself.
- She has tried to quit eating pizza, but to no *avail*; and this time she even ate a whole pizza all by herself!

089 下公車掉錢包
- Alan is a *commuter*, and he goes to work by bus every day.
- He is usually in *compliance* with the etiquette of taking buses.
- He always *presses* the bell before he gets off the bus.
- But today, he was talking on his cell phone and *simultaneously* taking a note, so he missed the timing to ring the bell.
- Alan got off the bus in a hurry and accidentally *left* his wallet on his seat.

090 看 3D 電影
- It's a *pity* that our children don't like to see movies with us, so my husband and I always go by ourselves.
- We like *science fiction* movies very much.
- We usually go to a movie theater located in a *skyscraper*.
- The movie we saw today was about *invasive* aliens.

312

▶ We were seeing the movie with a large popcorn and 3D glasses, and the movie was really nice!

091 健身
▶ Working out is very popular among modern people.
▶ As a result, currently there are many health clubs and fitness centers in the city.
▶ Albert is a muscular man, and he needs to do a lot of training to keep his figure.
▶ Besides doing weight training, he also uses treadmills and bikes in the gym.
▶ He usually rides stationary bikes to train his cardio.

Day19.mp3

092 研究時尚
▶ Ruby and Isabella are roommates in the school dorm.
▶ They became good friends, and they have a lot in common.
▶ For example, they both like reading fashion magazines to learn about the latest fashions.
▶ They are fond of wearing trendy accessories.
▶ They think fashion is a kind of popular culture, and everyone should know more about it.

093 生病就該看醫生
▶ Jack felt ill when he woke up this morning.
▶ Hence, he decided to see a doctor in a clinic.
▶ Dr. Lin is his family doctor, and he is a reputable physician.
▶ Dr. Lin checked his throat to see if he had a throat inflammation.
▶ He also used a stethoscope to check Jack's lungs.

094 打桌球
▶ I'm a sports fan, and I like to play all sorts of sports.
▶ My brother and I like playing table tennis the most.
▶ We go to our school gymnasium to play table tennis every weekend.
▶ People sometimes ask us how we can hit the ball so accurately.
▶ I tell them, "You have to concentrate on the ball and move your body nimbly. "

095 減肥不可能
▶ Mike is a couch potato, and he never does any exercise.
▶ What's more, he likes to eat desserts, like cheese cakes and chocolates.
▶ He cannot quit the habit of eating late-night snacks, either.
▶ They are the reasons why he gains weight so quickly.
▶ For Mike, losing weight is an impossibility.

096 勤洗手不生病

- In order to avoid getting sick, there are some rules that should be observed.
- For example, I wash my hands before eating to protect myself.
- There are a lot of viruses and germs on our hands.
- Good personal hygiene is one of the key elements of staying healthy.
- That's why I often urge my friends and family to keep good hygiene habits.

Day20.mp3

097 踢足球

- According to some research, soccer is the most popular sport in the world.
- Plenty of soccer players are not just athletes; instead, they are celebrities.
- Tom and Will are competing in a soccer match now.
- The match is very competitive, and both of the teams want to win.
- For Tom and Will, winning the trophy is the only goal they aim at.

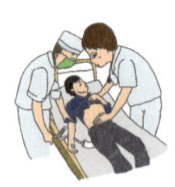

098 是時候健康檢查了

- I usually have a physical checkup every year.
- I always have a blood test to see if there's anything causing a blocking of my vessels.
- The doctor checks my abdomen through an ultrasound scan.
- I then consult my doctor about the results of the ultrasound image.
- My doctor is very thorough, he tells me every detail of my problems and gives me suggestions every time.

099 越算越嚇人

- Chris was walking down the street when he met a fortune teller.
- This man leaned forward and whispered to Chris, "Young man, you'll be in trouble soon."
- Chris was not convinced, but he still followed the fortune teller to his booth.
- After Chris hesitantly sat down before the booth, the fortune teller asked for one thousand dollars.
- At that moment, Chris knew the fortune teller was definitely a liar wanting to fool him.

100 減重有方法

- Bob likes tasty food, and he loves searching for new restaurants.
- This hobby has caused him to become fatter and fatter.
- His doctor urges him to lose weight and asks him to scrutinize what he eats every day.

- ▶ Trying to lose weight means he has to limit his daily calorie intake.
- ▶ His doctor also tells him that doing exercise should be involved in his plans for losing weight.

101 藥局拿藥
- ▶ Lisa went to a clinic because she had some skin problems.
- ▶ After examining, the doctor prescribed some medicine for her.
- ▶ After taking the prescription, she paid the fee at the registration desk, and got her receipt.
- ▶ She held a number and waited for receiving her medicine.
- ▶ The pharmacist gave her a tube of ointment and some capsules.

Day21.mp3

102 吃鮭魚很棒
- ▶ Eason wants to go on a diet, so he asks his friend for some advice.
- ▶ Eason also wants to keep fit, so it's important for him to eat right.
- ▶ His friend answers cordially, "You should eat more foods with high-quality protein."
- ▶ Eason asks him which foods are healthful.
- ▶ "You can eat more fish, such as salmon!", his friend answers.

103 導盲犬幫忙
- ▶ Lulu is a guide dog, and Jason is her owner.
- ▶ Jason is disabled because he can't see things clearly.
- ▶ Although Jason can't see, he still can give Lulu orders accurately.
- ▶ Lulu is a smart dog, so she can tell if a situation is hazardous or not.
- ▶ She can help Jason shun the dangers he encounters.

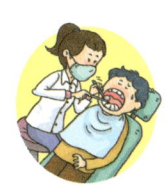

104 看牙醫
- ▶ Ivan is unwilling to see a dentist even though he has a toothache.
- ▶ He says that he can't stand the sound of the dental drills.
- ▶ But today Ivan went to the dentist's office, because his dental problem worsened.
- ▶ After examination, the dentist cleaned his teeth and filled the cavities caused by tooth decay.
- ▶ After the treatment, the dentist taught him how to brush his teeth correctly.

105 切洋蔥切到哭
- ▶ Steve cares about his health, so he wants to know what kind of food benefits him more.
- ▶ He looks through many books, trying to find the food he likes and that is also good for his health.
- ▶ He's not a vegetarian, but he finds that most vegetables are good for health.

- ▶ Steve bought one **kilogram** of onions, which was on sale, in a supermarket today.
- ▶ When he was **chopping** the onions, the poignant smell stimulated his eyes and made him tear up.

106 夕陽無限好

- ▶ Jamie is sitting on the beach and watching the **sunset**.
- ▶ She was not meant to stop to see the sun setting, but she **caught sight of** the beautiful view in front of her.
- ▶ The **warmth** and beauty of the sun were remarkable.
- ▶ Now she is **savoring** the peace and the splendid view of the sunset.
- ▶ The sun is just **like** the origin of life, and its greatness makes her feel small.

Day22.mp3

107 美好的海洋

- ▶ My family and I sometimes go to the beach nearby to see **marine** animals.
- ▶ We can see sea turtles on the beach, **not to mention** crabs and starfish.
- ▶ My kid likes to **dig** big holes on the beach, and then asks us to lie down in the holes.
- ▶ Playing with my kid and viewing the sea can make me change my mood from **distraught** to calm and happy.
- ▶ Looking at the sea also **evokes** a lot of beautiful memories for me.

108 璀璨星空

- ▶ "The **Starry** Night" is a famous masterpiece created by Vincent van Gogh.
- ▶ In reality, stars are **astronomical** objects appearing in the sky as sparkling dots.
- ▶ There are countless stars in the sky, but most of them are invisible to the **naked eye**.
- ▶ **Meteors**, also called shooting stars, are also attractive.
- ▶ Seeing a shooting star, I **kneel** down to make a wish right away.

109 種花很難

- ▶ Different kinds of **plants** have different flowers.
- ▶ Beautiful flowers are everywhere, but some of them are rare and can only be seen in a **botanical** garden.
- ▶ I once tried to grow rare flowers on my **balcony**, but they all died very soon.
- ▶ Without the right **soil**, water and professional skills, it's really difficult to make them grow beautifully.
- ▶ As a result, I sometimes go to a botanical garden to see the pretty flowers there and let myself indulge in the **fragrance**.

110 該重新粉刷了

- Making your surroundings clean and pleasing to the eye is everyone's responsibility.
- The appearance of my house was very old and dull, so I was responsible for making a change.
- The exterior paint of my house was peeling and faded.
- So I have hired a painter to repaint my house.
- The paint work is on schedule now and I think it's about to finish.

111 天乾物燥小心火燭

- It's terribly hot recently, and the average temperature is higher than normal.
- If the temperature is high, and the air is dry, then it's easy for wooden houses to catch fire.
- A house is on fire now, and firefighters are on the scene.
- It's truly horrifying to see the massive fire swallowing up the house.
- I hope the firefighters can put out the fire very soon, and no one is hurt by the fire.

Day23.mp3

112 梅雨季節溼答答

- In Taiwan, the "plum rain season" happens during May and June every year.
- During the plum rain season, stationary fronts cause extremely heavy rain.
- Sometimes torrential rains make many areas flood.
- Today John got totally wet on his way to school, even though he carried his rain gear.
- Now he is trying to dry his bag and books.

113 垃圾分類保護地球

- In order to protect our earth, recycling is important.
- To recycle, you have to sort out the recyclables, and put them into separate bins.
- Generally speaking, most of the recyclable stuff can be sorted into kitchen waste, plastic and paper.
- But some people sort them into combustibles and non-combustibles.
- In short, people shouldn't throw away their trash in a wanton way; otherwise the planet suffers.

114 過敏超難過

- I'm allergic to many things; having allergies is a part of my daily life.
- Do you know the symptoms of being allergic?
- Sneezing, coughing, and itchy eyes or skin are all the common symptoms of allergies.
- To get rid of allergies, you need to know your allergens.

▶ The clothes I am wearing today were on a shelf for a long time, and the dust mites on them are making me sneeze nonstop.

115 下雪好麻煩
▶ The sudden snow makes Amanda panic.
▶ That's because she is very bad at walking on slippery streets covered by snow.
▶ Plus, providing that it snows continually, it will be difficult for her to go out to buy groceries.
▶ Last time, a horrible blizzard even got her stuck at home for several days!
▶ That's why Amanda likes warmer climates more, and she even considered moving to a warmer place.

116 龍捲風
▶ A tornado, also known as a twister, is widely considered to be a kind of natural disaster.
▶ Tornadoes often take place in the middle states of America.
▶ Of course, they can also happen on any other continent.
▶ Tornadoes form when cold and warm air currents interact violently.
▶ When tornadoes happen in populous areas, they often cause devastating damage.

Day24.mp3

117 水資源的重要
▶ Water resources management is imperative to people all over the world.
▶ However, there are many places in the world still short of water.
▶ Drought is one of the reasons for the lack of water.
▶ In the case of water shortage, water rationing measures should be put in place.
▶ The restrictions will be suspended after there's enough rainfall.

118 颱風
▶ Incidents of a typhoon hitting Taiwan are recurrent during summertime.
▶ That's why we have to make preparations before the typhoon season.
▶ Typhoons will bring pouring rains and strong gusts of wind to us.
▶ Therefore, don't go out when there is a typhoon striking, or you may be blown away.
▶ Just stay at home, and make sure your flashlights and instant noodles are on hand, then you'll be safe.

119 淹大水

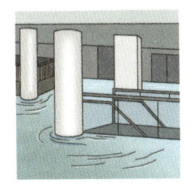

- The tropical storm has brought heavy rainfall to Taiwan today.
- In only one day, the rainfall has exceeded 500 millimeters.
- Because of the heavy rains, the sewage systems aren't working properly.
- Thus, some of the areas in Taipei have been inundated by floods.
- Furthermore, many cars and motorcycles have been breaking down on the roads.

120 害蟲

- There are various pests living with us every day.
- Flies, mosquitoes, cockroaches and termites are all common pests.
- Most people loathe cockroaches most.
- When they see cockroaches, they'll kill them with pesticides immediately.
- At any rate, pesticides are harmful, so we had better keep our household environment clean to make pests go away.

121 好老闆

- Linda is a marketing specialist working in a local company.
- She has to deal with advertising campaigns every day.
- She caught a cold today, but she still worked at her desk with a mask on her face.
- Her boss was worried about her sickness and kindly told her to go home and get some rest.
- Linda thought her boss was thoughtful and really cared about his staff.

Day25.mp3

122 技術好才能留住客人

- I attribute the reason a hair salon has good business to its staff.
- Perhaps you would disagree with my opinion.
- But in the hairdressing industry, customers do change their hair salons if their hairdressers quit.
- Although most of the hairstylists working in hair salons are well-trained, their capabilities and styles vary.
- That's why hiring good hairstylists is the key to building customer loyalty.

123 換份工作吧

- I always want to find a job with better prospects.
- My parents sometimes give me counsel, saying that changing jobs is a good way to get a higher pay.
- I do think that job-hopping is a nice way to get a better position with higher pay, so I started to look for another job.
- As a successful candidate, I'm answering the interviewer's questions now.

▶ The interviewer is interested in my work experience and the certificates I have.

124 網路購物

▶ More and more retail shops provide online shopping services.
▶ It has been a gradual process that people are getting used to ordering online.
▶ Besides, most people have grown a consensus that home delivery is really convenient.
▶ However, some problems of ordering online still exist, such as wrong deliveries.
▶ People have to contact the online seller to get what they ordered, which is much more inconvenient than buying in stores directly.

125 用電腦打字好難

▶ I am already a middle-aged man, and learning how to use computers to type is difficult for me.
▶ However, recently I have a new job that needs to utilize computers to do a lot of typing.
▶ I have encountered many problems, for instance, I can't find the right characters.
▶ To improve my typing skills, I have browsed many tutorial materials online.
▶ In addition, I have also practiced intensively to improve faster.

126 做一位演員

▶ I think every actor has their own angle to interpret a script.
▶ Some people may think that doing acting is boring, but I think it's extraordinary.
▶ To get improve, I have spent plenty of time altering the way I perform.
▶ Now I become a sophisticated actor.
▶ Besides that, thanks to those elaborate scripts, I have won several awards.

Day26.mp3

127 什麼都要排

▶ It's easy to get new information through online news or Internet communities now.
▶ Novelties, like newly released sneakers or new restaurants, always attract people to stand in line.
▶ A new pizza house opened nearby, and it excited me to stand in line for a taste.
▶ The pizzas there were worth the wait because they were really distinct and tasty.
▶ After standing in line for a long time, I was so hungry that I gulped down ten pieces of the pizza.

128 實驗人生

- I am a technician working in a laboratory.
- At work, I have to do a lot of different experiments to find the best formula.
- My job is to make new medicines, such as tablets for relieving headaches.
- It's a difficult job because we have to overcome so many hurdles before inventing a new medicine.
- Furthermore, we are always having a race against time to develop life-saving medicines.

129 同事之間的禮數

- Neil and Jeff work in the same corporation.
- Their chief financial officer's newborn is one month old, so they are discussing what gifts they should give.
- To protect the baby, though their CFO is usually hospitable, it's not suitable for them to pay him a visit.
- On the other hand, the CFO doesn't like extravagances, so it will be better to give him useful things.
- Neil insists they should give gifts together, so Jeff accedes to sharing the cost with him.

130 服務生不好當

- Molly is a waitress, and she is always tolerant to bad customers.
- Some of the customers are very captious, and they complain about everything.
- And some of the customers are arrogant, they even see servers as their own maids.
- There's a weird man sitting at the table, pretending he's reading the menu.
- The man is peering at Molly, and Molly is disgusted by his behavior.

131 在便利商店工作

- Angela works at a convenience store.
- The workload is heavy, but she enjoys interacting with her customers.
- She uses a cash register to do the transactions, and she bags the items for her customers.
- Angela was not born to an affluent family, so she knows she has to work hard.
- She thinks working hard is the only way that she can have a promising future.

Day27.mp3

321

132 包包維修店
- Alex has a good hand at repairing bags.
- He can repair wallets, handbags, pocketbooks and so on.
- He's also an ingenious man that can make his own bags for sale.
- In order to buy a workshop for himself, he has borrowed money from banks and had some liabilities.
- With his hard work, he definitely can settle all the liabilities and has his own workshop in the foreseeable future.

133 午餐踩到雷
- As an office worker, deciding what to eat at lunchtime is truly troublesome.
- There are so many optional places near my company.
- I usually choose from the canteen, cafeterias, and the food stands nearby.
- However, I went to a new restaurant for a change today, but the food there was really disgusting.
- I think I was too credulous that I believed the restaurant's sales pitch.

134 老闆愛監視
- Darla's boss likes to oversee his employees working in the office.
- He is just like a human monitor.
- Darla knows her boss likes to watch everyone, so she sometimes pretends that she's very busy.
- It's really a dreadful experience for Darla to have her boss standing by and staring at her.
- She is not exaggerating when she says her boss is an annoying man.

135 做房仲就是要會說話
- Natalia is a successful real estate agent.
- Actually, she won the Best Realtor of the Year last month.
- Now she is having an open house with the potential buyers.
- Her glowing descriptions of the house make all the potential buyers interested.
- It's out of question, she's a great realtor.

136 關心新聞
- Modern people often watch TV to get new information and knowledge.
- Furthermore, we can learn the latest news by watching news shows.
- Journalists report the news by observing, investigating and doing interviews.
- My family and I often sit on the couch, watching news shows reported by professional anchors after dinner.

Day28.mp3

▶ We want to keep abreast of trends by watching news shows.

137 最喜歡周年慶了

▶ I know some people like to shop at boutiques.
▶ However, I prefer shopping at the department stores, because there are chances that I can get great deals.
▶ Some of the famous brands in the department stores, like MAC or Dior, will merchandise their products when there's a sale.
▶ They even offer deep discounts the during the anniversary sales season.
▶ Besides, if I'm hungry, I can conveniently go to the food court for tasty food.

138 發生車禍了

▶ A car collision happened at the intersection of Park Road and First Street this morning.
▶ The car on the westbound lane lost control, and veered into the eastbound lane.
▶ The car on the eastbound lane couldn't react in time, so the two cars directly collided.
▶ The police and the ambulance arrived at the scene immediately.
▶ The roads were congested after the accident because they had to seal off the intersection for accident investigation.

139 銀行搶案

▶ A piece of sensational news was on TV today.
▶ A group of gangsters robbed a bank in the afternoon.
▶ According to the report, the criminals adopted aggressive tactics in the robbery.
▶ They were carrying and wielding lethal weapons to threaten people in the bank.
▶ Fortunately, the bank tellers stayed calm, and no one was hurt during the robbery.

140 解決停車問題

▶ The lack of parking spaces has always been an unresolved problem in our society.
▶ The average time for a driver to find an available parking space is twenty minutes at the minimum.
▶ Indeed, we don't have enough parking garages or parking lots.
▶ What we should do is reduce the amount of vehicles.
▶ Maybe we can do this by raising taxation on cars.

141 抽菸有害健康

- I used to indulge in smoking, but now I quit it for my health.
- My doctor told me that I may have bronchitis, even lung cancer, if I don't quit it.
- But to be frank, sometimes I still yearn for the taste of tobacco.
- I miss the sheer pleasure of smoking after meals.
- However, I know smoking is really bad for my health, so I do my best to restrain myself and completely quit it.

142 疫情衝擊

- Now the pandemic has changed our daily lives.
- The communicable viruses have made a huge impact on our behavior.
- For example, wearing masks is mandatory when taking mass transportation.
- Besides, people will be fined if they don't wear masks.
- Even though most people have already gotten their vaccines, wearing masks is still necessary.

143 排擠

- Human beings are social animals, and we like to stay in groups.
- In groups, people can get support and consolation from each other.
- However, if there are too many groups in one organization, it will have an adverse effect on management.
- For example, if a person doesn't belong to the group he/she is working with, then he/she might be frozen out.
- In order to avert the awkward situation, the management should do team building activities to keep the organization healthy.

144 線上教學

- Due to the pandemic, many schools have started to conduct online courses.
- For teachers who are accustomed to teach in real classrooms, it's not easy to prepare for online courses.
- First, teachers must have a laptop equipped with a high resolution webcam and a good microphone.
- Then, they have to share their teaching material with the students online.
- But most important of all, teachers have to remind their students to show up on time for the class.

145 月光族
- I just graduated from school, and I am trying to find a good job.
- Some of the interviewers asked me about the salary I had expected.
- I told them honestly that if the salary was less than 30,000NTD per month, then I couldn't live.
- I don't want to live from paycheck to paycheck, but it's risky to ask for a higher pay.
- Frankly speaking, an income like this is just barely enough for living!

146 在意的是品質！
- I have happened to meet some magnates' wives.
- Indeed, some of the rich people like to flaunt their wealth.
- Due to the gaps between the haves and have-nots in the society, some rich people might despise the poor.
- But most of the wealthy people I know are kind-hearted and willing to share their wealth with people in need.
- However, they do like expensive things, but what is foremost to them is the quality, not the brand.

Day30.mp3

147 別隨意穿越馬路
- Jaywalking is an illegal and dangerous behavior.
- Although Rocco had knew that, he still ignored the crosswalk a few blocks away, and jaywalked for convenience.
- A taxi almost hit Rocco, and the driver was so angry that he yelled at Rocco with coarse language.
- I think being respectful to each other is something that drivers and pedestrians should reciprocate.
- In short, for our posterity, we should respect each other and establish a safer environment.

148 貧窮問題
- Poverty in society is a big problem which may lead to crimes and hatred.
- Take Gary as an example, he comes from a poor family and lives in a shabby house.
- He is even a bit malnourished because he has little money to buy food.
- Sometimes he feels dizzy because he is totally famished.
- In order to make more money, besides his daytime job, Gary also works as a custodian at night.

325

149 藥物濫用很嚴重

- Drug abuse is a rampant problem in our society.
- Some dropouts are easily influenced by drugs from bad guys.
- They think they can get happiness through using drugs, but they are actually harmed by the drugs very much.
- I think our government should take drastic measures to stop drug abuse.
- However, it's not possible for us to eradicate the problem very soon.

150 華人的新年

- Nina and I have kinship, though I don't know much about her.
- Nina lives in a Chinatown, and she is a polyglot, who speaks English, Mandarin, Cantonese and Spanish.
- Once she told me how they celebrate Lunar Chinese New Year in Chinatown.
- Just like us, they also have dragon and lion dances, family reunion dinners and spring couplets pasted on their doors.
- However, setting off real firecrackers has been superseded by playing firecracker sound effects in some places.

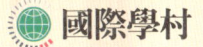

語言學習NO.1

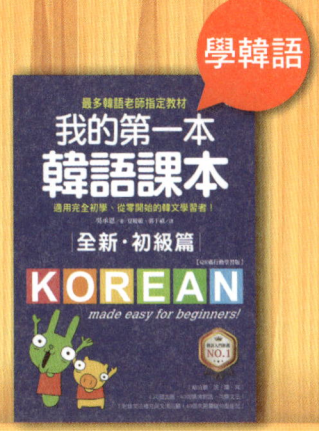

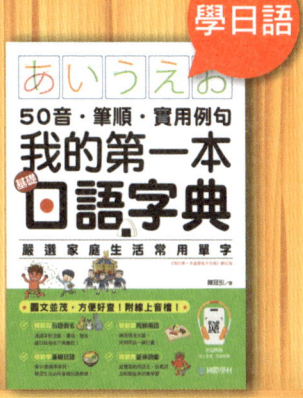

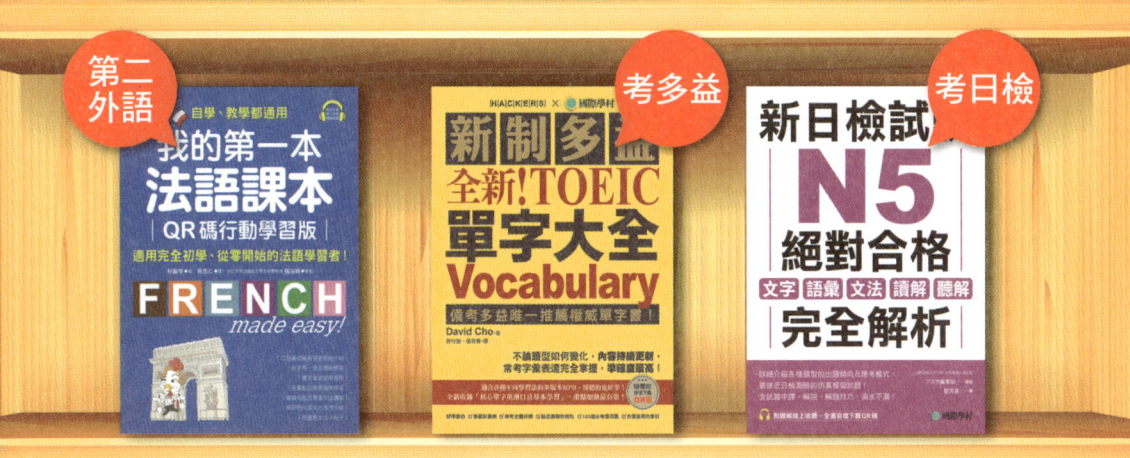

國際學村 | **LA PRESS 語研學院** Language Academy Press

學英語 — 1本就通 國高中英文

學韓語 — 我的第一本韓語課本 全新・初級篇 KOREAN made easy for beginners!

學日語 — 50音・筆順・實用例句 我的第一本日語字典

第二外語 — 我的第一本法語課本 QR碼行動學習版 FRENCH made easy!

考多益 — 新制多益 全新！TOEIC 單字大全 Vocabulary

考日檢 — 新日檢試驗 N5 絕對合格 文字 語彙 文法 讀解 聽解 完全解析

考韓檢 — NEW TOPIK 新韓檢初級應考祕笈 KOREAN Beginner Level Test Guide

考英檢 — 全民英檢 全新！GEPT 單字大全 Vocabulary 初&中級

想獲得最新最快的語言學習情報嗎？

歡迎加入
國際學村&語研學院粉絲團

台灣廣廈 國際出版集團
Taiwan Mansion International Group

國家圖書館出版品預行編目（CIP）資料

國高中英文單字加深加廣/陳頎著. -- 二版. -- 新北市：國際學村出版社，
2025.06
　面；　公分
　ISBN 978-986-454-424-0(平裝)

1.CST: 英語教學 2.CST: 詞彙 3.CST: 中等教育

524.38　　　　　　　　　　　　　　　　　　114004778

國際學村

國高中英文單字加深加廣

〔圖解＋敘事〕精選會考又實用的單字，解決看圖寫作及描述圖片的難題！快速擴充單字量，英文口說寫作能力同步提升！

作　　　者／陳頎	編輯中心編輯長／伍峻宏・**編輯**／徐淳輔
	封面設計／陳沛涓・**內頁排版**／菩薩蠻數位文化有限公司
	製版・印刷・裝訂／東豪・弼聖・秉成

行企研發中心總監／陳冠蒨　　　　線上學習中心總監／陳冠蒨
媒體公關組／陳柔彣　　　　　　　企製開發組／張哲剛
綜合業務組／何欣穎

發　行　人／江媛珍
法 律 顧 問／第一國際法律事務所 余淑杏律師・北辰著作權事務所 蕭雄淋律師
出　　　版／國際學村
發　　　行／台灣廣廈有聲圖書有限公司
　　　　　　地址：新北市235中和區中山路二段359巷7號2樓
　　　　　　電話：（886）2-2225-5777・傳真：（886）2-2225-8052
讀者服務信箱／cs@booknews.com.tw

代理印務・全球總經銷／知遠文化事業有限公司
　　　　　　地址：新北市222深坑區北深路三段155巷25號5樓
　　　　　　電話：（886）2-2664-8800・傳真：（886）2-2664-8801
郵 政 劃 撥／劃撥帳號：18836722
　　　　　　劃撥戶名：知遠文化事業有限公司（※單次購書金額未達1000元，請另付70元郵資。）

■出版日期：2025年06月　　ISBN：978-986-454-424-0
　　　　　　　　　　　　　版權所有，未經同意不得重製、轉載、翻印。

Complete Copyright 2025 © by Taiwan Mansion Books Group.
All rights reserved.